PENGUIN BOOKS

GOODBYE GIRLIE

PATSY ADAM-SMITH is one of Australia's best-known and best-loved authors. Awarded the OBE in 1980 for services to literature and the Order of Australia in 1994 for services to recording oral history, she has written thirty books, all of which have topped or appeared on the best-seller lists. Among her most popular books are *Hear the Train Blow* (the story of her childhood), *The Shearers, Australian Women at War, Heart of Exile, There Was a Ship, Outback Heroes* and *The Anzacs*, which was joint winner of The Age Book of the Year Award in 1978. *Prisoners of War*, her most recent work of non-fiction, received the prestigious triennial Order of Australia Association Book Prize in 1993.

PATSY ADAM-SMITH

GOODBYE GIRLIE

Penguin Books Australia Ltd
487 Maroondah Highway, PO Box 257
Ringwood, Victoria 3134, Australia
Penguin Books Ltd
Harmondsworth, Middlesex, England
Viking Penguin, A Division of Penguin Books USA Inc.
375 Hudson Street, New York, New York 10014, USA
Penguin Books Canada Limited
10 Alcorn Avenue, Toronto, Ontario, Canada M4V 3B2
Penguin Books (N.Z.) Ltd
182–190 Wairau Road, Auckland 10, New Zealand

First published by Penguin Books Australia Ltd 1994
This edition published by Penguin Books Australia Ltd 1995

10 9 8 7 6 5 4 3 2 1

Edited by Lee White
Typeset in Goudy Old Style by Midland Typesetters, Maryborough, Victoria
Printed in Australia by Australian Print Group, Maryborough, Victoria

National Library of Australia
Cataloguing-in-Publication data

Adam-Smith, Patsy.
Goodbye girlie.

ISBN 0 14 023507 8 (pbk).

1. Adam-Smith, Patsy. Biography. 2. Authors,
Australian–Biography. I. Title

A828.309

Contents

Acknowledgements

My children, Michael and Cathy, have come all the way with me, and their children, Rosie and Daniel, have brought me joy of the generations. I have been, still am, blessed by great friends, men and women, including those who encouraged me while writing this book: Albert McPherson, Greg Reinhart, Beverley Dunn, Dianne Ellis, Maureen Sheehan, Noreen Megay, and Jeremy Hammond, the physician–heart specialist who made it possible for me to go on. I was pleased to once again have Lee White's professional expertise as editor.

The Dancing Years

THERE WERE MANY RAILWAY PLATFORMS in my life, but the most joyous day I had was when I stood on the platform in the tiny country town as the train carrying away my parents gathered momentum. At last they stopped waving because we couldn't see one another in the distance and I jumped on my bicycle and pedalled pell-mell back to the little room that was to be mine alone in the baker's house. And there I took my corsets off.

Early in 1941 Dad was ordered under the Manpower Act During Time of War to move south as flying ganger on a single rail track into the Gippsland hills where timber was being transported out to build army barracks in the city. 'But I've got a music exam coming up!' I wailed – carefully, so as not to arouse suspicion in Mum. 'I suppose I'll have to give up music.' Mum wasn't a person to leave others to make up their own minds to do anything, but she could be trapped into thinking she did it all by herself. Within half a day I'd got it all fixed. Mr and Mrs Forrest, the baker and his wife, good Catholic church-goers of course (I planned this campaign thoroughly), would let me board in their house at the Penshurst town bakery. I could have my piano moved into their 'front' room to enable me to practise for the future exam.

And so I escaped across the moat to freedom. I stood on the platform, waving goodbye. Yes, I'd be a good girl for Mrs Forrest, yes, I'd go to church and yes, I'd have a bath every Saturday and always wear stockings. Back at my new abode, I took off my dress and began to rid myself of my armoury.

It had begun one day while my Mother was making a new dress for me. She noticed for the first time that my bosoms had begun to develop and my hips and abdomen to show signs of shapeliness. She set about right away to rid me of these dangerous attractions. First came the binder. My Mother had made this from a strip of very firm calico and it was bound round what she saw as my wickedly burgeoning teenage breasts, and joined by big hooks and eyes down the left side of the upper part of my body. Then she began on the corsets. These corsets had once belonged to Mum herself. She was almost twice my weight, and they had to be cut down to my size. When reconstructed, this masterpiece would have two walls, laced herring-bone style down the back, boned, with vertical whale-boned ribs the whole way around. The frontispiece could have withstood the attack of a battering ram of a medieval soldier. It was divided into an inner wall – nearest the skin, hooked on the left side from top to bottom – and an outer wall. The outer wall was the main defensive abutment: great big iron eye-holed hard loops which closed the gap by framing the loops over truly fearsome bollards that a ship could have tied up to. Because of the whalebone stays, Mum hadn't been able to cut the vertical length down to my size, so the top of this massive construction pushed up under my growing breasts and cut and hacked at me all day, while the bottom of the invention reached half-way down my thighs causing me no end of difficulty when I went to the toilet. The whole creaked like a sailing ship at sea, whether I moved or stood still.

I can honestly record that this fortress my Mother had erected single-handedly was never broached in the ten months I was obliged to wear it. Once, at a dance, a boy's hand slipped tentatively below my waist and when his fingers came in contact with the castle wall he whipped his arm back as if he had been bitten by a dog.

It was the war that got those corsets off me. I dug a hole out the back of the bakery and buried them. I have wondered if, in distant years, some archaeologist was to dig up Mum's invention, would it end up in a museum and would folks believe all girls in the 1940s were dressed in this strange way?

With that weight off me, I set off into the dancing years. The couple with whom I was to board were middle-aged, late to marry, and they had a little boy aged three years and another on the way. They were busy enough and didn't trouble me at all.

Freedom is the sweetest thing and I ran headlong into it. The same day that my parents left, I wrote to a shop in Hamilton to order a pair of navy-blue flat-heeled 'Wattle Derby' walking shoes, plus a pair of navy-blue medium-heeled courts that I'd seen advertised. Perhaps not exciting choices, but a change from my many-soled school shoes. Until now I had not been permitted to handle the money I earned - none of it, and sometimes it had been more than my father could earn in a week, what with my commercial enterprises of teaching piano to four children, serving and doing the bookwork at the bakery, as well as working nights at the newsagents during Christmas, Easter, etc. and playing piano in the New Mayfair Dance Band. The money, like the odd sums my sister, Kathleen, earned, was always handed directly to Mum. This I did not mind, it was what other young girls did in those days.

It never occurred to me to claim these monies for myself. Mum made all my clothes, mended my shoes. Dad was only good with boots. 'He should have stayed in the navy,' Mum said one day in a rare moment of wit. She did repairs around the house, leaving the heavier jobs to Dad. Dad always tried and usually failed. Once, near Christmas, he put up a shelf in the kitchen for the ingredients of Mum's Christmas cake and pudding. Mum was not overly grateful at the sight and walked past this slab of wood warily as if it might leap off the wall and hit her. The next night we were walking down the railway track in the clear hot air and we heard a terrific crash back at the house. Without missing a step Mum said evenly 'Your father's shelf.' Yes, it had gone, raisins mixed up with eggs, flour with everything else across the floor.

Dad didn't mention the navy much, but Kathleen and I got a bit of slang from him, always well-timed on his part. 'All shipshape and Bristol fashion' he'd say if Mum had us dressed up. 'Oh, very tiddly,' he'd say – nice and neat, or 'very pusser', otherwise. He woke us every morning of our young lives with the chant 'Heave ho! Heave ho! Heave ho! Lash up and stow. Lash up and stow!' And in our wee house we girls could always hear Mum's exasperated drawing-in of breath.

I cared for the bookwork of the bakery business as well as the shop part. Two bakers were in the actual baking area behind the living quarters, and I had my own little room – not that I was in the little room for any length of time. I had started work there after leaving the butcher shop. Next door to the butcher shop had been a haberdashery shop, with long counters, bolts of cloth, and all the trimmings needed for the home-made dresses of those days. By now, with money being so tight for so long during the years of the depression, very few women entered the shop. But I often went in and the owner rolled out bolts of cloth and described the material and how it was made and where, took down collars and ribbons that would match, and buttons too. In retrospect, I realise two things about this man and his shop: he had so very few customers my visits gave him the opportunity to fling a bolt of material across the counter and see its quality and comment on it, things he had done all his working life. The second was that the shop was soon to disappear. Indeed, it disappeared the day after he gave me the dress length of navy-blue crepe plus a white pique collar and crystal buttons to go down the front of the classic frock I would make, all for twelve shillings and sixpence. The shop burned down, and it didn't matter any more that no one came into his shop and he had moved away from the ruins and like others at that time, we heard of him no more.

It was the dancing years. There were great tunes and even greater words to sing to. Even in such a small town as Penshurst where the majority were poor, there was a dance at least once a week in the Mechanics Institute hall, an orchestra played, and crowds of people came along. There was even a debutantes' ball in which I took my place, although I was too young to be with such a group. Dad thought I may not get the chance again to wear a long dress and told Mum he thought I should make my debut. And, he was quite right, the days of long dresses, balls and such like would be swept away during the six years when so many of the young men were away at the war.

The dancing years were matched by the great songs of that time. We danced to 'Sweet Rosie O'Grady', swinging apart from our partners, joining again in the Pride of Erin; we slow-waltzed, fox-trotted, and did the quick step. We danced to the Tennessee Waltz and it was not only because it was a good tune that the boys went across the hall to the partner they had selected. In some mysterious manner we all managed to get the partner we wanted. We began very slowly: 'I was dancing that night to the Tennessee Waltz', the bodies swayed and got closer and closer. Our mothers must have near ruined their eyes trying to see what was happening; but that's what the dance was – a very slow, most seductive pattern of movement. Nothing that is danced today comes anywhere near a slow waltz to the tune of the Tennessee Waltz.

And yet, we were perfectly safe, no matter what it was we were being kept safe for. It was a valuable opportunity for us young ones, with body very close to body, sweeping to the side, back a little, forward again, at all times in contact with your partner's body, and I've always wondered if perhaps it was a very good way to get to know men generally. Sometimes, if the partner you had hoped to get wasn't at the dance that night, you'd be dancing with someone else and you didn't get this incredibly seductive experience; but when you did it was quite surprising. You wouldn't be going home with that person, and you mightn't see him again, but you had experienced something that probably warned us – or more probably, delighted us – that there were some wonderful things ahead of us in time to come. And I think the 'in time' part is the thing I remember of the most value; when dancing, you knew you had all the time in the world, you weren't going to be rushed off somewhere before you were ready.

There was a Highland Schottische which was fast and furious. We'd get more than a glow. The men would have a white handkerchief in case their hand sweated on the back of your dress, the music would be going at an enormous speed and getting faster and faster, and people whom we considered very old would leave the floor because they couldn't keep up, and the big thing was that you and your partner would be the last to give up – and even then, not to give up until the orchestra did. There was the Lancers which, of course, is a very old dance but it lived on until the war years. It was a wild dance; there were four men and their partners in each set, all controlled by a Master of Ceremonies. Nearly everyone was on the floor. The MC would call 'Gentlemen, salute your partners!' and the man would bow to the woman and she would curtsy to him and then we were off. You didn't stop moving, it was fast. One movement that was constantly repeated was the swinging. The skill of this was to go round and round as fast as possible, faster than anyone in the hall if you could, but never, as an old gentleman once said to me, 'never lose your feet'. And that was the skill of it. Sometimes there'd be great squeals of delight, a boy had swung his girl right off her feet, but the skill was to go faster and still keep your feet. It was a ballroom dance, not a square dance.

The Waltz of the Cotillions was a most graceful thing. I can't imagine anyone doing this dance today but it was a waltz which was done while one was moving around all the time to other partners in the foursome. To see the whole floor of dancers doing this set piece was quite elegant. When the music was coming to the end, you curtsied, the men bowed, took your arm, and took you back to your seat.

Near the end of the night a 'medley' was called which had many various dances with no break between. There was a wild Keel Row. The girls did a heel-toe action with their partner, going faster and faster, then there was the Three Hop Polka and the band would keep that going until there was scarcely a person left on the floor because it was so fast. Those who had become weary and stood back, now stepped forward when the music changed pace because it would be the last dance of the night – a waltz to the tune of 'Good Night Sweetheart' ('all my dreams are for you'), and the lights would be low and my Mother's eyes would be everywhere to see where I was – like every other mother in the small hall.

One night we were just finishing the dancing, the music was playing and we were singing 'Goodnight sweetheart, 'til we meet tomorrow, goodnight sweetheart, goodnight', and just as those words were hanging in the air, we realised there were huge rumblings out in the street and, oddly, a clarinet playing. We raced outside and there was the army going by. Well, not exactly the army, but it was the Light Horse on the way to train in Hamilton. They had trucks and had stopped to check the horses. When we rushed out the officers tried to keep the uniformed men in check – and we tried to get close to them (as close as your mother would let you). Somehow we found out they were going to be bivouacked in Hamilton and the camp would have an open day the following afternoon. It would be exciting to see these long rows of tents, and then the long rows of horses being watered, and women coming around with baskets of fruit. I knew in advance I'd be the only girl to arrive with Father, Mother, grown-up sister and her two babies.

It seemed that suddenly we were remembering 'Oh, yes, that's right, the war is on'. It had been a phoney war until that time, but here were men training and ready and outfitted to go to war. That night I recall many of us walked back into the hall and when we came out again we were much quieter.

At daybreak we heard the rumble of men moving and they went right down the main street, very slowly, and everyone was out to watch them. The clarinet player threw an artificial flower to me. I was probably thrilled by it then but didn't think any more of it until years later when men were being brought in to our hospital after returning from the Middle East or from the islands to the north. I always wondered if that man came back. The memory of him laughing and playing the clarinet out on the street stayed with me. There was no more to the story than that, but it did somehow let me know that men went to war and that life was going to be very different from now on. With Dad's transfer to Gippsland, like many a family in wartime we were split up for the first time, and forever.

The Last Christmas

THERE WERE SIX OF OUR immediate family at the table for that last Christmas, and numerous friends came in, and old Grandma Smith who had run away with a ship's bosun so long ago and now, at ninety-five, could still remember the excitement of it. Grandmother lived with us and, being a canny Scots woman, was telling the relatives she *always* got a sixpence in the pudding, though threepence was the going rate. I was out in the scullery with my Mother. She had put a two-shilling piece in the pudding and now she carefully got it out and put it on Grandma's plate. I said, 'But there's already a sixpence in there, Mum' for a piece with sixpence had been put on the plate, but she told me to just take it in to Gran. So we were around the table having home-made Christmas pudding and cream and for a short time we overlooked Grandma until she suddenly said 'Nothing! Not a thing!' We all stared because the word had gone around that there wasn't only a sixpence but also a two-shilling piece in her pudding. Mum said to me, 'Run down quickly to Dr Trumpy'. He was the son of a doctor who Grandma Smith had often ridden with to attend childbirth cases in the bush, she being a well-known professional midwife (who always exacted payment for her labour like any good Scotswoman would do). The doctor came straight away, had a piece of Mum's pudding, and kept asking Gran how she felt. 'No good at all,' Gran said. 'There weren't even a thrupence in it.' Doctor left after a while, saying to Mum 'If everyone had a constitution like Gran I'd be out of a job in no time.'

It was the last time we celebrated Christmas in the old style. Many of our extended family were at the table for that Christmas. There would have been one more but Bob, my brother-in-law, had been notified he was to join a troop train in Melbourne and we didn't see this brave young man again. But we were not to know the future, and the traditional celebrations were bright and happy. Bob had been on 'final leave', and he and my sister Kathleen had prepared the poultry from our chook house. For Christmas and New Year we would wring the necks of our chooks before we put them on the chopping block in the back yard. We would lop their heads off, then holding the chook by the feet, we dipped it in the tub of boiling water that could scald your hands if you were not nippy with the dipping in and hauling out, and pulled the feathers out. Then came the boring pulling out of the quills and we rubbed the now-naked chook with a sugar bag to clean it up, slit the vent, hand in, pulled the guts of the chook out, chopped off the feet and boiled them to get the thick skin off. The boiled flesh on poultry feet is delicious and gelatinous. You've never heard of anything so revolting? Perhaps not: we pay other people to do it for us these days.

There were still some of our young cousins at home ready to go to the war, some were already there. John Buick was home on leave from the navy for a week, but Raymond was already in the Middle East and about to go 'missing' during the debacle of Greece. Sheila Adams was in the army driving a truck, the two Buick girls were waiting for their call-up to the airforce, and the two Jackson boys and the two Simpson boys were up in the islands, we didn't know where. Most of the boys I'd known in Penshurst had gone before I left that little town to enlist.

No, I don't think we were any more patriotic than any other family (in fact, we as a family have none of that in us). What sent us to war was genteel poverty, lack of opportunity, and the never-ending grind of workingclass people – no matter how hard we tried to get along.

Being a 'battler' is, to Australians, akin to having some kind of courageous martyrdom swathed around you while you, the battler, beat your arms like wings to escape the invisible, cobweb chains that bind you. 'Oh, she was a real battler' we would say of my Mother – and this has been said often of Mum, even at her funeral, when discussing her never-ending labour. It meant not to 'get on' but merely to survive, to hold her family together, feed and clothe them decently, give them dignity while avoiding the do-gooders – those whose supposedly 'good works' were always repressing because of their firm belief in the social order of the rulers and the ruled. We, of course, never suffered from 'do-gooders', those who believed that sending the unwanted scraps left from their tables to the starving would find themselves on a pathway to heaven, or perhaps more importantly for them, election to the presidency of the local church guild or sometimes, merely the feeling of superiority when handing down an unwanted thing to another less fortunate.

Mum had none of that in her. When she sent us kids off with a big billy of soup it was the real thing – a thick, gelatinous stock made with lots of shanks, meat covering the bones, split peas, as many vegetables as Dad grew and everything always fresh, never left-overs. 'Tell her I made too much and if she doesn't want it throw it out to her chooks' she'd bid us as we set off down the road. Time after time we did this; sometimes it was cake, but mostly good nutritious stew or soup, and I recall that once it was hot cross buns made with yeast and I could smell the tempting odour all the way down to the woman with three little girls whose father was 'on the wallaby', as Dad described men who were tramping over the countryside looking for work – or escaping their responsibilities.

Living in the bush, the country, outback, woop woop, whatever we called it, had limitations but there were consolations, or so we thought. The smells of a country store of that time have gone: the grain for chooks, and out the back of the shop the currants and sultanas laid out on a piece of wire netting to rid them of weevils, the broken biscuits sold cheap on the counter, wheat ground in a handmill for porridge had a warm delicate odour, nothing packaged, even the sugar weighed out in front of you and the willow pattern china you could get 'free' if you saved coupons from Robur tea.

We had more pets – birds – than anyone I knew and all came to us after they had fallen naked to the ground when trees blew over in a storm or timber cutters rescued them. Mum mothered them by chewing grain and feeding them from mouth to beak. There was a white yellow-crested cockatoo, a Major Mitchell, a rosella, a 'smoker' (now called a Regent parrot) which a travelling priest gave me as well as a printed permit to keep this rare bird. They all lived to a great old age. Chu Chu, the pretty Major Mitchell, was perched on Mum's shoulder one day, nestling her head beneath Mum's curls. It was her favourite perch and she said 'Poor Chu Chu' – and the bird fell, dead. We mourned Chu Chu as the old friend she was. All these birds were free except on warm days when we wanted the doors open to catch any errant breeze and, of course, we children let the menagerie inside.

'The beasts' Mum would call them in a rage, when they used their razor-sharp beaks to chew the furniture, particularly the top of wooden chairs where they would perch like little old ladies and imitate our speech. The yellow-crested white cockatoo used to screech 'You'll get what for!' – and we did. Baby possums were brought to us and once a baby lamb, still wobbling on its feet. Mum raised them all.

A travelling show had a little pig but the owners couldn't train it to do anything at all except squeal when it was fed, so it was left behind for us. We fattened it up in a sty made of railway sleepers, but it escaped before we could kill it for bacon.

Mum accused Dad of purposely letting it escape as Dad was incapable not only of trying to kill a pig, but of hurting any living thing.

We always had at least one cow, sometimes more, and had our own cream and butter and buttermilk for making scones and making our skin soft (well, that's what we believed!). The yellow-crested cockatoo and the Major Mitchell, Chu Chu, would delicately nibble the froth from the top of the separated milk after we had removed the cream. The smoker and the rosella didn't go for that at all, and they didn't sit on the back of Billy, our white horse. But Chu Chu and Cocky did. When they heard Billy neighing with pleasure when Dad took bran and bread to him, they'd bustle off and share the spoils and when that was done they'd sit on Billy's back and pick and crack in their sharp bills: 'goodness only knows what!' as Mum said disapprovingly.

Like many another child, I keep memories of my Mother, not because I want to so much as because I have to: they are there. One memory that comes back to me is when, in later years, I drove her to a bush school back of Drouin where she and her brothers and sisters had gone to school at the close of the last century. She had told me how her father and the fathers of other children there had built the school themselves and the pieces of timber that were left over were given to the children to write on before they were able to buy slates.

This day, when the chairman of the organisation began to read out the names of early pupils of that school dating back to the nineteenth century, Mum startled me. Of course there weren't many people there who had attended that school in the early days, but as they called out the names of Jack Adams and Steve Adams, my mother answered for her dead brothers in Gallipoli in a clear voice: 'Present, sir.' And everyone later said 'She said it just as they would have done.' Mum looked almost joyous, as if she were back in those days when going to school was a very long hike, and the children would be met by their

parents with fern hooks to cut their way back to their home by
a different route each day, in the attempt to rid the land of the
clotted crowd of bracken in that area.

Dad's family were tall men, almost all above six feet and big
withal, except for Dad – the baby of thirteen children, he was
only five feet ten inches. The women were all tall, big-boned
Scots women. Aunt Isabella – Belle or Bella to the immediate
family only – was five feet ten inches, straight as an iron post
and gentle as a flower. In those days, we spoke of adults as aunt,
grandfather, mister and missus, but never by their Christian
names (or 'given names' as we now more aptly say).

Bella had 'married into' the Christadelphian religion. Her
husband, George, who was dead before I was born, was one of
the breakaways from a larger religion because their studies had
shown them another way, one that they believed was the true
path to whatever end they believed was theirs. Aunt Bella,
coming from the pleasantly uninterested-in-religion Adam-Smith
family, followed her man to the new faith and lived in it to
her death.

They built on Phillip Island in Westernport Bay and, here in
the tiny front room, they had shelves of books, all dealing with
religion, and I could go in there at any time to sit and read, a
thing I couldn't do at home as we had no books. The subject
matter didn't interest me much, but the beautiful use of language,
the choice of words, phrases and sentences was exposed, and I
submerged. On a separate shelf I came on a collection of simple
little privately printed books, all, of course, in religious vein.
The goodness of these people was manifest in their works. One
story of Gippsland adherents to the faith told of waiting in the
wilderness for their preacher to arrive, a man they called their
Brother. They had no church but were all gathered out in the
open under the gum trees, and they heard their Brother riding
through the ancient forest, singing as he came, ' ... the Good
Book in one hand, his horses reins in the other'.

The sincerity conjured up set me thinking about how many of us were wondering what and how and why we got here and do we go on to anywhere? But there came no answer. This aunt and uncle had no such problems, they never doubted. Sophistication, simplicity or intellect told me nothing that could solve the riddle, and I wasn't a being who could see or even imagine heavenly visions. Heaven was here and now. It may all have been so different if I could have seen – something.

In most ways this was a different household and ambience from any I had known. This family was *very* poor, the grey four-roomed square wooden cottage had no verandahs, no paint anywhere, not ever, bare wooden scrubbed floors, 'scrim' walls – newspaper stuck on to hessian were the room dividers. When aunt was dying the doctor came out from Cowes and he read the walls while Mum made him a cup of tea. 'Murder, love, despair, they're all here' he said. There was an outside washhouse where the horse harness hung, and where was kept the tin hip-bath that was carried into the kitchen on Saturday evenings. When we were visiting we took turns washing one another's back.

The lavatory was, according to my sister Kathleen, a bloody mile away, and we always formed a party to trek off with the lantern through the nights that seemed so dark and spooky with the koalas, that were in great numbers on the island, either grunting and thumping and roaring in their ever-sexy uproarious nights or crying so badly they sounded like babes lost in the bush. Indeed, first-time visitors would wake aunt through the night, insisting that a baby had been abandoned in the tree-filled bush. Some years later Dad and Mum moved the lavatory nearer the house, after filling in the six-foot hole at the old site. They dug a new hole for the wooden-paling sentry box to sit over. Dad christened it Parliament House and the name stuck, even aunt smiling gently at the title.

My parents later bought this property and ran the tiny, uneconomic dairy farm that was up the hill. Mum had this farm when I came home from the war. I loved it. She had always wanted to get back to the farming life she had been born into, and this wee, grey wooden cottage suited her well. My eye can still flash back to the charm of watching her wandering, in one of her always-bright dresses, down among the myriad flowers, shrubs and trees to the Hakea Arbour – and I swiftly stencilled on my memory that title which seemed so exotic.

The arbour consisted of five hakeas, all in deep bloom and carpeting the ground beneath. There was an unintentionally rustic seat made from one slab of wood resting on two tree trunks. There was always a running fight between sitters and growth or, as Dad said, 'Turn your back and more trees will sprout on that seat.'

But the truly unforgettable thing was the whole garden. There had once been long fences down either side and the back of the house, the fourth side being the waters of the bay. But the fences were no longer in view, hidden as they were in eight-feet deep walls of flowers, trees, shrubs, fruit trees and creepers. A memory remains of Kathleen and me, when we were children, crawling in under these great hedges, lying upside down and eating the white-fleshed peaches and the plums that had got to be part of this 'fence'. We'd scrabble in anywhere along its length and disappear among the wonderland that Aunt Bella called 'God's Benison'; the words sang in my head.

The purple buddleias were mixed up with blue plumbago and white lilac, lemon-scented verbena, herbs, red cherries, and white berries I never heard called by any name. Standing beside me one day Mum casually whispered the names of almost seventy varieties of flowers. In that garden all fought for recognition and they all won.

This richness had not come only by way of cuttings and roots from friends. When I was a little girl Aunt Bella told me she and her Sisters and Brothers (whom I understood to be the friends in her faith) did not use artificial fertilisers or sprays. Indeed, nothing could be called artificial in this woman's home, but she and her Sisters believed in 'propagating the beautiful gifts God gave us'. Thus they sought to give beautiful gifts to the earth. This house and the land had been named 'Ahava', a place of great peace, we were told, according to the Old Testament, and the nameplate of 'Ahava' was given to me later and is fixed on my own housefront.

The Duchess and Kathleen

BEFORE I WENT TO THE war I had travelled widely in the State of Victoria with my parents, living in tiny, isolated railway settlements. I was sometimes called 'the Duchess' by my parents.

The Duchess spent her childhood trying not to offend, to be invisible, which is tough when she was born an extrovert. Moving to a new settlement and unknown settlers and schools, with old feuds, habits and standards that were always unknown to us on arrival, was always a tense time. Of course, when Kathleen was still at school I had the world champion boxer-wrestler of all time at my side for protection, but with her being seven years older than me, and the school leaving age being fourteen, I did not enjoy her patronage for long. And being small I was unable to emulate her prowess in the ring.

Whenever I used a word not common in our surrounds, repeated some story I had thought beautiful, made a gesture with my hands or body, or admired anything that children in their ken did not do, my act was aped and the cry rang out: 'Oh! Hark at the Duchess!' To counter this I learnt slang and swearing and cursing, and had a repertoire that few country people to this day could enlarge on. Because of this 'bold' talk, as Mum called it, I was in trouble at home, and at the little schools I became feared because of my quick, sharp tongue which was the only weapon available to me.

The Duchess did try not to offend, not to be an extrovert, not to put forward solutions to anything until someone else stepped forward and then she could often manage, without stepping on anyone's toes, to proffer an easier or better way to approach a problem, even if it were only the words of a certain song. And that behaviour is real tough if you are a bouncy person. And I was: a 'goer' as the saying went. At little country schools I planned concerts and wrote programmes which included dances, songs, recitations, group and solo performances and poetry readings, and coaxed the teacher to allow us to present these entertainments in the school.

These 'concerts' must have been appalling. I can't remember anything about those at school, but I do remember one of my 'concerts' at our house which, at that time, was right on the railway platform at Monomeith. I drove our milking cow in through the side gate, singing:

Why has a cow got four legs?
I really don't know how,
I don't know, and you don't know,
And neither does the cow!

and by this time I had driven the milker out the back gate and later returned for my bow. I guess this was probably the standard set in my irregular eruptions of art. Mick Yates from Caldermeade railway station was often hauled in to perform in my plays when his mother, a station mistress, was visiting my station-mistress Mother. The ladies hopped on and off trains as if they were taking taxi rides in the cities! I could never get Kathleen to join my act and she has not been to a theatre, ballet or opera to this day and lives perfectly happily without such frills in her life.

From Monomeith railway siding we were only a few miles from Koo-wee-rup, a tiny town, but at least a town – which Monomeith was not. (Monomeith was only us.) At Koo-wee-rup I saw a musical, my first theatrical entertainment. Mum took me in on the railway 'trike' – in officialese a 'manual tricycle' – with her propelling by pushing and pulling the handbars (and sweating) and me sitting side-saddle on the back of the trolley. There was an element of danger here, because this line was busier than others we had lived on and men had to use manual power, not motors or a Casey Jones, to enable them to hear a steam train which may, because of some emergency, not have been scheduled. Outside Koo-wee-rup Mum pulled the trike off the rails and we set off on foot to the performance.

The title of the musical was 'Wait till the Sun Shines, Nellie', or something like that, and I recall the chorus sang 'We'll make hay while the sun shines, and make love when it rains', which appears a little more risque than one would imagine for the 1930s. 'Oh, take me where the daisies cover the country lane. We'll make hay while the sun shines . . . ' etc. And when it was over we went back to the rail line and Mum manoeuvred the iron three-wheeler back on to the tracks and off we set for home, singing 'We'll make love when it rains', and laughing and retelling the jokes which doubtless were corny but we repeated them for months.

In that same year my Mother carried me on her back from Flinders Street railway station to Melbourne University where I was to sit for an Australian Music Examination Board exam. Some weeks before the examination I had been running along the parapet of a railway bridge, lost my balance and fell off, tumbling down to the dry creek bed below. My ankle was badly sprained and ligaments were torn and I could not walk or lower the grossly swollen limb for some months. In the meantime, I had prepared for this piano examination and we knew we may not be so close to a city by the time the next exams would be held, so we went to Melbourne by train, my crippled leg sticking out like a fallen tree trunk. When we reached Flinders Street station, Mum asked for directions to 'The University' (there was only one university in Victoria in those days), and we set off, me clinging to her back, my arms around her neck and legs around her waist, and she bent over. After a while she had to put me down and 'have a blow', and then she set off again through the throng of city people who averted their eyes as though we were a freak show. Time and again she had to rest. We didn't speak. Once I tried to hop on one leg but this jarred the injury and I screamed. I don't know how far it is from the station to the university but there are quite a few tram stops but nobody thought to tell us then about the tram and, once Mum had set off, it was too late because, like a heavy-labouring man she had no energy left for brain-storming, she could afford only to remember to force her legs to keep going one after the other along that seemingly never-ending pavement. I look back now and remember this day some sixty years ago with a sort of horror that makes me feel faint and terribly sick.

I can remember the exhaustion of trying to hang on to Mum and even as a child knowing her own effort might kill her but knowing she'd never give up. She'd never given up any labour that needed to be done, the whole of her five-foot frame straining until she righted the problem, especially if it was to do with her children or her husband. So she was unlikely to give up this day.

Lindsay Biggins, the fine musician and examiner, discovered us sitting on the steps of the conservatorium, Mum's pretty hair dishevelled, her face pouring sweat as though it were rain. It is this woman I write about. Her actions may bewilder a person today, but she was unique, even in her day. When something occurred that she could not handle, was not able to carry on her back and she sensed harm of any degree to her children, she attacked like a lioness, but this wasn't always clear to outsiders – or to us children.

My title, 'the Duchess', was endowed on me when I screamed in fury 'I'm not going to scrub floors!' It was not only a social crime – there were outsiders visiting us at the time – but worse. Mum knew what I meant. Every girl we ever knew in our milieu went 'to work', and the only work that was available for women in the bush was housework or, as it was often called, 'being a slushy'.

'I'm not going to scrub floors!' There was no time for silence or shock. Mum had leapt up as if she had expected this. 'The Duchess, eh? Too big for your boots to scrub floors, eh?' And all the while she shouted it I knew it was something else that contorted her voice and twisted her face: she knew there was no other employment and there was no more schooling for me. I would have to go out as a slushy. Had we been alone it wouldn't have boiled over like this, she may have discussed it, said it wasn't real flash but what else was there? But now the lines were drawn. I screamed 'I'm not going to scrub floors!'

I had often scrubbed floors, like anyone brought up in a workingclass household, and thought nothing of it. All houses had a floor cloth, a very poor rag indeed for anything less ragged would have been put to better use. Down on your knees on the floor with grey, home-made soap which had been left on the splintery board that served as a shelf in the washhouse until it was hard as rock. The soap was made of old fat and lye and fit to take the skin off the hands as well as dirt off and out of the bare wood floor. It even wrecked the linoleum that was cut to fit so many different houses we lived in that eventually it would fit nowhere and congoleum was bought as times were hard, and when the next move came it proved its lack of mettle by refusing to be rolled into a cylinder and cracked across every fold. 'Cheap stuff,' Mum snapped in the frustration of loss.

But now I would stop. 'I'm not going to scrub floors.' It was a sort of inarticulate cry that had nothing to do with the scrubbed floor but more with the indignity and the sense that childhood could end at this point.

And I never did scrub floors, not for any but my own.

Kathleen and I couldn't have been more dissimilar. Most people meeting us refer to it – at their peril, for we two may appear to have nothing at all in common but any outsider who comments on it leaves with scars from both of us.

Writing didn't come easily to our Kathleen, but she was once moved to send news to Mum. 'Old Bill Leaf about a week ago.' It took Mum weeks of delicate enquiry to learn 'old Bill Leaf' had died.

Because she came into the family seven years before me she had some good years before the depression when there was enough money to have her taught music, voice production, Scottish dancing and what passed for ballet. But she had no talent for these things. Mum tried to get her to teach me the piano when she was seventeen and I was ten. We sat at the wooden-framed Bord piano. 'Put your finger here.' 'Which finger?' 'Any finger. Now: A B C D E F G H I J K L M N O P ...' and so my finger went to the end of the alphabet and the keyboard, and that was the last lesson I received from Kathleen.

When we were grown and away from home I didn't correspond with her greatly, she not at all with me. The roses didn't leave Kathleen's cheeks, they didn't 'fade away and die' as the old song says; her voice was never sad, it was often strident, barbing me until I screamed in temper. I cried but she didn't cry, I could never say that in her lifetime I saw 'tears bedim her loving eyes'. Not in the deep sense. Except, years later, at Mum's funeral where she stood weeping tears that fell like a waterfall and she could not control the flow. And her mourning was painful and long.

Mum loved company. We played and sang every Sunday evening around the piano and always included 'I will take you home Kathleen', the haunting melody with the tender lament. Kathleen had no singing in her, couldn't hold a tune or recognise one. I had and could, but didn't sing this song, couldn't see through the tears to read the notes so I played by memory. 'I will take you home Kathleen' I vowed over and over and over again. I didn't know then and I don't know now what it meant to me.

She had a rage in her. Her elder brother, Jack, (well, that's a puzzle, that is) became so insane with her behaviour one day when visiting us he chased her with a log of wood – which was his undoing and her saving. The log inhibited his speed and movement and after her head was split open she escaped and hid until Mum came home. Her taunting extended to teachers, aunts (she once belted Aunt Vera to the floor with her fists and Vera was a big woman), and me; which meant I got beaten for screaming and clawing at her while she, much taller, older and stronger, held me at arm's length. 'I don't know what's got into her' she'd say to Mum, who then got into me. But in a way for which there are no words, she was my champion. I don't know what she saw me as, perhaps just a little girl, although that can't be the only reason. When I was grown she would still protect me. Would do so to this day. We were all each of us had, and I still cannot hear that beautiful, sad refrain without tears bedimming my own eyes.

> I will take you home again Kathleen
> Across the ocean wild and wide
> To where your heart has ever been . . .

One night when Kathleen was away our gentle Dad said, as if in a dream, 'None of us will ever know what is in Kathleen's heart or where it has been.' And he was a man who loved her dearly for her madcap carryings-on and her courage and stalwart stance when life was not the thing the romantics say the bush and the depression were.

> But I will take you back Kathleen
> To where your heart will feel no pain
> For when the fields are fresh and green
> I will take you to your home, Kathleen.

But she found her home without my help, although she still

gives me hers. Her marriage – not her early marriage to Bob which was lost in the war – but her young man who came back from the war still a scallywag, a laugher, but with a severe speech problem from some shock he never speaks of, fracturing his words into a staccato stutter that was doubtless painful for him but painful too to those of us who tried to understand him because we couldn't help him. I knew Kathleen and he had each met their match when he came in one day and tried to tell her there was a market stall being set up outside their house. But we couldn't understand what he was saying. I tried the conventional 'it's alright' sympathy, which was quite wrong and made him angry and his stuttering worse. Kathleen showed no sympathy at all. She laughed with what seemed glee. 'Well then, let's make money,' she said. 'We'll set up a stall for the poor stuttering old soldier.' He stared, then began to laugh, they began to wrestle, I was laughing, we were shouting, near crying with mirth at the absurdity. It wasn't medical science that cured him of his affliction, it was Kathleen, over the years of teasing him, imitating him and both of them carrying on like ten-year-olds laughing, pushing one another around, having a beer, wedded as if they were Siamese twins. Now they are in their seventies but when they were younger they came out with some quite original hilarity to do with sex, never grubby but always side-splitting. From listening to them I learnt what ribald fun sex was. And also, what true love was.

And yet, for all that, there are odd, always unexpected moments when we two women – now so far away from harm, protected by friends and our children – can see 'the passing shadow on your brow' and we avert our eyes.

We are careful, we do not ever stand on a battleground or take up weapons, we never vent spleen. I sometimes wonder if she recalls the line, the haunting song:

I will take you back, Kathleen,
To where your heart will feel no pain.

Perhaps she has found that place but I never knew it. Perhaps it was only me looking for someone to take me home. But now I know no one does that. And why should they? We must each find our own way home.

And a life without Kathleen would have been no life at all for me.

Goodbye Girlie

THE WIVES AND MOTHERS AND fathers and the children on No. 2 platform at Spencer Street railway station, Melbourne, began to wave and cry out to us and to sing:

You are my sunshine, my only sunshine;
You make me happy, though skies are grey.
You'll never know dear,
How much I miss you,
Please don't take my sunshine away.

The civilians sang all the while as the long troop train began to pull out slowly from the empty No. 1 platform where no civilians were permitted when troops were being moved.

The other night dear,
While I lay sleeping,
I dreamed I held you in my arms.
When I awoke dear,
I was mistaken,
And I hung my head and I cried.
You are my sunshine . . .

The Regimental Transport Officer (we knew him as the RTO) and his men had directed the groups of naval men, army, airforce, nursing sisters and us – enlisted VADs (nursing aides) –

to the sections of the train that we would occupy for many days and nights to come as the steam train rattled northwards.

Many of us were escapees, young men and women happy to be leaving behind the memories of the depression, that period that had almost wrung the pride out of us, some of us were under-age, all of us were glad to be leaving.

There was little disorder, each of our groups had been given their marching orders before being bussed in, men in trucks and steam trains, nurses and aides in ambulances, each of us kitted out with tin helmet, gas mask, kit-bag, shoulder bag, waterproof ground-sheet, and emergency rations, as well as a small, splendid leather suitcase. And, coming from a heavy tea-drinking family, I had tied on to my kit-bag a 'silver' teapot – 'EPNS to prove it', as Matron said when she looked for the brand – and smiled as she came along the corridor to see we were safely packed in.

And packed we were. Some girls had already climbed·up and claimed the string-bottomed luggage racks, but they eventually swapped with us tinier, younger girls; there was much to be said for being small, nippy, fit and young in the army. As for the teapot, it stood me in good stead for the whole of my army days and I have it still, the broad-based, non-drip, sensible style symbolic of the great days of railway refreshment rooms.

There was scarcely room to move in the carriages, the floor was thick with kit-bags, the floor of the corridors just as deeply covered with gas masks, tin helmets and the rest strung up wherever we could manage. And then we were off to 'Somewhere in Australia', as we had been ordered to tell our parents to address our mail.

These were the singing days, days before television, video, and a-radio-in-every-household took the joy from the voice and threw it back canned. But in 1941 the families and friends were still singing:

Wish me luck as you wave me goodbye.
Not a tear, mother dear, make it gay.

Give me a smile
I can keep all the while,
In my heart while I'm away.
Till we meet once again, you and I.
Wish me luck as you wave me goodbye.

The train moved slowly. It was long and heavily laden, and it took a time to clear the platform. All troop movements were supposed to be secret but relatives invaded No. 2 platform at Spencer Street whenever a troop train steamed out. Coming from the bush, I had no one to see me off so I didn't push my head through the open windows to look out on to that platform like everyone else did. I looked out on to platform No. 1, empty now except for the station master. 'Good luck,' he called. As the train gathered speed he shouted 'Goodbye Girlie!' And he waved to me until I was swallowed up by distance. And only then did I know I was free.

The Second World War provided the greatest escape route in history for women and girls, while at the same time it exacted the most repressive and restrictive time for most young married women who were left at home with small children. I was one of the lucky ones – young, unmarried – I escaped. Kathleen had two tiny tots, one born just before the war, the other a few months after her husband, Bob, left for the war. Some readers of my earliest work (*Hear the Train Blow*) have written that the story of Bob in that book is the most poignant reminder of what the depression had been. When every attempt for a job had failed, Bob had got one day's work at a timber mill and, at the end of that day, put his hand under the circular saw and lost his index finger. With the almost £100 insurance money he and Kathleen were able to move out of our railway house into a two-room cottage on a rocky knoll on the outskirts of Penshurst, with enough money to pay rent and be assured of growing enough food 'until things get better'. But, as hindsight tells us, things didn't get better, but the war came and that was good enough. For many, it was their escape route from boredom, poverty and the fear that things would never change.

Unlike Vera Brittain, the celebrated, upperclass, young English writer who went to war in 1915 as a nursing VAD, I did not experience 'exasperation' at the breaking out of war in 1939. Vera Brittain saw her war, at the beginning, 'as an interruption of the most exasperating kind to personal plans'. She was 'going up' to Oxford. I, twenty-five years later, was trapped in the depression and was going nowhere. Like many another of my class and generation, I saw the war as my only escape, and I enlisted in the army as a nursing VAD as she had done a generation before me. Her book, *Testament of Youth* was my lodestar.

The only things we two young women had in common was that neither of us, at the beginning, saw our war becoming a superlative tragedy, and both of us perversely volunteered to serve in the most menial toil. And both of us lost lovers. Beyond that, we had nothing in common – or perhaps everything.

Being a VAD (Volunteer Aide Detachment) was an anomalous position. Like army nursing sisters, we enlisted in the Australian Army and could be sent overseas, but we were under the auspices of an organisation that had originally been formed in England.

Our leader had the title of Commandant. The Lady Commandant, a First World War nursing sister, Alice Appleford, was married to the Doctor Appleford at Lang Lang who 'fixed' my ankle when I fell off the parapet of the railway bridge when I was eleven years old, and so I knew her when she began recruiting girls for the VAD in Melbourne. She most certainly would have known my real age as she knew my Mother well, but nevertheless she enrolled me, one year under-age. Yes, I would study and get my First Aid and Home Nursing Certificates (in June 1941), plus working, 'getting in' 100 hours in a civilian hospital after my daily work. We country girls scarcely needed a reference: our community was our judge.

I'd already seen most of the young boys in the area escape by rushing off to war and I determined I would go too. There was a tiny private hospital in Penshurst, run by two sisters who were qualified nurses and midwives. Yes, they said, I could do the initial training as an aide here (after my eight-hour working day), and the 100 hours were spent mostly emptying pans and bottles and making beds, as well as studying for the certificates.

I went down to Gippsland where Mum, Dad, Kathleen and her toddlers were now living, and got a job in Wilkinson's grocery shop in Warragul. Mr Wilkinson asked me for assurances that I would not be enlisting. 'They just come to me until they're old enough to enlist and off they go as if they have heard a bugle blow.' 'Oh, not me,' I lied. But I had already enlisted and was waiting for my call-up, as had most of his employees under the age of forty.

But then, nothing happened. Months went by. I saw photographs in the Melbourne *Sun* of 'VADs Leaving For Middle East'. A double-page spread. It seemed forever, then my time came, I was ordered to report to an office in Melbourne, swore the oath of something-or-other, told I would be called up shortly, and sent off to the Myer store to have my uniforms tailored. We were being rushed now, hurried.

The uniform was very smart: white shirt, navy-blue straight skirt, belted jacket with a woven Red Cross on our breast pocket, classic felt hat with Rising Sun badge, black shoes, small soft leather clutch-bag and gloves, tie and grey stockings. Pale blue uniforms were worn in wards, and we had a fine blue mess dress for evening. On each shoulder were fastened the solid metal flashes AUSTRALIA, beneath these were our felt colour patches, the symbol of the battalion or, in our case, the hospital to which we belonged (the pale grey background indicated those of us who had enlisted to go overseas, as opposed to those who would remain in hospitals back home).

No one who has not been in the services could possibly know the tenacity with which men and women held to their colour patches, even to the degree that, on occasions, if one was transferred to another battalion permission was given for miniatures of one's original battalion or hospital to be worn as well as the new colour patch.

Insisting on miniature colour patches was, perhaps, a type of esprit d'corps, but beneath it was the ridiculous I'm-better-than-you syndrome. An example of this was if one returned from service from the Middle East and was then detailed to an army hospital that had not been away from Australia. That would have appeared 'infra dig' – it was vastly pucka to have been 'O/S', so the new patch was sewn on – and the miniature as well. Some of us moved around so many hospitals that, if we were silly about it, we could have had patches from wrist to armpit.

Behind and beyond this was a cruel jibe (but what is war but a cruel jibe at mankind?). Some men and women who had attempted to join up were unacceptable, usually because of health or infirmity. Some had been 'man-powered' and could not get a clearance. To many in the army this was seen as shirking – 'He could have got in if he wanted, could have gone over the border and told a good story there and got himself in.'

(As late as June 1993 I received a sad letter from a woman who said her husband had died recently, 'but he had really died many years ago'. He had gone in to enlist but was refused 'owing to being in a protected service – munitions'. 'He never got over it, he always felt people saw him as a shirker. And many did. He couldn't join the RSL, he felt an outsider. He carried the stigma for life.')

When we first came into the service we were billeted in a great Toorak mansion which had been turned over by the owners for the duration of the war. While I was there, waiting for my uniforms to be tailored, my Mother was permitted to visit and Aunt Anastasia came down from the country with her. Aunt had been out to visit her daughters, Victoria and Margaret, who had enlisted in the airforce. Mum was quite cock-a-hoop at seeing the opulent quarters in which her little girl was billeted, crystal chandeliers and all, while Anastasia's girls were in 'a stockade', as Mum described the spartan quarters those early aircraftswomen had to survive when they first enlisted. If Mum had seen some of my later quarters she wouldn't have been so cocky.

The VAD in charge of the hostel told me to 'run the hot water' to wash the dishes. Run the water? She must be pulling my leg! As far as I knew hot water came from a kettle on the wood-fire stove or, if for a bath, from the big copper in the washhouse outside in the back yard. 'It will take a while for the hot water to come through' Betsy told me as she left. I waited, wincing as the thick stream of sparkling clean water poured away down the sink and was wasted. I stuck my finger in a few times as water poured out of the tap, but it was still cold as I knew it would be – how could *hot* water come out of a tap unless the tank was out in the blazing sun, as it was back home up-country in summer? No wrigglers in this water! I waited. God knows how long I waited, but when Betsy came back she snapped, said, 'Oh, it must be turned off, don't just stand there!' I knew I looked a fool but didn't know what I had done wrong, didn't know what had been turned off. I felt like every country child has at some time felt: the universe no longer centred around the bush and it never would again for me. I grew up and exchanged one way of life for another, quick smart.

If I had thought anything at all about the army except as a place to escape to, I could never have guessed what a total change it would be from my life up to that time – for any girl's life, for that matter, because this war was the first that enlisted women other than trained nursing sisters into the services. In one sense you forgot your mother, father, sister and brother because they were now in the past and you were no longer under their control or within their ambit. You were under the total control of a machine that owned and operated you. There was no longer such talk as, 'I'll do that later, Mum.' You did it – 'Now!' There was no answering back – that got you detention in barracks. And there was much more along those lines.

You were now a number and required to recite it when called upon. Few men or women can forget their service number, it stayed tattooed in our memory forever. We women had to wear our identity discs around our necks on a leather thong, as did the men, the only difference being that the letter F for female was now added to the women's identification letters, that is, I was VFX: V for enlistment in the State of Victoria, F for female, X for volunteer for enlistment for overseas service. (My friend, Phyllis, had a heart murmur on enlistment, so was denied overseas service, her disc registering only VF.) Some called the discs 'dog tags', others 'dead-meat tickets'. They were durable and would last forever under any conditions: the shower, the sweat of the tropics, or be readable for identification on dead bodies.

There was a marvellous and ridiculous use of words, language and titles in the services. When I was at 108 AGH (Australian General Hospital) at Ballarat there were WAGS and BAGS courses for airmen – Wireless Air Gunners and Bombing Air Gunners – and these lively lads, 'Blue Orchids' as the PBI (poor bloody infantry) called them because of their smart blue uniforms, didn't really swagger as the infantry swore they did. When it was their turn to get a jab in the arm or the backside before leaving for overseas, all men were equal: as many tough infantry men fell flat to the floor as did the Blue Orchids before the needle went in, and many fell while merely standing well back in the line awaiting their turn.

We VADs did nothing courageous, left no mark showing that we had even been there, had worked so hard for such long hours and days and years but no, nothing marks where we had been. But like many other groups in that war and all other stupid wars, *we were there*.

In a period when a girl left her father's home only to go to her husband's home, these thousands of women in the navy, army and airforce had pioneered the greatest new movement in our history.

In one sense we girls were the lowest rank, but in another we were remarkable. You can't dismiss a bevy, a great big mob of young, healthy, fit girls, many in love with someone 'over there', and all believing they were, by their labour, perhaps helping men survive.

Them
and Us

WHEN I WAS EVENTUALLY CALLED up to report to the army doctor he said 'Right!' like a rifle shot, signed my medical record A1, and that was that. I was then taken to the army dentist and he whipped out my four front teeth from my upper gum. It was so painful at first I didn't have a thought for the terrible thing done to me, until I saw my face in the mirror. 'I thought you were going to fill my front teeth!' But, 'No, we don't do that for overseas enlistments.' It seemed that an army doesn't want a soldier who may be incapacitated with toothache at a time of great turmoil and movement. Had I not been enlisted for overseas service they would have filled the cavities. Instead, they put in a temporary plate where my own seventeen-year-old teeth had been and told me to go back to work, leaving the plate in my mouth for three days and nights. By the third day every patient I leant over must have near fainted from the stench. I mourned those lost teeth, and the replacements were no restitution. I wanted to write a letter about it but Sister Kirk said no one would bother, I must bear it, even if I didn't grin. 'They are "missing on active service"' Sister said of my wailing complaints of my loss.

We were billeted all over the pretty little city of Ballarat. I was dumped out of an ambulance into a private house, and the woman hadn't expected me at all: 'You've got a spare bedroom,' the sergeant accompanying us told her. 'My son is at the war' she replied, but she had to take me in, like it or not. Of course

I didn't mind at all; it was my first time 'out on the loose' by myself. The householder had no say in what I did, the army didn't bother to see what I did, so I did what I liked whenever the ambulance dropped me back at my billet after work (and sometimes that was after a ten-hour shift). A quick shower and I'd be off out the gate.

For these first few weeks of hectic settlement, although the hours were long and we worked hard, I had found heaven. There was no overt discipline and no one knew where we went once we left the hospital. Coming from a strict teetotal family I, of course, went straight to the hotels. These were the days of six o'clock closing, but our long day's work meant we weren't in public houses during the day. However, the back doors were open for servicemen and women for as long as the customers or liquor flowed. It didn't damage me at all, it merely taught me how to survive in such a society and a strong, young constitution can weather any amount of punishment. Times were different, and I never heard of a servicewoman being either hassled or violated.

We moved from our scattered billets to a large home, which must have made life easier for the ambulance drivers who had to pick us up for our shifts. (Were there any of the great homes left untramped by the army for those six years?) One of our own VADs ran the whole group of us as housekeeper and commander. There were twelve girls to a room, and I never heard a sound after we got into our hard beds, we were always exhausted.

First night, word came from Matron that a convoy of Americans was coming into the hospital and we were to return to work, to hop to it and wash and run all night. We'd none of us met Americans. We weren't too thrilled about it. 'Got in when they were pushed in' was the saying, referring to their tardiness in entering the war. The following night we arrived back at the home a little earlier, and six of us were promptly told off to accompany six American marines to an American Army concert – as a show of compatibility between the two nations,

I suppose. Matron turned up to see we were properly turned out in our blue neck-to-knee mess dresses and relatively high black heeled shoes. Even with this lift I could not have been compatible with my partner: he was six feet seven inches tall. I was five feet. Everyone laughed as we stood to meet these nattily dressed men. He was shy, horribly nervous, so I put my arm through his – 'Enough of that, nurse!' snapped Matron, and I took my arm away.

The concert was held in a big drill hall with a splendid USA Marine band playing. This night, we Australian girls heard for the first time the song 'Elmer's Tune'. 'Why are the stars always prancing and dancing around?' and the shy giant whispered, 'We brought the tune over with us. It's new.' I was offended. I didn't want an American to tell me they knew more than us. 'We've been in the war a long time. We haven't had time to compose songs!' Oh God. Even as I heard it coming out I winced, and began to apologise. 'No', he said, 'You're proud of your country. Our own country is always the best.' I tried to thank him but we were shushed as the music tumbled on and we never spoke of it again. We six girls shook hands with our partners at the door of the billets and went to bed to be ready for the quarter to six ambulance call.

A few weeks later things loosened up a little and I remember one night very well. I was with some of the girls in our rest room brushing my hair when two American officers were ushered in, with invitations to a mess dinner. One immediately took my hair-brush and began, most expertly, to brush my very thick hair. 'I always brushed my sister's hair back home' he said. He couldn't have been much older than me. He came from Butte, Montana.

Years later, in 1980, I was researching in America and was passing through Butte, Montana, so I asked the local paper if it were likely we could meet. I was there for only that one night, I must work all next day on official papers and be away on the evening Greyhound bus. And in the charming way Americans do these things, they produced the man, his wife and children. 'The Hair Dresser!' he announced, and in front of his family we had a cuddle and a kiss – which was far more than we would have managed forty years ago.

One of our girls had been gathering autographs on her cotton dressing gown, and would then embroider the name, which I thought to be a rather daring thing to be carrying around, and I bet Matron would have thought so too if she had heard of it. But our supervisor was a sensible, accomplished woman and ran a tight billet. The boy from Butte asked if I remembered the girl whose gown he had autographed and she was to sew. But, like so much we had forgotten, I didn't even remember her name. I was probably miffed, probably bloody annoyed in fact, because I had begun needlework autographs on a luncheon cloth and this now appeared a pale thing against a dressing gown!

Until they got their own hospitals going we had American patients, and I once went by train to Melbourne and met, by arrangement, a young American GI on a day's leave from our hospital. He was irritable, irritated by his uniform rubbing the burn scars on his back, the day was hot, and he pushed his cap back just as an American army provost patrol came along. They snapped at him for being 'unofficially dressed' or for one of the many stupidities of army etiquette, and he snapped back. They could see his wound stripes but they, with no service chevrons, decided to bully. With my usual quick temper tamped down to sweetness I said, 'Please sergeant, I'm taking him back to hospital. This is my job.' Me! The lowest pan handler 'taking' anyone anywhere! But it worked and we plodded off, the day ruined. We went to the movie we had planned to see, but as we entered the already seated audience saw our distinctly different uniforms and began to sing 'When a boy from Alabama meets a girl from Gundagai', the latest Jack O'Hagen song – a 'hit'. 'Very soon they're walking out together, a new day has begun.' That embarrassed us and we sat rigid, not even opening the candy he had got specially from the American canteen for me. At interval we left, took an early train back and parted at the railway station, he to travel back in a US ambulance, me to wait until a tram came by. I don't recall meeting again. I imagine those years were like that for most people.

In 1987 I was interviewing Jack O'Hagen for a TV documentary I was doing for the BBC and told Jack the story. 'Poor children' he said, holding my hand. I told him we were never desolate. We lived for the day, in all truth, that is what we all did. We moved, always suddenly, and I never again met American servicemen although I later often saw them when I came down to Brisbane. Out of a lopsided loyalty to our own men, whose uniform looked poor against the extraordinarily splendid American uniform, I refused to dance with them, or indeed, to acknowledge them in any way. So much for partners in wartime! When we would have to go through Brisbane on 'marching orders' to somewhere else, we always had to stay overnight and embark on another train in the morning, and so we had the night free. We always went to the Brisbane Town Hall dance, with its unique circular dance floor. Here the 'Yanks' – as we disdainfully said – were jitter-bugging. We, who spent our war years away from big cities, had not learnt this dance. Neither had the Australian servicemen. Naturally, we therefore all agreed it was disgusting.

THE VAD's 'IF'
by 'One of Them'

If you can work all day without your make-up,
Your snappy hairdo hidden 'neath your veil,
If you can serve up umpteen dozen dinners,
Then wait on Matron without turning pale;
If you can wash the everlasting dishes,
And then turn round and wash the trolley too,
And when your mess jobs are all finished,
Tidy up your tent for inspection and review.

If you can track down your elusive orderlies,
And make them help you when they'd rather shirk;
If you can run on countless errands for the Sister,
And still be up to date with all your work,
If you can make the orange drinks and egg flips,
About the diets knowing all there is to tell,
And get the MO's morning tea and heat a poultice,
And maybe sponge a man or two as well.

If you can take a 'ticking off' from Matron,
And realise she doesn't mean it – much,
If you can bear to see your rec. leave vanish
When you thought you had it safely in your clutch,
If you can take the trials and tribulations,
The good times and the bad all in your stride,
If you can do all this and keep good tempered,
Then you're not a VAD, but a saint who hasn't died!

Thinking back, I believe we young women in this quite humble and laborious VAD service could never, then or now, have gathered together a greater group of women than we had in those years.

The system of using VADs worked smoothly and well. Our Commandant in each State cared for us and saw us as *her* girls. From this distance in time it could be seen as an exclusive group, and it was in one sense: all had volunteered to work under any circumstances and hours under the discipline of army orders. There never was any need for discipline - mostly because we had all enlisted in our home town areas where everyone knew one another, or in the case of city girls, were known to the group they had enlisted with. We were proud of our distinctive uniform and shoulder flashes and Red Cross on the upper arm.

And then, in 1942, an announcement: we were to discard all VAD uniforms and the bits and pieces that went with them and don khaki. You could almost imagine you heard the cry go up from Hobart to Port Douglas and across to Darwin. No! We most certainly wouldn't change our uniforms. Khaki! Even the men of our hospitals were against it. We were adamant. We would stay with our time-honoured uniform. We were still outraged when the next blow hit: we were to go into Darley training camp in Victoria, as did the soldiers and the service-women, and we were to learn to march and, God help us, salute.

I honestly tried. To salute you had to take a swing of the arm and elbow that could decapitate a stander-by; and worse, you could almost tear out an eye with the nail of your middle finger with no difficulty at all – I bore witness to this. For the whole of the three weeks we tottered up and down the parade ground my bloodshot eye was bloody, hideous and embarrassing. Everyone, including the poor First-World-War sergeant-major whose charges we were, did a poor job of sympathising. There was more, worse, and everyone said 'But how did you manage to do that?' How would I know how I did it? I thought I'd executed a perfect about-turn. I didn't do it on purpose, as many accused me. None recognised that I had believed I would surprise them all – including the sergeant-major – with my dexterity. When four or five girls fell to the ground I had assumed it was their doing, not mine.

I didn't have time to wreck any other army convolutions for the following day we, the staff of the First Orthopaedic Hospital, were marshalled and told to be ready at 6 am the following morning to entrain to go north and set up our hospital in Queensland. That night, Phyllis, my mate, and I had an unplanned celebration behind the latrines. Phyl's mother had died recently and her father was remarrying and Phyl had been given the day off to attend the wedding. This sudden remarriage had upset the young girl greatly. That night on her return she smuggled in a bottle of champagne and a cake and we had a secret party. In retrospect, it seems a rather ordinary event, but the business of getting in and out of your hut in such a training camp was quite difficult. An AWAS (Australian Women's Army Service) corporal slept at the end of each of these big barracks and one had to wake her for permission to visit the latrines after 8 pm any night. Phyl and I so confused ourselves with how to get out and stay out for a decent time that we finally couldn't work out how we'd get back in until the corporal herself had to relieve her bladder and left the door unlocked for a moment, so we shot in and slipped into bed, fully clad.

There was some antipathy between the women's services in the same way as there was in the men's. In our case, the VADs (the name had already been changed to the Australian Army Medical Women's Service, but many of us refused to accept the change for some time) had an aura of superiority because of the long tradition that shaped us.

I had two cousins in the Women's Royal Australian Air Force and another cousin in the Australian Women's Army Service, and when we met again at war's end we laughed at the stupidity of it. But we agreed that women were narrow-minded only to the same degree as were the male services, and both sexes flashed their colour patches and stripes equally proudly.

In retrospect, I am surprised at the ease with which we slipped out of civilian life and into army discipline without looking back. To us, leave was a matter of filling in time until we could get back to our hospital and the men and women there. This was our home, no matter where the hospital strayed and settled for a time, that was our place and its inmates were our charges, the staff our compatriots. There is no other explanation of how we bonded. We saw civilians as people in no way related to us. As Sergeant Margaret McLeod ('Mac') said, 'They are them and we are us.'

On joining up we each had been issued with a carton of cigarettes which were replenished each fortnight, and I imme-diately lit up as if by order of High Command. From then on I chain-smoked 'for the duration'.

We were given no instruction on how to fit into this new

life. I only once heard a lecture on venereal disease and even that talk was as much a joking thing as a serious problem among troops. Phyl and I came out of the lecture saying 'but what's that to us?'

The 1 AOH (1st Australian Orthopaedic Hospital) was first formed at Mount Eliza in Victoria, then moved to Queensland. There was a large contingent of physiotherapists there and although they marched in as officers we aides got along famously with them. They were adaptable women: one day I saw one twist a bit of fencing wire to haul a leg up in traction while waiting for equipment to arrive. The 1 AOH, although not the ubiquitous AGH (Australian General Hospital) most aides worked in, nevertheless dealt with a great variety of diseases, wounds and sickness, as well as serving its general purpose – the repair or removal of bones, restructuring of everything from ligaments to supplying missing bits and pieces of bodies.

Most of us very young aides were, quite rightly, kept from the theatre but one day when a convoy came in with more patients than expected, I was hauled in – feeling very important as I dressed in a white nightdress that fell to the floor, the length of my five-foot body – but like most things in life or war, the bigger you are the harder you fall. Sister Kirk 2 I/C (second-in-charge) saw me hovering and ever so silently but with terrible menace in the only part of her body that could be seen, turned eyes of ice on me. 'Stand over there,' she somehow hissed without making a sound, 'you shouldn't be here.' 'I was told ...' 'Keep quiet.' 'But Matron said ...' 'Shut up and keep out of the way.' Well, she got her come-uppance when the surgeon, Colonel Colquohoun, who was in charge of the whole hospital, called 'Nurse!' Me? I wasn't sure, could anyone possibly want this theatrical outcast in a gown so long it swept the floor as had those of Florence Nightingale's girls eighty years before? 'Nurse,' our bulky surgeon called. I raced over, holding up my gown so I wouldn't fall over it. 'Mop!' he snapped, not even turning sideways to see that I was in place. Mop? 'His forehead!'

hissed Sister Kirk. His forehead? For god's sake, who would want anyone to mop their forehead when they were fit and well enough to do it themselves? But the lights blazed down and the heat up north defied the crude cooling machines of the day. Sister pushed a wad of gauze into my hand while directing a laser beam of fury down on me and I leapt into my most important task in the war, mopping my leader's copious sweat that poured down as though he had a malfunctioning cistern on top of his head.

Dr Colquohoun always said 'thank you'. 'You are very good at mopping' – and I always thought I was, too.

My peripatetic life had left me with many friends and relatives scattered over the continent and I heard of many of their movements, wounding, illness or death. While we still had boys to write to, I wasted my time by writing silly, flippant letters. I recall asking the Jackson boys, Pompey and Doug, who were a little older than me, 'Are you both still as bushwacky as ever? Surely at least one of you will come back having learned *something* besides flirting with girls!' And to the two Simpson boys I wrote 'It will surprise me if you don't get lost over there as you did when we were coming home from the dance at Jindivick.' (Only one of these brothers came home.) When you are young you never contemplate death, never think that three out of four boys would never come back, never flirt again.

From the time you put on uniform until the day you are ordered to remove it, you are a person so removed from anything that came before, a new persona has enveloped you, and civilians, family and acquaintances are aware of it.

We had a portable gramophone in our mess but, except for the officers' mess, I never saw a **wireless** set in the hospital or quarters and, of course, there was no television at that time. The gramophones were said to be 'both restful and cheering' for the men in wards. I know only that they were blaring and the musical taste of both the patients and the good people of Red

Cross who brought the records was in their boots. At the beginning of the war, the songs we sang were from the First World War; some, such as *Goodbye Dolly Grey*, were actually from the Boer War:

> *Goodbye Dolly, I am leaving,*
> *Though it breaks my heart to go.*
> *Something tells me I am needed*
> *At the front to fight the foe.*
> *See, the soldier boys are marching*
> *And I can no longer stay.*
> *Goodbye darling little Dolly,*
> *Goodbye Dolly Grey.*

No one appeared to be surprised to find us young girls living within a community peopled by a great preponderance of young men scarcely older than we were. Before we left our parents' homes we had always been separated from boys, even at dances our parents or older sisters had chaperoned us home. But now we were on our own, and if our working shift hours allowed it we could go out of the grounds until 10 pm (2200 hours, army talk) every night, and one night a week until 2359 hours (one minute before midnight). We younger girls used these hours to the full, running pell-mell back to camp from the nearest town or army camp, getting on to our palliasses by the skin of our teeth before an inspection party came around. For almost all my time in the service I lived in tents within a whole encampment of tents lined up in rows. Accommodation was spartan, no furniture apart from a low locker, our uniforms hung from the tent walls. We had two grey blankets and a change of bed linen was issued once a week.

We set up hospitals all over Queensland. Some places had no name until we trundled in. We were at one hospital running right down to a lovely beach. Here on night duty we could hear the tide come in and go out, and when our shift ended at day break we'd go to sleep on the sand in the sun. When it got too hot, we'd move like somnambulists, dragging the groundsheet back among the tea-tree and take up where we'd left off sleeping. I had a small alarm clock Granny Smith had given me when I joined up. 'Dinna lose it!' her still-Scottish voice snapped. 'It cost me two shillings and sixpence.' It had a ring on the top big enough to hang it on a twig of tea-tree and during the stay at that hospital, if I wasn't using it for an alarm it was out on almost semi-permanent loan. Sadly, the day we were packing up that hospital – always an horrifically army-style You! and You! At the double! sort of day, ending with 'Men to the trucks! Nurses to the ambulances! and off we'd go – this time the wee clock was forgotten and it may hang to this day beneath the tea-tree near a golden beach.

One is aware of the lies, the dishonesty about war, but also the challenge of endurance. Vera Brittain rightly believed that those boys and girls who have just reached the age where love and friendship and adventure call more persistently than at any later time are drawn to it. 'The glamour may be the mere delirium of fever, which as soon as war is over dies out, but while it lasts no emotion known to man seems as yet to have quite the compelling power of this enlarged fatality.'

Both my grandmothers died while I was away and it was strange, when I think back, how close we all were in that family of Adams and Smiths yet their deaths meant no more to me, and indeed, meant less to me, than did those of the men who died in our hospital. Grandmother Smith died in 1942 aged ninety-five and my mother wrote me that my father, who had been the youngest of Grandma's thirteen children, was desolate. I knew he'd been the pet of the family but somehow I'd never thought of my father being disconsolate at the death of his mother. The young see death so differently to the old, and we were young and we were now in a different sphere.

Grandmother Adams died shortly after, and I had leave at this time. Her coolness towards me had not pained me greatly, and watching her slow dying in the bed at home gave me time to think of the hard life she must have led, with ten children and a husband who had never been gentle. My leave was up before she died and I had gone into the room where she was lying at her home, and my great-aunt Anastasia (not to be confused with my younger Aunt Anastasia) was sitting at the bedside holding a lighted candle in my Grandmother's right hand. She had placed her left hand in the brown burial habit representing the passing of life to death. I only saw this briefly, and then ran with all my accoutrements to the train which would take me back north again and away from the life that seemed no longer real to us. The life of the hospital and the comings and goings of sick and wounded men were the whole of our life and our families were in retreat, left behind us emotionally as well as physically.

Chauvinistic jargon of the day was slanted in a way one would hope the men of today would never do. We can pity the men in their fear, and their frustration at being separated from their woman and/or women in general, or no woman at all. But some of their reactions were unforgiveable.

Our mail was always left on a rack in the VA's mess, and we'd pick it up at lunch. You saw some sad things, although most reports of relatives being killed or taken prisoner first went through Matron's office. But mail was usually glad tidings of someone being safe or on their way home, or just letters like young men and women back home would write to one another when separated for a time. One day a VA in her mid-twenties opened her mail and collapsed, falling straight across the table with the open 'letter' in her hand. The girls began to resuscitate her while one ran for Sister Kirk, the Deputy Matron. The 'letter' lay open on the table for all to see. 'She' had written, according to the anonymous sender:

I'm sorry dear, I missed the lights, the fun,
I couldn't wait until this war is won.

It might mean years, and youth is very short,
My friends kept urging me to be a sport.
I tried, but I was powerless to resist –
I want to live, I couldn't just exist.
I'm far too young to make you a good wife,
I'd never settle down to married life.
Forgive me dear, it's hard to write you this,
So I shall end it with a farewell kiss,
To wish you luck, and hope you'll soon forget
The empty little playgirl you once met.

'He' had supposedly written in answer:

Your letter reached me when I straggled back
Dog-weary from the old Kokoda track
And something died; something I'd had was gone.
The thing that kept me sane and spurred me on
I know you'll find it hard to understand,
The way you helped, the way I schemed and planned
When things were tough; I didn't mind the war,
I felt I had someone worth fighting for,
You say you're too young, perhaps you're right.
I've aged, I grew to manhood overnight.
Goodbye my dear, may you be happy in
The peace we're fighting night and day to win.

signed Hal Percy

Sister Kirk rose to the occasion as she would always do (she had already served in Greece and the Middle East until she was evacuated). 'Oh you little sport' she mimicked the letter. 'I'm far too young to make you a good wife: I'm really just an empty-headed little playgirl.' And then she roared to the rest of us: 'Eat your lunch and get back to work.' But she took the pale, trembling, mousy girl who we knew never went out with boys, and with her arms about her led her away to her own quarters to comfort her. And we, left at the table, could hear the rasping, choking sobs of the poor plain girl disappearing into the quarters and not until then did our rage burst wide open.

I think our Sergeant 'Mac' got it right, as she usually did do. 'We must understand men who are away from home, but that doesn't mean we should bear their cross – because we are already carrying our own crosses.'

We were ignorant of the great events affecting the war and our troops – so were the folk back home but it does seem odd that so much was kept from those of us who were so very involved. Once our old surgeon, Colonel Colquohoun, saw a long line of ambulances trundling down the dirt road towards our unit and he swore: 'I don't suppose the buggers know how to send a signal that they're coming.' I loved this old man - I suppose he was in his forties, but to me that was very old indeed.

As time went on some of us tried to continue with our pre-war interests. It had never worried me that my friends had said 'Woof! Woof!' when I told them I was playing Bach, or that Kathleen went into a fit of coughing when I played Prokofiev (kof, get it?), but at least it wasn't my family who, after reading the title of their child's new music, forever more referred to her as playing 'Choppin' – and with great pride. And why not? To play any instrument in bad days and bad places was an achievement, no matter how it was pronounced. It is all very well today for folk to ridicule the 'way backs', but what they need to know is that these people, we people, isolated by time, distance and lack of education, were at least trying to get by with, if the gods were kind, a small step forward.

In a tiny wooden-walled cottage, bereft of comforts of anything of beauty, except love, the playing of classical music, scales and exercises, even if badly, gave a dimension that relieved the hard, cruel, dreary monotony of the life most people were sealed into as inexorably as had been the generations before them.

I was stationed for a while at one hospital on the outskirts of the city of Toowoomba, and promptly found a music teacher. 'But you won't be able to practise' she said. 'No piano, or even a room to yourself where you could continue to study your violin.' But I already knew that. I would continue my work on the theory of music and harmony and could be examined at the end of the year as though I were a civilian. The precision, the elegant phrases of this study were a joy; at the end of the year the hospital was moved, lock, stock and barrel, and I couldn't get to a city to sit the exam but that didn't cause me any pain. It was the doing of it, the purity of the progression of notes and harmony, the excitement of little skittish bits of relief, even humour in a score, and the unending possibilities of notes on staves that gave me pleasure and rest from every other thing around me.

Ginger

THE HEART CAN BREAK; I know – I've heard it. Once only, and I doubt one could survive the hearing of it a second time. It doesn't crack, it crumbles like the fragile egg-shell of a tiny bird, and leaves a shadow on the palm of an outstretched hand and sometimes you think you see it there, long years after the body that had surrounded the heart has gone to dust – or wherever lost boys go, and young girls yearn for another chance.

A girl of seventeen – or seventy – would today be so much more sophisticated, worldly, practical, and may not hear the tiny egg-shells shatter, or feel the bluish dust in the palm of her hand for the rest of her life. C'est la vie, yes, that's life, baby, and half your luck if you missed it. But we, us, certainly me and the girls I knew in the 1940s, took life differently. At the very least it could be said of us that we did *take* it, grabbed it and ran with it, unafraid. There was a thrumming in the air, an excitement, an ephemeral but warning drum that presaged Armageddon, and a short life: so kid, make it a merry one.

I was an older lady, seventy years old to be exact, when I heard my heart break and the years tremble backwards to when I was eighteen, cheeky, sparky, game for anything, in love with every boy I met and they with me. We ran hand in hand up the hill outside our camp, yelling and hurrahing like the wild young, mad things we were, us girls in our indoor uniforms of pale blue and white veils fluttering behind us, the boys in army hospital garb of shapeless navy-blue dressing gowns. 'God help you lot if you're caught,' an old man called out to us one day.

We sang, and we recited aloud as we ran. 'Though poor and in trouble I wander alone, with a rebel cockade in my hat' – we all knew it in those days. Henry Lawson. He was 'home' to us much more than the darling of the drawing room, Banjo Paterson. 'Though friends may desert me and kindred disown, my country will never do that.' We were naive - innocent and very young. And the civilians, knowing we shouldn't be out, would laugh and waggle a finger at us for being naughty girls and boys.

We knew all the Australian songs and poems:

> *They can sing of the Shamrock, the Thistle, the Rose,*
> *Of the three in a bunch if you will,*
> *But I know a great country that gathered all those,*
> *And I love that land where the waratah grows,*
> *And the wattle blooms out on the hill.*

Oh yes, we were corny, but we embraced life as if we knew it was the only one we would have:

> *Though the battle be grim 'tis Australia that knows*
> *That her children will fight while the waratah blows,*
> *And the wattle blooms out on the hill.*

And we kissed and ran down the hill again. Not just once, and not just with one boy.

When we grow older we revere our bodies, protect them, lead them away from danger, but youth laughs easily at death or danger. One day I came to my place in the mess and there was a note for me:

> *Maiden who readest this simple rhyme,*
> *Enjoy your youth, it will not stay;*
> *Enjoy the fragrance of your prime –*
> *For oh! It is not always May.*

I never knew who wrote it or why it was left there; it meant nothing to me as I slipped towards being eighteen years old.

A batch of girls were being taken down to open up a new hospital, 108 AGH, in a hurry. Matron said 'Step forward all the country girls.' It was the middle of the night. 'For God's sake!' said Betsy who ran the hostel we were billeted in. A few girls stepped forward. 'Nurse!' Matron said to me, 'You're from the country aren't you?' (How could anyone mistake it?) But I replied, 'No, Matron, I'm from the bush.' My word, did she puff out her proper pigeon bosom. 'Get out here!' It was all very well for the girls to laugh at me, but it was all Dad's fault. He had always told us that the rich came from the country but that we poor came from the bush.

We 'country' girls were not being singled out for any medical skills – we had little – but there was hard physical work to be done quickly, with the need for each girl to tackle whatever seemed necessary without troubling the professional nursing sisters who had their own long hours of work. Matron had been born up-country and she believed we who had had a less pampered life than city girls were what she wanted. We were to go in a train of ambulances to Ballarat, a beautiful inland city in Victoria: fast.

It was now early 1942. We had not heard from the young men we knew must now be in battle – dead? Captured? There was no way to tell. The newspapers were silent and gave no clues, the silence from the islands and Singapore was intense. No letters came. The last I'd received from our Simpson cousins was a Christmas card with a palm tree painted on it; Pompey and Doug Jackson who, up till now had written regularly to me, were silent. I had known for a time that Jack Page from Penshurst and other country boys we knew had been captured by the Germans in the Middle East, they could write to us, but from those young men in the islands north, west and east of northern Australia there was only an ominous silence we all tried not to speak of. Until now: now the wounded were coming in. Who?

We were not told, but we were to get the beds made, match up pyjama tops and bottoms, unpack cooking gear – do the many menial jobs one did on the run if one was a VAD.

It was late at night when the patients arrived. We heard the first few ambulances stuttering up from the gates where the big sign 'Ballarat Lunatic Asylum' hung. A few boys lifted the canvas flaps at the back of their ambulances and saw the sign and quickly passed the word: 'It's a bloody lunatic asylum!' And a whole batch of them leapt out and ran for the trees. It took time to round them up and assure them they were in a totally secure, new building in Australia and when daylight came they could see what a beautiful setting they would be in.

They were all too sick and weak and tired to be much trouble, but they needed a sponge and were hungry. Matron came to me and said, 'Get them something to eat!' (I don't recall her ever speaking without ending it with an exclamation mark.) 'But I can't cook, Matron,' I cried. She said, 'Get out there and cook enough food to get these men to sleep.' Well. That was a problem. Not only could I not cook (my Mother was too good a cook to have me or my sister in her kitchen, except to wash the basins, etc.), and worse than that was the obvious fact that, this being a brand new, empty hospital, our food supplies had not yet arrived. I ran out and round to another ward and there I found rice, milk, bananas. As that ward was empty I ran off with them, taking a dixie with me which, I learned later, was big enough to feed sixty men.

When I got back with my booty there was a young, red-headed boy about my age in the kitchen. He was really good looking, even when dressed in the hideous army pyjamas that came only half-way down his legs. I said, 'Matron would kill me.' He said, 'Blow Matron!' and stoked the wood fire. 'Where are you from?' I asked, meaning what part of Australia. 'We're not allowed to say at the moment.' And I suddenly recalled that none of these patients had colour patches, the small insignia all troops wore on their upper arm to identify their battalion. 'Who are you and the others?' But he wouldn't say, and I knew I should not have asked – they must be men who had escaped from islands we had lost up north, and the government would fear that Australians might panic if they knew how close to defeat the country may be. That was how I saw it. The young man/boy sat down by the stove and we talked and laughed and I stirred the porridge-like mess of rice, bananas and milk and when I considered the whole mess to be cooked, the boy, whose name I learned was Ginger, carried it into the ward for me and put it on a trolley. The patients came over and I began to ladle the food out into each individual's little dixie and within the time it took for them to taste one spoonful the man next in the queue had got a glimpse of the food and said 'Hell! It's rice and bananas!'

The dixies were put down and the soldiers got back into their beds. I was shocked. I had no idea what was wrong until Ginger came over to my trolley and wheeled it and the big dixie back to the pristine kitchen. 'It's all we've had to eat since we went on the run,' he said to me. 'You couldn't have served them worse.' And he in his poor army pyjamas and me, between rage and total distress, sat down on wooden crates and stoked the fire in the stove and made a cup of tea. And I learned that night of his battalion. Isolated on the island of New Britain from any other 'friendly' troops, they had been swamped, overwhelmed by the Japanese invasion force. Those who could, ran. 'We call ourselves Curtin's Harriers.' (John Curtin was the Prime Minister of Australia at the time.) They had crossed and recrossed the mountainous island, looking for transport to make an escape, but they were being hunted too hard for many weeks before some of them, including Ginger and his mate, Jimmy, got off in little boats and managed to get across the Japanese-held waters and arrived in New Guinea, and eventually, Australia. I didn't then know that many of these men – including Ginger and Jimmy – had been witness to the grisly Tol massacre, some escaping after being left for dead, their thumbs tied behind their backs, their wounds including bayonet stabs from the upper cheek down through their mouths. Ginger was crying. 'I'm sorry' he said, 'I'm sorry', and stood up and I took him into the ward where most of the men were asleep and the remainder were shivering and shaking with the effects of malaria and the various worms that had afflicted them in the damp, hot, sweaty crossings of this fetid island where they had slept on the ground.

We were not encouraged to befriend patients, but it would be unbelievable to think we couldn't get around this. When decent food and medication were administered, the young men soon recovered, even though they would be troubled regularly with malaria and the worm – either behind the ear or the big, long one in the stomach.

We never knew what prank they would be up to next. Once, when I was on night duty, the sister in charge of the ward went off to another ward to chat with a friend and I was half dozing when the phone rang. It was a sister from the civilian hospital down in the city. 'We have two of your patients here and we want them out,' she said. 'Not from this ward' I replied. 'What uniform are they wearing?' 'Well may you ask' said the civilian sister. 'They are in pyjamas and the blue flannel dressing gowns of an army hospital and wearing digger hats.'

There could be no doubting that they were ours. The civilian was a decent woman. How did they come to be in beds in her hospital? 'Oh, they had had a couple of drinks they said and needed to lie down, and they saw an open window and climbed in and went to sleep. I nearly dropped dead when I saw them only a little while ago and realised they were not ours.'

The ambulances were lined up ready to take us back to digs when the night shift ended so I told a driver about the two scallywags and how the civilian sister only wanted them out of her ward – there would be no charges. So off the ambulance rumbled and returned with the lively lads before our ward sister returned. And, for the first time in my life, I could 'read the riot act' and truly frighten someone.

In those years Ballarat still had trams and when we were on day shift we could trundle up to the hospital or down to the city, and because of our long hours we were usually nodding asleep as the tram rumbled down past the lake. When the 2/22nd men first arrived it was a common thing to have a woman or man on the tram approach us and softly ask what battalion had got home, or 'Is it true some men have got back?' 'Have some got home?' 'Are any alive?' We, of course, could say nothing, but it was very sad and this approach must have been multiplied all over the areas in Australia where army ambulance trains rumbled into a hospital.

I was at Ballarat for only a short time but it was the coldest billet I ever knew. As more patients were rushed in, big canvas tents were erected in the grounds and, because of the mud, we VADs were issued with gumboots. We slipped and slid in them and, with the continual hurrying around, our feet perspired and the odour was revolting when we took the boots off when we were going to bed.

Ginger and I had 'gone' with one another for two months while we were in Ballarat. He called me 'Lik Lik' – native for 'little'. When he was well enough we hired a rowboat from the Lake Wendouree boat sheds and he and I and his mate Jimmy spent a day rowing on the calm water with curious swans about us. Within half an hour of us being there both the boys were lying flat in the bottom of the boat, shaking, shivering, sweating with malaria. Almost every man who lived to get home from the islands had malaria, so this was 'no great panic station'. This day I had brought with me two bottles of drinking water and their atabrine tablets; they had bought a bottle of rum, the only grog on the shelf of the nearest hotel in those days of strict rationing of beer when almost no top-shelf stock was left 'for the duration'. The boys had been ecstatic about the rum. 'What a beaut publican!' But a few swigs from the bottle and they had begun to shake, shiver and shudder and sweat until it dropped off their faces and wet their summer uniforms. There was nothing to do until the attack wore off.

First Ginger lay down with his deep-red curly head by my feet, and next Jimmy. I gathered the open bottle of rum and had what can only be called a swig. Then another. Tremendous! I rowed to the miniature island in the lake and, hidden among the reeds, I had a truly decent drink. I then rowed out on to the lake and had fun learning how to steer while rowing but, as the hot day wore on, I needed more liquid and the bottle of rum supplied it until, to my surprise, I found the bottle empty. Coming from a teetotal family, it was the first time I had drunk alcohol 'to excess'. Eventually Ginger and Jimmy woke, one after another, with a slight fever but no worse than usual. I was worse than I had ever been before or after. I was so affected that when I got the boat to the sheds and the boys hopped off to secure our painter, I managed to let the boat drift back out in the water and it took a long time to get it back in, with me getting one oar in the water and one in the air as the craft swirled round and back again. The boys were calling out, a civilian took a photo of me. (I know he did because he presented it to me forty-three years later.) And the instant the boat got near enough to the jetty I stumbled off and hurried to the nearby toilet where I was as sick as sick can be. And then I blacked out.

I remember no more until I woke up in a bed I'd never seen before, in a house I didn't know, with the two boys holding my hands and begging me to wake up. I didn't want to wake because each time I did pains slashed across my eyes and forehead and I was sick again. I slept, and when I awoke this time I was alone and darkness had fallen. I didn't know then that it was the day after yesterday.

There was no one in the room, no sound in the house. The boys didn't return until much later and then I was told everything. Ginger and Jimmy had been caring for me in between dashing back to the nearby hospital to cover their tracks – and mine, although I was officially off for my three-day-a-fortnight leave. Behind the bedroom door I could see my uniform, clean and splendidly starched. I felt around under the blankets and found I had been left in all my clothes, except the uniform. I looked up at the boys, little older than I was, and then we all began to laugh – except I didn't laugh long because it hurt too much. That bottle of rum had left me very sick and I have never drunk it since. 'Poor Lik Lik VAD' Ginger crooned as he stroked my forehead.

And the house? Well, several families had got to know the young men who had escaped from the beleaguered islands up north of Australia. They had given them door keys and the thoughtful offer to relax, drink tea, listen to the gramophone, cook a meal. Suddenly I panicked. 'What day is it? Is my leave up?' No, there was still this evening and I would be back on deck at 6 am tomorrow, clean uniform and all. They had even polished my shoes.

And the story never got around to Matron, nor anyone else at that time. (But, forty-five years later, when I was dining with the Anglican Bishop of Ballarat prior to my dedicating a new library to the college, he said to me 'Did you ever get dragged over the coals for taking those boys for a row on Lake Wendouree?')

Ginger and his mate Jimmy would go walking in the grounds of the hospital when they were first out and about but, as soon as the available drugs began to lessen their malarial attacks, we were all able to run off freely. Ginger and I got a three-day leave pass and went down together to see my parents. And a month later we got another leave pass and went down to Ginger's parents 'in the wildwoods' as he said. But time was short, and we had to get a train down to Warrnambool and stay overnight, ready to get on the early morning train to get us back to Melbourne then on to Ballarat.

The publican at Warrnambool said yes, he did have two empty bedrooms, and took us upstairs and asked 'The one key

will do?', leering at Ginger who said, 'Yes, one for the Lik Lik
VAD and one for me'. It was late in the evening. 'We'll have
to go to bed right away' I called. 'Beat you!' said Ginger, but I
got into my pyjamas and into his room as he was buttoning up
his pyjama top. 'I won' I yelled. We cuddled, and murmured on
his bed and then he said, 'I wish we were married, don't you?'
and I said, 'Yes', and in a short while I went off to my room
and left him in his. I didn't wonder whether we were being
virgins. I didn't think of it. I just loved him, cuddled him.

When we returned to the hospital a communique had been
posted giving the number of men taken prisoner of war. '23 258
Australian troops in Japanese hands and 12 819 missing, of
whom no news has been received at all.' We were still taking
in patients and patching them up so they could be sent back
up north to fight again. The obscenity of war is never more
evident than in an army hospital. It was not acceptable for a
young man to cry 'Enough, I've had enough!' and yet, never
silent in his psyche and his trembling heart is the whispered
'must I go again?' This is not a thing that is spoken about: the
way boys/men have been brought up makes it almost impossible
for them to cry 'enough!' But they could say, 'Nurse, you get
on well with my doctor – I see you laughing with him, joking.
How about trying . . . you know . . . tell him I'm not cold-
footed . . . but I'm not sure I can do it again.' And you would
tell the doctor, in a jokey way, of course, and he would tell
you firmly you must never, *not ever* listen to or speak of such
a thing. But though the young doctor does spend time talking
to the boy in the bed, one day when you come on duty the
boy has gone and a new patient is in his place. Boys just disappeared with their patched-up bodies and you knew they had
gone north again.

Ginger disappeared in this way. One day he was telling me
about how his father had pioneered a soldier settler block after
he got back to Australia from the first big war, and Ginger and
his brothers had lived in a lean-to beside the small house until

they left to go to this new war – and then he was gone and a note was brought to me saying 'See you soon'. But no mail came from New Guinea to me. Everyone I knew was asking 'Got word from Ginger yet?' The older nursing sisters always told us 'They forget a pretty face when the rifles are cracking.' But Ginger! I would have thought Ginger would have remembered me.

I never saw him again. There seemed to be an awful lot of people you never saw again. One day you're as thick as thieves and declaring love eternal and the next day it's 'See you soon.'

Ginger, who had been a friend, mate, a simple young country boy with whom I had got along fine, had just gone. Everyone in the hospital knew that he and I were a partnership. However, there was a saying in those days when things were difficult to explain: 'It's the war'. Yes, it was the war and we had made no spoken arrangement. Indeed, when he was sent off he had gone before I got word that his battalion had left on a ship 'going north'. And I received no word from him, not one letter. I pretended I didn't care, but I was heartbroken.

Fifty years and two months later, I was speaking with one of the men who had been with Ginger in New Guinea. This man was one of the few remnants of the battalion and didn't know that Ginger and I had had this almost childlike friendship and innocent love. He began to tell me about things that had happened after the men in our hospital had recovered from New Britain and, once patched up, had gone on to New Guinea. He said, 'We had a bad thing happen there. Did you ever know Ginger?' I said, yes, I knew him well. He continued, 'One night we were sent out on patrol up in the Wewak area – the colonel was all for night patrols, which was a bit of a joke as moving around in the dark in the jungle you made a noise like a bull elephant. He was burning up his troops with night patrols and all sorts of tricks. This night he sent Ginger, a corporal, out with his section, and it was Ginger's understanding that we were the only patrol out. But this night was a real bit of a mix-up. You don't send a patrol out unless you know what other patrols are about and exactly where they are. But our patrol was sent out. So Ginger and his patrol were out there in the black jungle and in the course of the operation Ginger thought he spotted a figure silhouetted in the dark.

'We had a whispered conference, some of the patrol said it must be one of our blokes: you knew the configuration of men and the clothing they wore, some said it was just the shape of bushes, and the rest of the patrol said it had to be a Jap, there's no other patrols out but us. Ginger, through long experience in jungle warfare, both in his escape across New Britain from Rabaul and his time in the hinterland of New Guinea, knew that there was a split second between sighting and shooting. He said, well, if he doesn't have a go, I will. So Ginger lined up the figure and fired. Of course, he didn't miss, he had been in this game for too long to miss.'

And his bullet hit Jimmy, his mate who had been in the boat with me and Ginger that sunlit day on Lake Wendouree, and who had cared for me when I was sick during the ensuing days.

I learnt from the ex-soldier – who had no idea that I had known these men so well – that Jimmy had been out on patrol in the opposite direction and when he reported back to base and was told that Ginger had been sent out into a particular area, he asked could he take his patrol out again immediately because he was aware that there was a Japanese patrol headed in that direct line. Jimmy's men later reported that, in the thick jungle, he was unsure whether the patrol he had come on was Ginger or a Japanese patrol and he couldn't take the risk. He raised his rifle, but Ginger was faster than him.

Hearing this story fifty years later was a most terrible thing for me. When I returned home I just sat there with tears raddling my cheeks. I couldn't stop crying – I don't know where all the water came from. And I couldn't help but remember that Ginger was noted for his great care in planning everything he did. In particular, his jungle patrols had to be 'spot on', as he had once told me.

The ex-soldier who told me this story had no idea of the effect the telling had on me and he said, 'Ginger had been becoming more daring and pushing his luck at that time. He was still respected as being a leader who cared and protected his men, but he would now take chances – always when only he himself would be involved. It could have happened to anyone in that area. Most of the men on patrol could see nothing at all, hear nothing, but Ginger had had years now in jungles and he had sensed through the bush the shape of a man, that was all. It was just his own acute sense of danger, and when one of the men said it might be one of ours, he had said "And it might not be." And fired.'

Because of my peripatetic life in the Australian Army Medical Women's Service, my mail was scattered all over the place, and some I didn't get until months later. One bundle didn't arrive until I was on my way down south to be married. As the train was about to depart, the kind and thoughtful WO II, Mac McKellar, came running down the platform waving a bundle of mail tied with string. 'All the same handwriting!' he called as he thrust the letters through the open window. 'Looks like New Guinea to me!' And it was. 'Stored away on *HOLD*,' Mac called. And the train rolled on as I opened one letter and I didn't open any of the others. Not ever.

The letter on the top of the pile was numbered '6' (the letters beneath were 5, 4, 3, 2, 1). 'Dear Lik Lik VAD' it began. 'What has happened? Today I was playing football and my opponent said, 'I hear your girl is getting married to a 9th Divi bloke.' This can't be true Pat. We were the happiest little couple in the whole Aussie Army.' I folded the letter back with the others, unread, as for four days the train jolted south, and I only remember confusion and bewilderment and a sadness I'd never known. I told no one. I have never mentioned it until today as I write. And a huge and horrible wave of confused emotion floods over me.

The wedding had been arranged by long distance and the

guests invited and the witnesses had applied and got leave to attend and – I never could see any of it clearly. And I still can't.

In 1993 I saw a photograph of him in a journal, announcing his death. And I wished . . . I wished we had stayed in the one bedroom that night, a half century ago. And I still wish it.

My
Mate

EACH OF US HAD A mate, you can't survive in the army without a mate. 'You need a mate to guard your back' they said. I don't know whether the same applies in other services but this has always been true of the army. Phyllis O'Brien was my mate. Before we met, each of us had had a casual mate or belonged to a small floating group unconsciously waiting for a mate to turn up. But once we set off together we were a twosome and were recognised as such, and the connection survives to this day. All around Australia there are hundreds of pairs of women who, fifty years later, still see themselves as army mates.

The first time we met Phyllis was leaning, slumped against a barracks wall near Matron's office, a strange pose for a rather timid, 'well brought-up young lady' as she obviously was. I had seen her around for some months but had scarcely noticed her. She was quiet and I was rowdy. I passed by, then doubled back. 'You all right?' She replied 'I don't know which one.' She wasn't weeping, distraught, distressed. She was in some other state that my own youthfulness had not encountered. 'Have you been called in to Matron?' That, of course, was always our worst fear. 'Yes.' 'What have you done?' Her hat was skewed across her forehead where she had slumped. 'Matron called me up, she told me my brother had been shot down, dead, over Britain. But she didn't say which one.' Phyl had three brothers and all were pilots.

Matron, for all that she terrified us, would have been kind, loving and caring, as at all times when she must tell one of her girls such news. But she hadn't known Phyl had other brothers in the airforce. 'I don't know which one' Phyl repeated. Together we went back to Matron's office and, after phoning the ADC room for details, this woman who habitually terrified us now put out her arms and cuddled us both into her ample bosom. She told me to take Phyl away 'and care for her'. We lay on my palliasse, our arms around each other, both weeping, not saying a word, and that night I moved into her tent, dragging my straw-filled palliasse down the lines, with a couple of orderlies coming along behind, carrying my cyclone-wire stretcher and kit bag. And we have been mates ever since. She is aunt to my children, I am aunt to hers.

It was not just that sad, sorry episode that bound us. Mateship, like love, is an amalgam of coordinates. We were both too young to be away from our homes and suddenly exposed to horror in that still-sheltered age. We needed one another, we fitted. To the camp and the hospital, we were just Pat and Phyl. A third girl was put in our tent once and we did our best about it, but without mentioning it to one another we knew she didn't fit with us. We two went everywhere together. If one was off duty she waited for the other before leaving camp. When off-duty leave was permitted we would gallop up the hill to get back to camp in time, rush from pubs that we should never have been near (most pubs were out of bounds to young nursing aides).

One day we came off duty at 2 pm from a 6 am shift and found Robin lying on her bunk reading – naked except for her army bloomers. Gee whiz! Phyl had the courage to photograph her but when the time came, none of us girls had the courage to collect the print. Weeks went by before Phyl, the quietest of all, plucked up the nerve to go and get it. Speaking with Phyllis fifty years later, I learned that until then she, too, had never seen another woman's breasts.

During my time in the army I didn't think much about religion, except for the time when Phyllis and I decided we would 'do something' for Lent. What this would be was hard to decide because Matron told us we were not to go off food – she wanted the most out of our labour. Eventually we two girls decided we would say the rosary each night, kneeling on the floor of the wooden hut we were billeted in temporarily, along with twenty other aides. The nights were bitterly cold in this camp, wind whistled through the gaps in the walls, floorboards had been laid down directly on the grass and were wet. The first night was hard, the second worse.

At first the other girls thought we were play-acting and they partly went along with our Hail Marys and Our Fathers, and chiacked us no end. The second night the 'joke' had worn thin: *everyone* wanted us to shut up and get into bed. So we prayed quietly, quickly, mumbling away 'Blessed Mary ever a Virgin' (so were we, for that matter) and 'at the hour of our death' and 'pray for us sinners'. It became a little embarrassing, we could see the girls' view but our view was equally urgent – we would have given it up willingly but we had made a vow to say this rosary each night during Lent for 'the missing, and the boys we've nursed who have gone back to the war'. We couldn't back out now.

With the doggedness of youth we stuck it out, kneeling on opposite sides of my stretcher, the straw palliasse making us sneeze and our noses run, the cold draughts and damp ground making us shiver, and all the while wishing we'd never made the vow, the promise, in the first place. When Lent ended one of the older girls came to us and said not to worry about the chiacking, that the girls thought it was fine that we'd stuck to our guns, but we must consider the whole, the total mateship and camaraderie that alone could render our work effective. That gave us amnesty for the rest of the war.

Though religion didn't loom large in our thoughts, Phyl and I once went to the local convent for advice. We had both met the men we were later to marry when they returned from New Guinea. We two girls were worried: 'What do you do when you get married?' I asked Phyl. She said she didn't know. So, after worrying about it for a couple of weeks we decided to go to the nuns and ask them. Phyl phoned and the nuns said they'd be delighted to have us to afternoon tea. Off we went, certain that all would be revealed before evening fell. Well, of course it wasn't.

The nuns had pretty pieces of needlework and the odd embroidered amulet done for us as gifts, and lots of gorgeous cakes. They were curious to hear of the way we travelled and lived in this new, strange world we young women inhabited in 1942. But they said nothing at all about bed. Phyl and I exchanged looks and took it in turns to try to bring the bright, friendly conversation round to what happens when the lights go out. But the nuns said nothing about it. Neither had we. We said nothing that would provoke a discussion on virginity, intercourse and pregnancy – and no wonder. We had never thought of it, or spoken to one another or any other person about such matters. Our mothers had certainly never spoken about sex to us, and I imagine very few girls of our age at that time would have been much different from us.

Eventually, three hours later when the sunset had already faded, we said our goodbyes, gathered together the gifts these good women had given us and set off back to camp. It started raining and we had nowhere to shelter except for a children's playground. We hadn't spoken to each other since we left the convent and we sat on two children's swings and went silently backwards and forwards. After a while Phyl said: 'They didn't tell us, did they', and I said 'No'. And they hadn't.

By the next Lenten period Phyllis and I had been parted – not for any disciplinary reason but because I had been given rank. *Rank?* I was only eighteen years' old. I was wild and wayward, as Matron had often told me, but now I'd given her a real headache. It came about this way (and it was one of the few things in life that Mum did for me that was wrong and nearly got me into trouble). I had enlisted for overseas service and now a batch of girls were to be sent to Bougainville. I wrote and told Mum. She asked her priest to pray for me (people did lots of praying in those days) but the priest said there must be some mistake, I was too young, and that Mum should write to army headquarters and tell them about their being mistaken about my age and that I should be sent home. At this time Dad was in charge of a 'flying gang', a chosen group of railway-line repairers who were on call 24-hours a day to patch up the havoc caused by massive overuse of the rail tracks because of wartime traffic. When he eventually got home he was told about Mum posting this letter and, of course, being an old navy man of the First World War, knew that such a letter could drop me into it. But there was nothing he could do, it was all too late.

I was called into Matron's office and our senior surgeon, Colonel Colquohuon, was standing beside her desk, both looking monstrously big and fearsomely sombre. I thought – nothing. I was stricken. I was inside all the terrors I'd ever heard of, from the Siege of Mafeking to the execution of the Tsar and his family. Matron's bosom, high above my head, was swelling and swamping over me. She was very cross indeed, probably more so because her routine had been interrupted. Routine was her alpha and omega.

The colonel had always been good to me, I was his pet. When the hospital staff had had an official photograph taken he insisted I should sit at his feet – and when I squinted because of the brilliant Queensland sun, he roared 'Get it done with! This little girl's being boiled!' But now he seemed not to remember me, he was looking anywhere but at me, while Matron looked nowhere but at me. By God, she hated her brilliant routine to be interrupted – doubtless more so for being interrupted by one of the lowliest cogs in the Australian army. She was making huffs like drumming-out noises. I expected her to say 'Your parents will be disgraced if you are dismissed'. She was reading from a document in her hand, and it said that my family had had honourable records in two wars and two had been killed at Lone Pine and three others wounded and four 'missing' since February 1942. Colonel Colquohoun said slowly 'We'll have to hide her for a while; where can we hide her?' Silence. Then he said something about being too busy to be wasting time on something so stupid and to let him know when she's been hidden. 'She'll be eighteen in three months and everything will be all right then.'

The warrant officer brought up the answer within the hour. I was to be sent south to a Warrant Officers school and I would have to leave that afternoon by train if I was to get down to Brisbane, to Sydney, and out to the school at Liverpool before the course opened in three days' time. 'You might even come out as a Warrant Officer Class II.' 'What?' 'That's the school we've got you in.' There was another different school beginning in six weeks' time but the colonel had said to 'get her out today'.

I decided to wear my khaki uniform that afternoon when I set off to Sydney. There was no point in flogging a dead donkey. Like many early VADs, up until then I had been rebelling when the title was altered from VAD to Australian Army Medical Women's Service (AAMWS). Worst of all, our blue uniforms had been changed to khaki, with big pockets like the Diggers had. Being short, I looked like a burnt dumpling. Now the time had come to be sensible, there was no way we could get back to the old days. Our small revolt was over. Yet strangely, there was an unspoken bond between those of us who enlisted voluntarily before the date when women, as well as men, must enrol for labour if not in the armed services. It was, and is, silly, but there you have it. War *is* the silliest thing.

I gained third place among thirty-five professional men and women, and came out of that school with two stripes on my arm and the opportunity of going on to the rank of Warrant Officer Second Class (or WO II) as vacancies came along. But I would have happily swapped those khaki uniforms, including the knickers, and the stripes, for our much-loved navy-blue uniform.

With my two stripes I was given more responsibility and I was sent with four VADs to a small hospital that was being set up near a Military Provost Centre for 'incorrigibles'. I thrived on the challenge of more responsibility. The four girls with me had their own work to do in wards and I organised the general duties rosters and the kitchen, and the myriad things that crop up. It never seemed to be any different to what I had been doing before I began to go up the ranks. But I was working harder and longer than ever because, apart from all my other tasks, I must now see to the comfort or problems of the four privates in my care. We were a very happy lot and Phyllis came over to stay when she could get leave. I had a good big tent for me alone, with hanging wardrobe, chest of drawers, and boards for a floor.

But I did hate this place. From the lip of the hill we could look down and see the men brought in for punishment being dragged out of the back of trucks and sent off in the terrible, humid heat to run till they dropped, round and round an area as big as a football oval, in full army kit of great coat, kit bag, heavy boots, the lot. And when they fell they were kicked till they got up and began running again, and this was repeated until they collapsed and were dragged into a barracks in the compound. I was not so naive not to know that there would be some of the worst men in Australia enlisted in the services, as there would be in any army, but it seemed a terrible thing that it was Australians bashing Australians, even though they may be incorrigible. I asked for a transfer, and got it.

I fitted in well wherever I was sent. I like to think it was my country – bush – upbringing. I could turn my hand to most things, was strong and willing, and would happily work day and night when necessary. But the constrictions and restrictions of working in wards eventually were not for me. It wasn't the boredom of bottles and pans and sponging that bothered me, but the nursing sisters who, doubtless piqued at our youthfulness, could play merry hell on a VAD. (Shades of Vera Brittain's experiences some thirty years before.)

Few ex-VADs (now AAMWS) speak of the attitude taken by nursing sisters on the use of our service. It was strange to find, when re-reading *Testament of Youth*, that Vera Brittain could write: 'The sisters hated the necessity of using VADs and they showed it plainly. Whatever training or experience she had, they were determined she should not be permitted to imagine, even for a moment, that this entitled her to any kind of status. The longer a VAD performed the responsible work that fell to her, the more resolutely her ward sister appeared to relegate her to the most menial and elementary tasks. I was never allowed so much as to attempt the simplest of dressings, I was sent, together with the rest of the VADs to that multitude of soul-killing, time-wasting tasks so dear to civilian hospital tradition, and so infinitely destructive of young energy and enthusiasm . . . ' Vera Brittain believed that the 'holiness' of the nursing profession was its worst handicap, that the 'sanctity' of the nursing profession was such that people forgot that nurses were just human beings. She wrote at great length about VADs and the treatment of them in her day. She claimed that the rigid sectarian orthodoxy crushed the gaiety and independence out of the young women who had gone nursing so hopefully.

I suppose not much had changed from her day to ours. She would have had exhausting rounds of bed-making, bed pans and bowl washing, cooking, cleaning: all of them part of the VAD's work. I got along reasonably well and none of this really bothered me. If a VAD was complaining to me about a superior, I always said 'Don't get upset about it, it's only because they're older than us and the young boys won't go out with them.' This always brought a laugh.

I was personally never troubled by any sister, but I saw and heard the stories of other girls and that disturbed me. One day I hinted to Colonel Colquohoun (what a cheek one has when young!) that I would like to do some other task and he said 'How about doing the officers' mess?' 'I wouldn't be a flunky for anyone!' I snapped. 'Well, go away and cook,' he said laughing at me as he walked off. 'You get a shilling a day more for cooking.'

I didn't know if this was true, but asked the adjutant and he said it was true, my pay would go up to seven shillings a day. The officers' mess had lost their cook who had gone on leave and the replacement had failed to turn up. I could transfer immediately.

Well, I had fun. The young doctors would come to the kitchen and warm themselves at the wood-fire stove on early chilly mornings, and they experimented with cooking, and flirted and laughed with me. The older surgeons came out and shared a bottle in the evening, and it was very homely. I loved it all – except I couldn't cook. When I was stuck for an idea or had ruined a dish, I'd race over to the general kitchen and the real cooks always helped me out.

I began to like the idea of being my own boss. I had a full-time offsider for fetching and carrying, preparing vegetables, cleaning and running errands. Half the time I couldn't find him but we got along well when we did meet. Later, when the cook came back from leave, I was transferred to various places where it was considered I would 'calm things down a bit'. Seemingly I did, but from this distance in time I can't remember how I could do this as I was noisy, always in trouble for forgetting rules, laughing, flirting with patients and staff, always late (I still am) – but could manage to get on with nearly everybody. That was no great qualification, but not everyone had that ability.

That
May Morning

ONE DAY A TELEGRAM ARRIVED to say that the man who had decided I was to marry him, Bill, was on his way down to Brisbane from the islands in a hospital ship. It said I was to meet him at the wharf. This telegram came at midday and I was on duty until 6 that night, so I spoke to Warrant Officer McKellar, who had been very good to us young girls, and he learned that the ship was due before daybreak – twelve hours away if I could get away from the hospital. As it happened, things went surprisingly well; there was a concert party performing outside the hospital that evening and they would then pack quickly as they had to be in Brisbane the next day to set up for a concert there that night. Mac spoke to one of the drivers and arranged for me to travel in the truck, so I would be in Brisbane by daybreak.

The concert party was like several others of the time – good quality. Some of the best entertainers in Australia performed at these concerts and this one had American and Australian stars. I introduced myself to the sergeant driver, he got me a good seat and told me he would be leaving the instant the show ended. But I still had my hours to work. Phyl said she would starch my collar. In those days collars were not attached to the shirt and we had to mix up a paste and dip in the collar, then iron it – quite a job. It was the sort of thing we bush girls could do well, but I didn't stop to think that Phyl wasn't a bush girl. When I came off duty I rushed to the tent to get things together.

Phyl had everything ready so I went to the ablutions block and, as usual, there were long lines of girls waiting. Eventually I got back to the tent, but when I began to fasten the collar it was sharp and when I had a good look at it I found it was covered with blue lumps as Phyl had tried to make it stiffer, but she hadn't mixed the paste properly so I had to go with this appalling collar scraping a hole in my neck throughout the concert and all the way to Brisbane.

The concert remains in my memory as one of the best I've seen. A tenor sang the last item, then the whole concert group came back on stage and started to sing softly, so we could scarcely hear, 'There'll always be an England . . . ' We all leapt to our feet and joined in this song which had an enormous effect on the troops at this time, when British people were being bombed mercilessly and we still believed England was 'the motherland'. We stood as if it were the national anthem. Then, as the lights came up, I grabbed my haversack and ran to the truck.

We rumbled through the night and when we reached Brisbane daylight was still an hour away. However, the ship was already in the Brisbane River and we could see the glow of cigarettes all along the ship's rails where the wounded men were leaning. I learnt from people in the great crowd there – so much for secrecy of military movements! – that the wharfies had refused to bring in the ship. I asked what would happen and they said that probably at about 9 am the wharfies would go back to work and permit the ship to berth, so I decided I would go to the VAD hostel. These hostels were in all major cities for nursing aides in transit. I knew roughly where the hostel was, but hadn't allowed for the fact that the trams had stopped running. It was 3 in the morning. When I saw a tram coming I propped myself on the track to make sure it stopped. The driver was cross, he asked what I was doing and I explained I wanted to go to the hostel; he explained that this wasn't a regular tram – it was a track cleaner, trams had finished for the night and he was returning to the depot. I hopped on anyway and stayed there and wouldn't get off, asking him to drop me wherever was near the hostel. This he did, but he was very sulky. I reached the hostel, rang the bell and the Matron came. I told her what had happened on the wharf and she got a bed and a cup of tea ready while I had a quick shower. She said she would call me later and not to worry. When she did call me, she put her hand on my shoulder, shook me and said, 'Your friend is here.' She told me not to bother to get into uniform but to put on my dressing gown and come to the vestibule where my 'friend' was waiting. I did this, but there was only a very thin, yellowish-looking man there who smelt quite pungent and gave off an appalling odour when he moved. I went to the kitchen and asked Matron where was my man she was speaking of and she said he was in the vestibule. But I said no, that wasn't him. Then she spoke his name and said it was the name he had given, so I went back and he put his arms out to me and I realised it was him. I learnt later that the smell was not just from the ship, it was from the incredible eruptions he had in his armpits and crotch which were like running boils, caused by the damp heat, the poor and meagre food, and debilitation. Matron was as professional as one would imagine, she said for him to get in and out of the shower before the other girls awoke (this, of course, was ordinarily definitely forbidden).

I was bewildered. I had no idea he would be in this condition, although I had seen other men like this after returning from fighting in the jungle. When he came out of the ablutions block I had to tell him I had no leave, was due back on duty the following morning, and the driver who had brought me down had said he would fix for another truck driver to let the two of us travel together back to the hospital so I would be in time to go on duty at 6 am the following day. This we did, and it was unfortunate that amongst the cargo of this truck were coffins. At the time it didn't seem alarming, I had seen coffins and took no notice, but Bill had been reluctant to board the truck so I offered to sit in the back among the coffins and let him sit in the front, but he said no. It wasn't the happiest of meetings and when we got back to the hospital area we weren't sure what to do as he didn't want to go to hospital.

I took him to a small hotel, he fell on the bed and went to sleep immediately, and I went off to the hospital to get into my day uniform. When I was free later that night I went back to the hotel and realised he was very sick, so I returned to the hospital and asked the warrant officer what I should do. He said he would get him into the hospital, although it was irregular. Bill was indeed AWL (absent without leave). He should have stayed on board the ship until he was granted leave, but Colonel Colquohoun and the warrant officer fixed this up between them, they were two splendid men. Bill was put to bed in the hospital, a sick, ill, disoriented and debilitated man. When he was well enough, he was sent down to be discharged to go to his home in Tasmania. He wrote to me constantly, telling me I must come down immediately, must be discharged and care for him, and that we must marry.

I had never intended this. I was still mourning the seeming desertion of me by Ginger. But the concert was over.

I can't remember, never could, how I had first met Bill and, given the preponderance of men over women – at least twenty to one in the Queensland military areas, and all aged roughly between eighteen and thirty-six – it still surprises me that he was able to cut me out from the noisy, cheeky young boys I so happily gambolled with.

He never said anything beautiful to me. He was tired, not just because he was so much older than me but because he was war-tired. He had been away almost from the day war started. He had fought on the Western Desert, El Alamein, Tobruk, the whole shooting match, and when the 9th Division was sent home to 'face' (as the saying went) the Japanese, he was first sent to our hospital to be patched up. It was there I came to

My cousin Margaret Buick (left) and I could never have guessed in 1933 that in a few years we would dress up in a different rig – she as an aircraftswoman, me as an army nursing aide.

Kathleen had two brothers who were not mine – then neither was she my sister. But it was a story too long to tell.

Mum, a keen Box Brownie photographer, took this in 1938 with light from the kerosene lamp – Kathleen, Dad and friend Rene. (My music certificates hang on the wall, along with Dad's naval discharge, dated 1918.)

A visiting warship was a curio; the young newly-weds saw no omen in it. Dad, Kathleen and Bob, 1938.

After this family holiday at Black Rock, Victoria, in 1939, my cousin Margaret (top left) and I (top right) did not see one another until war's end.

Dad and six of the laughing cousins (me centre, Bob to my left) in 1939. When war came, six of us from this snapshot became mixed up in the three services.

The threat of war seemed to cause an outbreak of marriage. Kathleen and Bob were swept along – to disaster.

Bob, Kathleen and children the day before our last Christmas.

Grandmother Isabella Adam-Smith, wearing her naval service brooch issued in the First World War to mothers with sons at sea, and Aunt Bella from 'Ahava'.

Mum and Dad taking a rest from 'laying the foundation stone for Parliament House, at Rhyll', Phillip Island. The farm was bought while I was away in the army.

In my VAD uniform, 1941.

The war swept us all away. The life we had known was gone forever.

This Melbourne *Herald* cartoon was not too exaggerated in its depiction of the earliest enlisted women returning home on leave for the first time in uniform.

I loved life in an army hospital – the drama, tragedy, fun and friendships.

Phyllis O'Brien. 'My mate' – still is.

Our sergeant, Margaret ('Mac') McLeod, was one of the greatest women in our service.

Our tent lines.

We three topped the Warrant Officers' school in Sydney.

' ... in love with every boy I met and they with me.'

'Ginger and I had "gone" with one another for two months while we were in Ballarat.'

In 1988 a gentleman handed me this photograph of my attempt to get the boat ashore on Lake Wendouree, Ballarat, after the rum episode with Ginger in 1942.

Mum wrote on the back of this card, 'Until my girl comes home'. She had never worn trousers and it surprised me to learn many civilian women had to work so hard.

When Grandmother Adams died it seemed unreal to me – our army life seemed the only thing we now knew.

This snapshot and the one below at left have always been a joke to young relatives – and were a source of dismay for my parents. After posing for this photograph on the day I was to be married, my parents made their way to the church, wondering if I was going to show up. May 1944.

A neighbour came by with her camera and saw me still standing at the gate and coaxed me into the 'bridal' outfit.

May 1944.

I made all the children's clothes as well as my own. This dress I made from old curtains Mum gave me. Money was scarce but by now (1950) more and more of my writing was being accepted.

Having kids when you are very young is great fun – here Michael, born in 1945, is aged one. After the short cuts of the army, I let my hair grow long and wild.

One is fun, two is double fun – Cathy Danae was born in 1948.

Returning to Tasmania one more time. My parents tried to save my marriage and often encouraged me to go back to Tasmania.

In the late 1940s I began travelling Tasmania gathering research for my writing. My Dutch friend Hans Maree became a wonderful travelling companion. Here Hans (centre) and I pose with one of our piner friends, Frank White, in Strahan, 1952.

The Abel brothers in the dense forest with which the south-west Tasmanian piners had to contend. The Splits, Gordon River.

I went below with the miners in the last of the original mines in 'The Silver City', Zeehan, Tasmania.

The cook threw this fly net over me in this south-west Tasmanian miners' camp. The flies were worse than I'd seen anywhere in a lifetime in the bush.

Gordon Abel and I relax after a strenuous trip up the Gordon River with piners in 1953.

After buying my Linhof Technica from the chemist in Devonport I was able to supply photographs to illustrate my stories.
I practised on my children, who graciously (mostly) posed for me. Cathy was my favourite model – still is.

I played with the Linhof as if it were the most gorgeous toy and a great challenge. Mostly I had to photograph 'on the run' but sometimes pulled in a photograph I was proud of, such as this one on Bruny Island, Tasmania.

East Coast CRUISE

VISIT
TASMANIA'S HISTORIC
EAST COAST
ON THE
"NARACOOPA"

Sailing from Hobart weekly

My life changed forever when I accepted an assignment to write about a cruise on the *Naracoopa*. I couldn't have predicted then that this small wooden ship would become my home for almost six years.

know him, before he went into battle again. He was tall, blue-eyed, had straight, streaky blond hair, was sun-tanned – and looked awful. He was wearing the nosebag we hung on men from the desert war whose antrums had been scoured by the blinding sand-storms. Many Middle East veterans had this operation and their dripping noses were not a sight to delight; for weeks after the operation they looked like sad-eyed horses snuffling into chaff bags.

Except for the few days when Ginger and I had visited his parents in Victoria's Western District, I can't recall ever having gone out alone with another boy, until this older man came along. Sometimes I would be with two boys, more often groups of us who were off duty at the same time tore off together.

One day I was passing by the antrum ward and Bill said 'Hello nurse. I've been watching you for some weeks.' I gave an 'oh yeah' or whatever the equivalent expression was in those days. And then he said a thing that no one until that time had said to me: 'Would you like to come to dinner?' In those days the ordinary folk didn't 'go to dinner'. We might have had tea with someone – and that didn't mean afternoon tea. His way of asking me out must have interested me because I said yes, I would be off duty that evening until 10 pm. There wasn't much in the nearby town in those days, and I suppose there weren't many eating places anywhere in Australia where ordinary people went as it was so much cheaper to eat at home. The working class was not used to dining out. I thought it was fine to be in a place with fresh flowers on the table and a good-enough menu. I asked Phyllis to come with me.

We talked about tanks, battalions, hospital ships, and then he became more personal and asked me if I had a boyfriend. I said yes. 'Where is he then?' 'I don't know. I thought, and he thought, he'd be going to New Guinea and up the Kokoda trail but I doubt it now, I think something different, I think they may have pushed on further. I haven't had a word from him and they sailed three months ago.' I had written to Ginger and had waited and watched for letters from him. It was an ominous thing not to have received a letter after so long but I didn't want to discuss it with this man. I was thinking of Ginger, not of him.

The next day I spoke with the regimental sergeant major and told him I hadn't heard from Ginger. He said, 'Oh, that's funny because there have been several girls here who have got letters regularly only a week after the men sailed.' I asked if he knew if they had been in action and he said yes, they had been, but he'd not heard of any of the men who had gone through our hospital recently having been killed, missing or wounded, although he said this might not yet be in the newspapers 'but the word gets around quickly'. I went to one of the girls who had a boyfriend 'up north' and she said her boy even got a letter away just as the ship landed in New Guinea and he had been writing regularly. She said it was magnificent how the army postal corps got mail back to Australia so quickly and expertly. She then asked, was I serious about Ginger? and I said of course, I had visited his parents with him and he had visited my parents and I had been taken to meet his sister who was serving in a canteen at Spencer Street station. This girl was some years older than me and she said, 'Well Pat, there's only one answer, isn't there?' I said I didn't know what she meant and she said, 'If everyone else is getting letters, don't you think it odd he hasn't bothered to write to you?'

I was desolate in the sort of way one becomes when you are busy, far from home, have no time for tears, and certainly wouldn't shed them in front of your compatriots. I saved them for my pillow that remained damp throughout the night until a burning sun would heat the tent enough to dry it.

I felt rejected, and thoroughly so. There was no one to talk to and if there were I was too proud to let anyone know I had been rejected. There were still fragile parts of my psyche that could tolerate no damage, no pain, nothing. I had no word for this but I knew it was so within me. So I forced myself to forget all those merry months Ginger and I had had, and I recall that I felt great embarrassment that I had sent him letters almost daily, even some small gifts to cheer him and let him know I loved him.

I walked straight through the ward to Bill and said 'I've got the day off tomorrow'. I can hear now the cheapness of the way I said it. 'Good' he said, 'we'll go off and do the town.' And so it began, this new relationship that spawned so much sadness and so much joy of children.

We went out to the few things one could go to there, and then he went on leave to see his parents in Tasmania and I promptly went out with the group of young people I used to be with before Bill came along. In this group there were men almost as young as me, and we were never less than three together, rarely more than five. We had a lot of fun and there was extraordinary comradeship amongst us. Then I heard a rumour of the battalion that was going up to the north coast of New Guinea and realised Bill would most likely be sent there. And he was. He came up north to embark and he brought a ring his Mother had given him, a heavy gold ring with three emeralds, put it on my ring finger and I felt the weight of it and I was trying to tell myself 'Who cares?' Then he sailed away and with him went Shy Bill.

Shy Bill had been his mate and would be until his death. Shy Bill had been through the same battles in the Middle East, Greece and Crete. 'My' Bill had asked if I knew someone to make a foursome and I said my girlfriend, Phyl, would be off duty and maybe we could go to the pictures. So we four went out together, never again did we go in pairs. Shy Bill was a blacksmith in civilian life on the west coast of Tasmania, and he was so shy he didn't kiss Phyl until he was due to embark for the battlefields again. They always walked apart, Phyl would be by the fence and he would be near the kerb. Only on the day he set off for New Guinea did they walk close together.

And so, once again they sailed off to war. And we waited,

Phyl and I. I received letters, she none at all, not a word. I asked our RSM what he thought about that as he knew Shy Bill, and he said Shy Bill was 'true blue'. The letters I was receiving from 'my' Bill were heavily censored with great strips cut out of them, and the areas that hadn't been cut didn't mention Shy Bill. I wrote to 'my' Bill once I realised so many letters he wrote had had large amounts cut out and asked him what was happening? He replied, and had cleverly written on the top of the page: 'Censor: my letters are being censored heavily and I had written these things because there are two young nurses who are awaiting news and the friend of one is dead and has been dead since the second day of our landing.' So I had to tell Phyl.

She was on duty and I asked Matron what I should do and whether she would tell Phyl. She said no, I was old enough to handle it and to tell her the best way I could as her closest friend. She said she would give us leave for the rest of the day. I went to the ward, got Phyl and told her, and I recall there were quite a few young boys in fold-up chairs outside the ward in the sunshine and we had to pass them to get back to our tent lines at the back of the hospital. I could hear them calling out 'What's wrong with the young girls? They're crying. Nurse, what's happened?' And we went on with our arms around each other, sobbing our hearts out.

Shy Bill had died in a strange way. He had been only slightly wounded when they advanced and he was taken to a Regimental Aid Post and 'my' Bill then went forward. He returned two days later expecting to take Shy Bill forward and found he had died the previous day. Shy Bill had been given the wrong blood group, the wrong serum, not an unlikely event in those days when transfusion was a relatively rare and new medical aid.

Phyl and I wandered about when off duty, each stunned, though from a different cause. Her short acquaintance with Shy Bill and his bizarre death, and my confusion over the seeming indifference of Ginger and the even more confusing possessiveness of Bill, had moved our erstwhile gaiety and security into a phase we could neither understand nor deal with. We were, after all, still very naive and young. And the heavy work load and long hours often drained us of the sparkle of our years.

And then, everything brightened. A soldier I had met in the ward asked me if I'd like to 'go to the pictures'. I hesitated. 'My cousin is just back from the islands' he said. 'He could come with us.' And I told him of Phyl's loss and before any time at all Phyl and her Gordon were in love, and I greatly approved (and I still do!). But the man who initiated this meeting was a sick man, mentally and emotionally. As Gordon described it, the young man was trigger-happy, his long spell in action had tripped his reason and he was taken by ambulance to the Army General Hospital in Brisbane where he would stay for much of the life that was left to him.

Life in a busy army hospital had an immense variety of characters and conditions and there was little time to ponder on the sorrows and the unfairness of life, and nobody wanted to hear about it anyway. The emotions of the young do not differ between nations. Vera Brittain, the English girl who was a VAD in the First World War, wrote: 'I walk in ways where pain and sorrow dwell, and ruins such as only War can bring, Where each lives through his individual hell.' She was 'worn with tears, For he I loved lying cold beneath the stricken sod' and she wondered as she grieved, 'If when the long, long, future years creep slow, And war and tears alike have ceased to reign, I ever shall recapture, once again, The mood of that May morning, long ago.'

Bill and I would never have met had it not been for the war. He would have remained on the island of Tasmania where his family had been born, for generations since they came to Australia, and never sallied forth across the water to the 'mainland'. In his thirty-three years until he left for the war, he had never been off the island. I, eighteen, coming from an outgoing, dancing, singing, cuddling, peripatetic, laughing railway

family of the Australian bush, was swept up by the excitement
of the periphery of war and the whole dramatic, unbridled,
dangerous, wild, blood-stirring atmosphere of the times. And
there was another thing: when we first met, the war was still
near us, threatening Australia; the 9th Division who had fought
at Tobruk had been sent home. There were boys from training
camps nearby who were suddenly ordered overseas, there were
boys I had known who were now dead, and boys I knew who
had disappeared, not heard of since February 1942. Life was a
flighty thing, and in our hearts we knew it.

Bill and I would walk along the fragrant frangipani-lined
streets on my off-duty hours, and other '9th Divvy' men, seeing
his colour patch in the shape of a T (for Tobruk), would call
out across the road: 'Ho! Ho! Ho! Ho!'. It was a cheeky,
comradely greeting meant to resemble the droving of sheep
across the paddocks (which is what they later did do - not
sheep, of course, but they did drive the Japanese back and out
of New Guinea). Sometimes they would call out 'See you up a
tree', referring to the way it was said the Japanese fought.

Something within me should have sent a signal but no message
came and I didn't notice its absence. Looking back, I can't recall
if I even noticed the different tenor of our days when the young
boys had left to go to the fighting areas of New Guinea. I didn't
notice that I wasn't having as much fun any more, didn't admit
that things were different when a tired man in his thirties was
hanging round the hospital grounds, waiting to take me out.

You
Make Your Bed

WHEN BILL RETURNED I GOT compassionate leave and came down to Warragul in Victoria and we went through the old ceremony with not a word between us as to why we were going to 'join in holy matrimony'. Aunt Sarah's husband, the urbane English-man, Eric Anderson, drove me to church. Well, he seemed urbane to us because twice he had received an inheritance from England (and each time had blown it on the gee-gees, 'even flying interstate to race meetings!' Aunt Alice and the rest of her sisters gasped). Anyway, in those days of rationing he was the only one in the family with enough petrol in his car to get me to the church.

Uncle Eric was a rather decent sort. Everyone else had gone on ahead, including the two witnesses in their army and airforce uniforms, and we set off later but a train held us up at a rail crossing. 'Do you really want to get married?' Uncle Eric asked.

That was a peculiar remark, I thought, what with me in a long white dress and carrying flowers. Eric asked me again and said, 'I could turn the car around and drop you as far away as you want to go.' I was silent. 'Get back to your battalion or whatever you're in?' But it had gone too far. I couldn't back out. I was never a good backer-out, I never have been. Mum always said I was 'staunch'. I wish I wasn't. Who would? Could? And suddenly we were in the church and the organ played 'Jesu, Joy of Man's Desire' And it wasn't too bad, all the fuss, frills and the long veil lent by Mum's cousin Anne. The bridegroom set this veil on fire when he lit a cigarette as we left again in Uncle Eric's car. I belted the flames out with my bouquet of nerines, and on we went with him singing 'I'm going to buy a paper doll that I can call my own.' Bill had begun to sing this while we were walking out of the church:

> *A doll that other fellas cannot steal . . .*
> *When I come home at night she will be waiting,*
> *She'll be the truest doll in all the world.*
> *I'd rather have a paper doll to call my own*
> *Than have a fickle-minded real live girl.*

The aunts must have saved up months of their butter and sugar ration cards for the 'breakfast': Alice's cream-puffs were known for miles around, and there were butterfly cakes, jelly and chocolate-covered lamingtons with real cream. The collection of gifts was just as difficult to find in those times, there being nothing frivolous produced during the war and yet I still have, and use, many of those gifts my family searched so diligently for over fifty years ago.

We sat side by side in the train from Warragul to Melbourne. By now I'd got back into uniform, and he talked to his airman friend and I talked to Anne whom I'd known from my first day of enlistment. It was all rather nice, the four of us yarned about troops and who was wounded and who was on their way to New Guinea – by now nobody was going to the Middle East – and time went quickly. Once in Melbourne, Anne went off back to her hospital unit, and the airman ducked off, and we two got on the Burwood tram to get to Aunty Julia's house (Dad's sister). And the party was over.

I went to the altar a virgin and I've been preaching ever since that it is the most damnable thing a girl can do if she expects or wishes to live a life of what is euphemistically called 'conjugal harmony'. No one should be exposed to that – not just the tearing of the membrane and the blood, but the trip to the chemist the next day, giving the semi-whispered order for Vaseline 'we only got married yesterday', and the wink from the chemist and the smug return of a semi-grubby grin. Then back to the room, walking with your legs apart, and the yelp when it started all over again because the Vaseline couldn't protect the tender parts.

The next morning my Aunt Julia said 'What do you think of being married, Jeannie?' laughing as old women have done for centuries, a sort of historical chain, adding a link each time another victim joins the initiation ceremony. Julia wasn't a nasty woman, she was usually fun, but this was tradition.

Bill and I sailed that night on the old *Wairana* to Tasmania to stay with his parents in their little, thin-walled, rented cottage. It was winter, bitterly cold. I thought of Queensland and wanted to get back there, or at least to Sunset Country where I was born. It snowed. Snowed! I hated it, had never seen it before, feared it, like I subconsciously feared most things in this place of old people as opposed to the vital warm youth I had lived with for so long. I thought there was only one good thing going for me: no one knew my thoughts. I was fun. 'You're always laughing' Mr O'Day, the bank manager, said. But, 'You must join the CWA' (Country Women's Association) said the mother of the man who told people we were married.

I never knew, and still don't know, what 'marriage' meant or means. The wedding ceremony that became popular among the working classes towards the end of the last century is still the one where the girl wears a white dress as evidence of her virginity and a veil over her face which will later be thrown back as the symbol of the breaking of her hymen. The man then places a ring on his captive's finger as evidence of ownership. When Bill's mother explained this to me I took off the gold ring with the three big emeralds and threw it over their back fence. Search as they did they never found it and I didn't care. What a farce the whole thing was – and is. Until my first real lover and I joined, I thought fucking was the greatest historical exaggeration since John the Baptist resisted the unparalleled temptation of Salome.

After four days of 'marriage' I bolted back north to my hospital – with the assistance of my army friends who had sped to my aid when they received my telegram asking to have my two weeks of compassionate leave rescinded. Swiftly they telegramed that my leave was cancelled and I was to report back to lines within the next five days, the time it would take for a person to travel from Tasmania to Queensland. And so my first journey to Tasmania was brief and unhappy and full of foreboding, but it was not crippling. I was still in my teens and the resilience of youth is instantly refreshed.

I marched back in past the guard on duty as if I'd never been away. The five days of travelling had been like a dream. Happy, I slept, got off every three to four hours when the train stopped for recoaling, watering and inspection, and for the hundreds of hungry men on the long troop train to get a meal. 'Ho! Ho! Make way for the nurses!' some soldiers would shout, and you'd push in for a hot pie and sauce and sometimes, if it was a real outback place, there would be home-made cakes, but they went fast. The big mugs for railway coffee moulded into your hand as you pushed back out to the platform with your booty.

One night, following a stinking, hot, high-humidity day on the Sydney to Brisbane run, there seemed to be no air at all, the heat just swamped us, crowded as we were in the carriages – and me in winter uniform I'd been wearing down south. One of the crazy things about the army (and navy and airforce, for that matter) was uniform and how it must be worn. For instance, if you were in winter uniform you did not remove your jacket – and on this occasion I was in winter uniform of woollen jacket and skirt, long lisle stockings, heavy shoes and felt hat, gloves in my little army-issue wallet. The men in the carriage were, like me, all odd-bods, returning from leave or on transfer. A sergeant said 'You!' to two corporals, 'move into the corridor' and 'You!' to a great big private, 'stretch out on the floor', and to me he said, 'Nurse, you can now stretch out on the seat'. I didn't waste any time. I put my feet up, put my head on his lap and went to sleep until we got to the border and I never once thought 'what would Matron say?' I was going home to my unit.

The uniform conceals the man – or the woman, for that matter. In war the uniform reveals nothing of the personality, honesty, or the background of a man's true life. Marriage under these circumstances is much more bizarre than the marriage of some races where women do not meet their man until after the marriage ceremony. It is often said that marriage is a gamble, but relationships forged in wartime are even more so.

By late 1944 the war had moved away from Australia, Americans were in total control, and the egocentric General MacArthur determined to get all the glory (if glory there be in war – I for one cannot and never did see it). The Americans raced on to take Japan while Australians were left to 'mop up' – truly, they do use these awful expressions in war. Where once we laboured day and night, now we could get a discharge with very little trouble. Married women were being encouraged to get 'de-mobbed'. Pressure was used, none too subtle, even outright demand from marital partners who were now discharged.

I didn't want to leave, I wanted to stay in the best company I ever knew. But a letter from Tasmania changed all that. Pinned to it was a doctor's certificate stating the soldier had neurasthenia which was being exacerbated by the absence of his wife. Was that me? I had never thought of myself as being a wife. 'The Wife of Bath?' I scribbled over the discharge document.

I wasn't even working with my own mob when I left; damn the promotion, the increased pay and the stripes. But a great body of old army friends saw me off as the train passed through Brisbane, young men and women singing and crying in equal quantities. We had all loved one another.

Mum, Dad, and the two boys, John and Albert, who were

being brought up as part of our family, met me off the train at Melbourne. After I'd used up my army deferred leave I went to Royal Park in Melbourne to get my discharge, feeling strange in my new civvy clothes. I felt even more strange when a group of young recruits in neat new uniforms, marching down the avenue, assumed I had come to enlist and called out 'You'll be sorry!' – the old army quip we'd all used at some time. 'You'll be sorry!' I was now in mufti and my smart new clothes suddenly lost their glamour. No more Stand To, no more reveille, no more girls, no more boys.

My parents accompanied me to the ship which was to take me to Tasmania. Mum had knitted me a dress of vieux-rose wool, the very prettiest thing I had seen for over three years, and men and women on board the old ship commented on it. It fitted my seven stone five pounds figure like a soft glove. I adored it and wore it for years. Now the lines were parting, the ship's screw was turning, and all I loved – the people and the soil – were down on the wharf and I was off to somewhere, and someone I had no feeling for. It wasn't hate, not even dislike, it was – the war. It had turned all of us upside down.

I cried all the way to Tasmania, always did, sobbed and sobbed. As often as I forced myself to return to that island state I sobbed with great gasps. It was as if I was exchanging paradise for perdition. I wasn't even embarrassed by my tears, they were only the outward symbol of my total distress. I cried and cried inside and out, as the coast of the mainland of Australia faded behind and the island threw its loneliness at me.

On another return trip I was flying back to Tasmania and a portly lady sitting beside me offered her handkerchief. 'Have you lost someone dear to you?' she asked and I said, 'Everyone. I've lost everyone I love.' It was the first time I'd admitted to myself that that was what distressed me when I went south to Tasmania. After a while I blew my nose on her handkerchief and talked until this stranger said, 'There are things you can do to ease this.' I was bitter. I said, 'I know, I've been told to "Grin and bear it" and I've been told over and over again "You've made your bed, now lie on it".' 'No,' she said, 'work.' And that was how I became a sort of loosely tutored waif of Australia's fine female politician, Dame Enid Lyons. 'You will grow to like this little island, come to me whenever you like,' said Dame Enid, and I did.

But I hated waking to days of dreariness and nights where there was no love. My mind was cluttered with words and ideas I daren't utter. I wished I could be buried like the boys who had died in our hospital. I wished I was back with my friends, boys and girls of my own age and style.

My parents, desolate with despair at my situation, sent me the piano, brought me a wireless on one of their trips – and they made several voyages in an attempt to stop me from running away to God-knows-where. They had so little money and even the freight for the piano must have been exorbitant, but still they tried to make my marriage work.

It was 15 August 1945. There was a rumour on the wireless but the men went to work, it was hard to believe war might be ending after six years. Then the bells rang out and the shops shut and everyone ran on to the street. The war was ended, finished.

I was home alone. It was particularly painful for me and the feeling remains clearly. I wanted to be with the mob of girls and boys in the army, not the people who took to the streets down south. Anyway, I couldn't go anywhere. The little bells of the several churches in Ulverstone clanged away all day and I was alone. I walked down to the river, clambered down the bank where violets grew and gathered a great clump. The man, Bill, was home, drunk, his battered years overseas gave him no strength and I thought, they shouldn't have done that to him, left him lying with his face in a puddle of muddy water for me to drag him out. Later he had a bath and went off with old First World War diggers who had made me put my army jacket on. I played old songs on the piano, hoping some of the revellers would stay but they all ran off to the pealing bells and pubs and left me playing 'My Darling Clementine'. I thought: what were the girls and boys doing up north? Were all the sick and wounded wheeled outside? Given beer?

A girl came with a box of chocolates she'd kept all through the war for just this occasion and, as no one in the town cared for her, she came to me and we sat in front of the fire and ate the chocolates. So the war ended for me.

When I went to live with Bill I went straight back to teaching piano. My students' fees paid for the rent for our miserable house. When we first left the in-laws' tiny, shared, rented cottage we were still to share a house with others, a recently married (for the first time) sixty-year-old couple who were bitterly anti-drink, anti-Catholic, anti-sound and voluble about all three. Here was the echo of the men who came back from the First World War and wanted to marry, only to find there were no houses for them, no hospitals for their babies, and not enough schools for the baby boom that followed.

Because of the Second World War no accommodation had been built for six years. Living as we did was well enough, if whispering was your idea of private conversation. We moved to three other equally unpleasant houses before we were able to build a house of our own with the help of the government scheme for returned servicemen. But in the meantime, we were living in rooms behind a funeral parlour, and in other unlikely shelters including one decent house – though the owner wanted to evict us to enable her to get a higher rental than the government's fixed rate which we were paying legally. She came to our gate daily and shouted 'Aren't you ashamed to keep us out of our own house?' But this house did have one mighty bonus for me: we were near the seaside. Bass Strait rolled by near enough for us to hear the sea change in the night, and every day I inhabited the magic shore. *Every day*. Sometimes I just sat and stared at it. Like Billy Wilson of my childhood who, when first taken to the seaside on a bush school excursion had whispered it, I almost whispered 'What a bloody lot of water'. After my upbringing in the dry-lands country it was unbelievable to gaze at water as far as the eye could see.

I was visiting 'Ahava', the place of Aunt Bella's benisons, when I learnt that I was pregnant with my first baby. It was just before the end of the war and I had been staying in this enchanted place with my parents for a week when I realised I was pregnant and 'as happy as Larry'. I went back to Tasmania immediately. There was only one thing wrong with that lovely time while waiting for the baby – I was surely the champion thrower-up of all time (and repeated the performance when my little girl was on the way in 1948). I am a small woman and remained so during pregnancy, at one time taking part in a parade of 18th-century dresses wearing an 1820s yellow taffeta gown with a twenty-inch waist. I was happy, entirely.

My only surprise was that I had taken so long to get pregnant; after all, I had married and had then 'had sex' and, with the ignorance of most of the young women of my generation, I had been under the impression that one became pregnant immediately after intercourse. But we didn't use those terms: I was 'in the family way'.

I had not only been enchanted to be pregnant but relieved that I could be so. When my first period came after marriage I was so embarrassed I tried not to let him know. I wasn't pregnant! I had already worked my way out of much religious belief but now, suddenly, I prayed, not just because I wanted a baby but because I thought I must be odd not to have conceived 'at first blow'.

When I was pregnant I 'had the fancies' for rice (which was not easily available to civilians). I wrote to the girls up north and they replied by telegram: CEASE THY CRAVINGS WENCH. RELIEF AT HAND. ALL SEND OUR LOVE. SIGNED MAC AND CO. The rice arrived in a beautifully wrought box made by John, the carpenter. I learnt later that it was a concerted effort by the cook, the carpenter and the army postal service, and it brought me immeasurable cheer.

Five days after the peace bells rang out the baby came. The following day Mum arrived on the boat and I was happy in the way one never ever expects to be. To hold my own baby, someone I knew to be mine, so dependent on me; to see my Mother hold the baby and whisper to him, his father pleased as punch at the infant, and me engrossed by his thick black hair tousled in the crook of my arm, and I without a care in the world.

Perhaps it wasn't as magical, deeply and heavenly as I thought, it may merely have been that, for the first time in eight months, I was not vomiting.

Five months after my healthy, laughing son was born I miscarried with another babe at home, in bed at midnight. It didn't hurt as I remember, but I was mystified: what was happening? Something was coming out with the blood from my 'front passage', as we females called the vagina in those days. 'You are miscarrying' my children's father said. 'You must have been pregnant again and we didn't know.' I thought I wasn't as silly as that and told him so: 'The *front* of me. Not the *back*.' It was his turn to be mystified. 'You have a baby out the front, not the back, you must know that, you've already had one baby. They come out the *front*.' Oh! In those days chloroform was given when the babe was 'coming' and you were well on the way and yelling ferociously, hurting and terrified. In the 'private hospital' in our town (it was an old house), Nurse Stuart, Proprietor and Accoucheur, administered the liquid when she thought proper. A pad was stuffed over your face and chloroform poured willy-nilly over it and you went out cold and stank of it. So how could you be expected to know where anything came out?

When this second pregnancy ended in the babe deserting me before I was taken off again to Nurse Stuart's establishment, I didn't have anything except a stench of chloroform around me, hanging particularly heavy in my long thick hair. That afternoon

when my five-month-old son was at home yelling for a drink
and was brought to lie on my breast he promptly inhaled the
fumes and went to sleep. I had to scream to have him taken
out of the room to air. The father came in and he was affected
also. How could a girl expect to know what came out of where
in such an era?

My children were 'baby-boomers', as were the children of the
hundreds of thousands of servicemen who poured back into
civilian life at the end of the war. My darling little daughter
(yes, I was besotted by the pretty, healthy, wee thing – still am)
was born with great ease and no chloroform in 1948. A young,
fresh-from-medical-school doctor had come to our town, and
although Nurse Stuart was permitted to retain her establishment
until retirement, a certificated nursing sister must now be
employed on the premises. Yet it wasn't these medical advances
so much that changed the terror and pain of childbirth but the
erasing of the myths and old-women's tales. Trevor, the young
doctor, talked to me about this. 'Some won't listen,' he said.
'Some say mum and gran know best.' He promised me a pain-
free childbirth and I did have this. He also promised – and
did – 'fix up' the damage done during the birth of my first child.
Being a tiny woman I had torn badly and had not been stitched
properly, and the ragged gash healed in a lumpy fashion causing
urine to trickle out sideways.

Later I had yet another miscarriage, and again I didn't know
what was causing my pains although by now I was knowledgeable
about what went out and where from a woman's body. I read
all I could find but there was little of sense about childbirth
and pregnancy, illustrations in books were mystifying to a degree
that if you weren't told what the drawing was you wouldn't
know it was part of the human body.

This miscarriage slipped away (out of the *front* passage!) while
I was in hospital for treatment for bleeding, non-stop vomiting,
a cancer on my cervix, and fainting. The man I'd married then
got condoms – I never saw them. He used them, lying flat on

top of me, and then put them in his shoe at the bedside. I
didn't move. I hated it all. Four pregnancies in three years was
enough. If the pill had not been made available in the early
1960s I would have remained sexless. But some years went by
before that happened.

Not having lived near water until then I had the delights of
walking on rocks at low tide and peering into sea anemones
which opened and closed like tiny gumnut babies in tutus. There
were living things walking and sliding and stealing the homes
of other living things, crabs as small as my smallest fingernail,
and things I didn't know at all. I spent hours every day down
there on the edge of Bass Strait, never knowing the
unthinkable – that I would some day live on that water and see
it more as my home than I had any other place.

I had spent almost more time down there on the fringe of
rocks and water when I was pregnant than I had in the half-a-
house. When my son was born I had carried him down and
bedded him in dry, soft seaweed where I would watch him and
he me. When he began to toddle he too took to the rocks and
islands made by the departing tide. When my baby girl arrived,
she was soon following the two of us and was just as much
enchanted by the to-ing and fro-ing of water, and the excitement
of 'rocks walking Patsy!' and 'flowers!' when a sea thing showed
off its temptation to its prey.

But I was not a good wife, or so I was told. The rages when
I was late with the lunch were icy. I would run home, one kid
on my back, one holding my hand, and try to get inside and
have something cooking but often I was caught coming in the
gate. Then it would be a bit 'bedlamish' with his pushbike
seemingly intent on tripping us all up and his bicycle clips being
severely snapped on to the handlebar of the bike while the eyes
accused me. Oh well, the lunch hour would eventually pass and
off we'd go again. The sunny days in Tasmania are few and we
made the most of them. Come what may and come what did I
remember that little town beside the sea with affection.

As a newcomer I saw what those who had lived there for generations took for granted, and I wanted to tell the world. It wasn't quite the world I eventually told, but it was a start. I wrote to ABC News (Australian Broadcasting Commission) in Hobart and told them I was disappointed they had not mentioned the centenary of Ulverstone which was being celebrated soon. They wrote back and told me that no one had told them and could I tell them, and what was my telephone number? I didn't have one – telephones were not yet universal among the poor in the 1940s and '50s and I had wedded a *very* poor family. And there was another reason: 'You'll be wanting to ring your mother all the time.' *He* had never lived in a house with a phone whereas I, of course, had lived on railway stations where my Mother used the phone daily. So I went to the post office, phoned the ABC in Hobart, and said if they put a telephone in for me I would . . . hell, what would I be? 'A stringer?' Hobart asked me. 'Yes' I said, as if I'd known the word forever.

I was to receive 2/6 for a local item, 5 shillings for a State item, and the rare one, a national story, earned me 10 shillings. I phoned in an average of three items a week, but when the split in the Labor Party came in 1953–54 this leapt up considerably. The State Labor Party's annual meeting was to be held in Ulverstone at Paddy Bourke's Hotel. I knew and liked Paddy, and he was one of the few people in those most stringently limiting days for women who noted my rising success and my increasingly long absences from the town. Paddy guessed I might soon be in a position to clear out permanently.

To tempt me to stay, this solid man coaxed me to do the local reporting of the Labor Party conference. He taught me how interesting, vicious and dirty politics could be. He reminded me that my Grandfather had walked home to Gippsland from Queensland in the 1890s when the squatters locked out the union shearers. 'You must do this' Paddy said. So I did. I phoned the ABC, they said they were sending up a reporter and he would do the reporting, I would do the stories and features. And

I loved every hour of it, on my toes all day grabbing stories, national radio phoning to ask for interviews with politicans; there were the long nights drinking at the pub when rumours – and sometimes even the truth – would be exposed.

The Labor Party was splitting. Eric Reece, the Tasmanian Labor Premier who had always visited my home in Ulverstone, asked me to drive him to Devonport: 'I have to talk to George Cole.' George was going DLP, the new Democratic Labor Party that would eventually keep Labor out of parliament for many years. My few years of writing features for the top magazines of the day stood me in good stead, but politics was not an exercise I admired or wanted to be part of. So this foray ended at the time of the momentous split, and my days in the little seaside town were ending too.

The Argonauts

THE 'ARGONAUTS' SAILED INTO MY life at the little seaside town of Ulverstone while I had one toddler at my knee and another in the womb and all the time in the world, when women were expected to do nothing, think nothing, and indeed had nothing but housework to do. And in this breathing space I got my introduction to education.

The impact of the 'Argonauts' children's session was great. Previously there had not been a specifically children's show on ABC, but that wasn't what launched the 'Argonauts' and kept it afloat. There was a great variety of interests discussed, serials for young as well as older children, a running correspondence that some children used for years, but I don't believe any of this was enough to blow the 'Argonauts' across the oceans that many another ship has foundered in. I think it was the conscious belief that children needed and wanted a quality product.

The 'Argonauts' took its name from the *Argo*, the mythical ship rowed by Jason and his men in their search for the Golden Fleece. Each Argonaut – any child who joined this radio club – was given the name of a classical figure. So many joined that they ran short of names and had to add numbers. A very short time was given to the history of the ancient legends, but they so gripped the imagination of the listening children that to this day you can come upon men and women who promptly say 'Oh, I was Athene 41', or 'I was Ulysses 23'. Painters, singers, musicians, writers – all were catered for. Thousands sent samples of their work. Ida Elizabeth Jenkins led the 'rowers', along with 'Mac' and 'young Jimmy' and they all lacked the condescension that, until then, had been meted out to children in such shows. The children were named on air only by their ship and number as a 'rower'. The original *Argo* had had a fine crew, and nothing in the history of radio or television in Australia has had the quality and the impact that the 'Argonauts' had.

I was doubly riveted because I had read 'stacks of books you couldn't jump over' (as the Ulverstone librarian said), and to actually hear the characters in these books being spoken about as men and women who could have lived on our planet blew my brain into top gear. I read and read and read and read. When the baby girl arrived she was named Cathy Danae – Cathy from *Wuthering Heights* and Danae from Greek mythology. As I suckled her I read, as I had with Michael Julian three years before. Now he said 'That naughty man won't chain Danae to the rock, will he?' and brandished the iron poker beside the open fire like a little Trojan warrior. These were the most contented, happiest years of my life. Cathy, from the beginning, had a time clock that set off its alarm at 4 am regularly every morning in the chill of a bitter Tasmanian winter. I'd change her, talking and singing nonsense songs all the time to coax her to quieten so as not to waken her father. Then I'd light the wood-fire stove in the kitchen, make a pot of tea on the hob, and with a blanket around me pull up a chair and settle her on my lap. And with her tugging away at me in that fashion that babies have I would contentedly drink my tea and read. And then I began to write.

I always wrote, even when I had had only a slate to write on. Sometimes it seems to me unreal, a dream, that I got to do what I always wanted to do. Few have that luck. Sometimes I think it is someone else doing it. No. Some*thing* else. I work hard, not only for the long hours I have done since I first began to write, but even when I am ill I have pen and paper brought to the hospital and if my body is not too clogged with pain or pain killers I get some words down. I've been driven since birth.

I remember Mum came on me at the kitchen table writing on our little tablet of paper. 'What are you doing with that pad?' 'I'm writing a story about the man who came to our school today.' 'I don't care about the man who came to the school, just don't waste good paper.' And I had the pad taken from me, and rightly so. These things cost money and we were just 'hanging on'. Words failed to match the speed I desired. I scrawled everywhere except on or in our house – I had great respect for railway property!

Telling stories and folklore had been a part of our household from birth. All of us could tell a story well – except Kathleen. She was happy to be reading *Peg's Papers*, *True Romance* and any other such literature that came her way, surreptitiously of course. She was a humdinger at concealment and was rarely caught out. Even then she went searching amongst her friends for more such magazines as soon as the razor strop was replaced on the wash-house wall and her current reading matter burnt. A thesis writer may find an interesting paper in comparing the difference in the reading material of two girls brought up together, each with the same lack of opportunity, yet each reading different, diametrically opposed material. And why not? It's what suits your needs in life that should be the only arbiter of our taste, and particularly what suits our thoughts.

I loathed Freud, adored Kant as if he had written just for me alone. Then there arrived a book in the local Ulverstone library which included the letter written to the *Sydney Morning Herald* in 1890 by a Sydney Presbyterian minister referring to the death of Father Damien Parer who had gone to live on Molokai Island (Hawaii) to minister to the lepers, and the reply by Robert Louis Stevenson. The Reverend Dr Hyde had implied that Father Parer's love for a woman leper should negate the public sentiments of affection and admiration being given this man who had given his life for others. Stevenson's reply was majestic.

Surely no one after reading this letter, I thought, could ever again be so misguided.

People were, of course, but I had learnt a lesson of tolerance and love in that intolerant, strangely convoluted and cruel tag-end of many centuries of using 'love' as a weapon. For the first time I began to relate to cause and effect.

I turned on the wireless every afternoon, and as I listened with my small son to Jimmy, Elizabeth, Mac and the rest of the crew of the 'Argonauts', stories that would delight my own son tumbled out of my head. I rushed to the piano and began to play 'train music'. Michael immediately began chuffing and whoop-whooping around the dining-room table – and so 'Pufftah' was given the green flag and sent on his way. It was a simple story of an engine that picked up its train as it went: a freight train, and a lion from Sydney Zoo (he couldn't speak our language), a passenger coach that left the rails and went overland whenever he smelt bananas in Brisbane, a cattle truck that ran amok in Darwin, and so on. It was funny, it made kids laugh. The lion ate hay. 'Lions don't eat hay' said the adults; 'don't be silly' said the little kids whose imagination had not yet been crippled by education.

The local librarian, working in a room as big as a bedroom, was interested in me because I kept asking for books I had read about in *Books and Bookmen* (which took two months to come out from England). I owe her. Eventually she was ordering up to three books a week for me from the State Library in Hobart. Some I chose, many she chose for me. She said no one else asked her to order such number of books to be sent from the city. She was excited to have 'real' work. Sometimes she led me to works I'd not known of. Well, of course I didn't know of much except for the books in that wartime ever-travelling armed services library – which was surprisingly varied, carrying all of Dickens, Jane Austen, the Brontes, Howard Spring, *All Quiet on the Western Front*, even *Mein Kampf*. The 'Jeeves' books were tattered with wear but, surprisingly, so were philosophical works.

I wrote the story line of 'Pufftah', the script, the theme song and music for beginning and end of each episode, as well as the music and songs for the whole of the eight episodes that constituted each series. I'd never known anyone who wrote, knew very few who read books, and knew no one who had done anything as audacious as to write a letter to the ABC (Australian Broadcasting Commission).

For each episode I received three guineas (£3/3/0, for which, in fact, there was no single coin. A guinea was a very gentlemanly term in those days.) The ABC's reply arrived only two weeks after I'd sent my first two episodes up to Sydney. (The librarian at Ulverstone had phoned Hobart to see if anyone in the State Library knew how to go about such matters, and by the greatest fluke in my career someone *did* know that is was usual to send only a short example of the work.)

We – the pregnant me and my toddler, Michael – were on the front verandah carving animals from potatoes, carrots and white turnips while waiting for the mailman. Mum, Dad, and Phyllis wrote to me constantly to help 'keep my pecker up'. The scene is one each of us has in our memory box, we do nothing to hold it, the moment has registered itself, is indelible. The scent of crushed nasturtium leaves brings it back to me as nasturtiums clambered all over the little front garden. (The garden remained, as all my gardens have to this day, harmonious, rambling, a joyous refuge where flowers and trees are not tortured into the shape mankind is usually made to conform to and, by extension, makes all things do so.)

Michael's little feet stirred the cream and tangerine flowers as he scampered off the verandah to meet the postie at the gate and came back brandishing a letter above his head. 'Big' he said. I read it, and shouted aloud 'They've bought "Pufftah"'! Oh Michael! They've bought "Pufftah"!' Cathy was a fine, healthy foetus or she would have vacated the womb on the instant. She always seems to me to have been my talisman of good fortune.

'They've bought "Pufftah"!' Michael shouted, leaning on my

knee, laughing and leaping as if he too knew the whole impact and import of the letter. 'They've bought "Pufftah"!' he said in wonder, as I laughed and hugged him. To this day, it is a family saying when something good happens, even if I have the rare success with my cooking – 'They've bought "Pufftah"!' as a sort of Hurrah! Miracles do happen! The ABC bought three serials from me, Radio 3DB bought two: all for children under seven.

I was asked for more when 'Pufftah' ended. I wrote 'The Silver Jacket' because Michael, by the time he was four years' old, was a fisherman. He fished in the Leven River near our home and brought in fish as often as not. 'Do fish have babies?' he asked in the forthright way kids have when they expect a forthright answer. 'Yes' I said, and hoped he didn't ask for more because I didn't know how fish had babies. I'd seen bubbles come up from where he caught fish on his line, but for all I knew it could have been fish farting.

So, back to my librarian who sent off to Hobart and within a week she had a book on fish which explained their life, habits and spawning. It was too academic for me to explain directly to a child, so I immediately found names for fishes running out of my finger-tips and Michael was asking 'And what next? Why don't they drown down there under the water? Why can't he have a silver colour like the big fish?' Oh God: it was back to the librarian again.

When the series of 'The Silver Jacket' was running the librarian said to me, 'I think the way you treated the spawning in such detail was splendid. No beating around the bush, children don't like being fobbed off. Congratulations.' That woman helped me more than she could know. No one else mentioned my writing to me. I thought Ulverstone had become a mean little town, but Ida Elizabeth Jenkins, when I told her about it in a letter, quickly wrote back: 'They may not know how to address you now you are a national figure. It isn't easy for people outside their own realm to realise their friend or acquaintance is still the same girl she was before her name was mentioned every night on national radio.'

The friendships remained and all seemed the same as ever but — the locals never mentioned my work.

In 1952 a letter came to me at Ulverstone, headed Victorian State School No.3805. The only good teacher I had had during my wandering childhood had written to me and 'the years rolled back'. He had driven back to Waaia 'for old time's sake' and:

I must admit that my chest puffed with pride when I read that my prediction of your ability with the pen had come true. There are so many things, which, predicted, remain as predictions only, that it is a real incentive to find that there still exist those who can by their own efforts bring out what is inside. Congratulations, little Dreamer, and may you continue to dream your way to the highest rungs of the literary ladder. (So, I didn't whack you for dreaming, did I? Why should I when your dreams were so well placed.)

He remembered my childhood playmate, Kevin Young:

Some six years ago, Kevin Young called to see me at Rye. He was studying medicine, and had retained that charm of manner he had when a boy. Two pupils, therefore, from Waaia have given me a thrill. That is very good when it is considered that there were only eighteen pupils in that school.

Perhaps one of the best moments of a teacher's life is to find that his work has succeeded. It has always been my belief that no measure of success or failure can be gauged until the pupils have taken their place in life. So, I had great Pleasure (with a capital P) when I called in to Waaia yesterday and read your charming letter. A little girl 'dressed in a gown of blue brocade' (remember?), a little girl who went to a little bush school remembers her teacher after fourteen years. No wonder the old fossil is pleased, and so he sits down at the same old typewriter which ticked out the Magazine in 1937, and says 'Many thanks, very best wishes, and remember me to your father and mother.'
Yours sincerely
Gus Schmidt

I was embarrassed that the thick-spectacled librarian might learn how very little education I had had. 'But' she said, 'You embarrass me with your learning.' I dared not tell her I felt, and still in a way feel, totally uneducated. Leaving school – a one-teacher bush school – when you are thirteen years of age can scarcely be called an education, no matter how well read or travelled you become. Yet, for all that, I have never wanted to go to university. I like to study and listen and then make up my own mind.

In between times I was writing short stories, some for the English magazine *Argosy* – such a coincidence that the title was related to the 'Argonauts'. There were plenty of outlets for short stories in those days, providing they were good enough. I wrote two short stories about boxing – my Father and his Father had both been interested in amateur boxing and Dad had quite happily let me trot along with him to the few bouts held in the bush. Invariably I had believed the man throwing a flurry of punches would win but no, Dad said such men merely knock themselves out while their opponent used his skill to wear him down.

Dad had known Ambrose Palmer, one of the greatest boxers Australia produced. 'He humped his bluey all the way to Sydney in the bad days. No one deserved the titles he won more than Ambrose.'

Such experiences added to the knowledge I believe every writer must have – you must know as much about mankind as you possibly can learn. To be narrow in interests, to assume some part of mankind is less worthy of your study than another, is to narrow your view to a pin-point. There are few with the erudition and rare scholarship to carry that quality. Can man read Kierkegaard and Kant alone? Does he not wish to know how the rest of his world faces up to each day?

My lack of formal education never worried me, perhaps because I was going too fast to know I was uneducated. The Council of Adult Education in Melbourne advertised a Summer

School dealing with, if I remember it rightly, Acting and Theatre. Mum helped me make a dress and cut my hair, and on one of our rare trips to Melbourne I managed to attend the sessions, conducted by Robert Morley, the British actor.

The class was bouncing along with enthusiasm when he asked us to come on stage, one by one. I was last in the line. He asked me to read, but I hadn't brought a book so I spoke: Macbeth. We'd been told to be brief. 'Glamis and Cawdor' I said, but no one heard 'Cawdor', they were too busy shouting with laughter at my pronunciation of 'Glamis'.

What had I done? I went to leave the platform but Mr Morley held me back. He asked the audience why they had laughed and he didn't look surprised when all but me pronounced 'Glamis' correctly. 'Why did you pronounce "Glamis" in that manner?' he asked me. 'I read it in a book,' I replied. 'Have you seen this play on a stage? Heard anyone pronounce these words?' 'No.' 'Who told you to read this play?' 'No one. I found it and I liked the story. So I read it.'

Robert Morley faced the audience and intoned: 'She liked it. She found it. She read it. Does anyone of us in this building so love literature as to have first read Shakespeare without having been told to? Without being forced to? And know it by heart?' There was a shamed silence and I crept back to my seat.

I wrote my first book in partnership with the husband of my friend Hans Maree at their home 'Lonah'. Hans was a folk artist who became my closest friend, until we both escaped from Tasmania some years later. Her husband, Piet, owned a publishing house in Holland. The book was a sort of descriptive, historical thing that was to carry advertising. For an additional sum I volunteered to get the advertising. I had no experience in this field but I was still young and keen and game for anything. I went up and down the north-west coast by train and visited business houses – from little shops to big companies – and in two weeks captured all the advertising we needed. I wouldn't do it again, but it taught me that every adventure opens up a little more of life.

When I began writing books I had, of course, no idea about how to go about getting them placed with a publisher. I looked along the bookshelves in the Ulverstone library and saw the name, Ure Smith. I liked that, so I posted my manuscript of *Hear The Train Blow* to Ure Smith in Sydney. The following week Sam Ure Smith replied – could I come to Sydney, fare enclosed. What a stroke of luck! I had, with all my ignorance, struck gold: the best and kindest publisher one could have. I knew nothing about publishers, publishing, the history or, more importantly, the stance and reputation of publishing houses. There was no one in the society where I lived who discussed literature. When I met Sam Ure Smith my delight bubbled out and with it my need to talk. 'Go on doing what you've been doing, don't let anyone talk you out of it.' And I did just that. For years there were nights when I'd have to wait until the children were in bed and settled down – only then could I write uninterrupted. I still write at night, many times switching off the electric light and continuing to write in the light of day. I don't do so well in daylight as I do at night, when all is silent and I am alone with my story.

The children's father hated my working – he saw it as defiance on my part. It wasn't. I did what I did because it was what I wanted to do. The children were happy and well cared for and I could see no reason to spend my days sitting down with women in the village, drinking tea and complaining about life. In the end, he just sort of accepted it.

Hans Maree was, of course, more sophisticated, as was her husband, and appreciated that if I had a talent then I must exercise it. Hans and I once left our children in the care of her mother, Mrs Gregorius, at 'Lonah' and took off on a train journey down the north-west coast of Tasmania (there were no roads there in those days). There were no other passengers on the trip to Zeehan and the guard promptly said 'Hop up

into the van with me, love, because there's a heater there.'
Like all West Coasters, he had lived there forever, and Hans
and I were both great listeners and 'nudgers' any time the man
drew breath. He knew this rare strip of earth and leant out
of his window and pulled in pieces of trees and creepers we'd
never known existed, as the tiny engine on the three-foot
gauge wobbled and shook its way southwards, pushing through
the ancient forest.

Further down, the engine slowed and a blast from its whistle
sent birds shuddering away from us as two Davy Crockett
prototypes pushed their way through thickets of growth. Both
wore possum-skin hats, as much for the warmth as for the fact
that they had no other head covering in this wild, wet area.
Their occupation was hunting possums. Any kangaroos? 'Lord
luv us no, they wouldn't be able to push through the bloody
undergrowth if you'll pardon the expression.' But the two men
had done so. Hans did beautiful wood-turning and was surprised
and charmed with the splendid timber. 'Oh gawd, you ain't seen
nothing' one of the men said. 'You hang on a bit' he told the
train driver and, turning to Hans said, 'Come to our camp' and
off he went with Hans in tow. She was a magnificent woman,
she had exhibited her art work in Europe, was cultured and
beautiful, yet she didn't hesitate and in a second had disappeared,
swallowed up by the vastness where the sun never touched the
forest floor.

I spent the interval on the footplate with the driver and
fireman and learnt the peccadilloes and peculiarities of driving
in mountainous land where tunnels and carved-away cliffs were
unknown. I was already gathering folklore and I filled in my
time well until Hans came back in view, pushing her way
through a maze of blueberries. The men were laden with long
logs of nine varieties of wood. 'Aw, that's nuthin. She ain't seen
the blackwood, the celery pine, the Tasmanian h'ash.' His mate
edged in, 'She ain't seen nothin until she sees the huon pine.
Golden it is.' Like all true outback men who live and work in

total isolation, these men had a speech unlike any other and the written word cannot convey it.

Then we went on to Tullah. Until the early 1960s there was no access to Tullah except by a little two-foot gauge rail line, and the railway engine was called 'Wee Georgie Wood'. Wee Georgie was named after a music-hall singer, and when Hans and I got to Tullah there were still posters in the Mechanics Institute for 'East Lynne' which had been performed there in 1912. You could almost hear a honky-tonk piano tinkling away.

We couldn't stay this time. Wee Georgie Wood huffed and puffed and threatened many times to run off the track – a thing we later learned was quite common. 'Actually, whenever she feels the urge' her driver said. When Wee Georgie stopped for water we two women would help haul the buckets up from the little creek down below the bridge.

When we reached Zeehan the railway men helped get Hans' car off the flat-top truck of the train and pointed the way in the blackness of night to a hotel in this once-booming town of silver lead. We went in, coo-ed, but there was no sound. No lights. We listened, we could hear the footfalls of a man's boots. It was the engine driver. 'Thought youse might be a couple of city slickers' (city slickers, from Ulverstone?), and he brought matches and candles and said, 'Take your pick of the rooms.' 'Are they all empty?' 'Every one.'

By daylight we were downstairs, our sleeping bags rolled and packed away, when a lady came to ask us to breakfast. 'There's nowhere to get a meal now, but once we were famous like the American movies. I'm Lil.' Staying with Lil was a helicopter pilot who worked for a mining company down in the southern area. While a hairy man took Hans off for yet more rare timbers, I went off for the first time in a helicopter which taxied down the main street of Zeehan a little after daybreak. After a long time of looking down on the unbroken vista of tree-tops the pilot roared 'Want to go down?' Sure I wanted to go down, but I hadn't thought of climbing down a rope ladder! The pilot held the chopper steady while three of us slid down a rope and had lunch in the small clearing the company had scraped out of this terrible tangled growth that grew thirty feet in height. The blowflies were so thick that the men threw a sheet of mesh over me. Men sat eating with one hand and waving the other frantically, grabbing flies by the handful off the food. In all my years in the bush I never saw anything to equal this revolting battle.

There was no reason for me to take that trip, but that was often the case – I got to places and came home without a thought of danger of any kind. When the helicopter landed at Zeehan that night Hans was waiting for me. 'Squeeze in most tightly' she said as she motioned me to her tiny car. Well yes, I would have to do that as she now had the boot open with timber sticking out and more timber in the car, leaving so little space that I must sit on part of the driver's seat.

We went to Strahan, a tiny port and I was invited to take a trip up the Gordon River with piners, the men who for almost a century had gone up-river and harvested the huon pine. When they began casting the lines off a young woman came running down the wharf and threw sheets and blankets on deck. 'If I'd known a woman was going to be on board I'd have made them make it more comfortable,' she called to me. I was mystified. Not until dusk began to fall did I ask what time we'd be going back and they answered 'In a week or two'.

Hans was a magnet and people flocked to her with rare wood, they loved her. And I had gathered enough folklore, local tales and myths to keep me busy. We returned to Ulverstone and our children, though later we were each to leave at different times, neither of us knowing where we would end up and we lost one another for many years. We both altered our surnames back to our free state – me to Adam-Smith, Hans to Gregorius – and, of course, we had many different addresses. Years later I received a communique from Red Cross International – and we two old friends were reunited. She flew to Melbourne to see me, I flew to Holland to see her, and our friendship had not altered at all. We travelled around Holland in springtime to galleries and music recitals, orchestral and chamber music, and old churches. She was as imaginatively innovative as ever and as strong as an ox: 'Oh Patsy, do not say that. An ox is not a thing to say!' She had bought a small traditional farmlet and had her weaving gear in her house. It was a lovely little place with beds let into the walls in the way of little historic homes in that area. On a second visit with her several years later, she had built – alone – an upstairs section with two bedrooms and, with help, an outdoors weaving room for her students. But eventually, to my joy, she returned to Australia and remains here.

I had lived a lifetime of wide open spaces: 'land, lots of land and the starry skies above' as the Americans had sung during the war. But now I was earthbound, pegged out like a sacrifice, I thought dramatically. I was told 'You are bound by the law, and the church, to come to bed with me.' I asked the priest and he said yes, that was right, and added that I should go home and 'stop being silly'. I said bugger the law and bugger the church, and he told me I was damned for eternity – and as if a great trumpet was blown I heard a terrified scream: it was my baby in the pram outside the door. A nun had put her big, black-bonneted head in the pram to talk to the child and the blacking out of daylight had been frightening. I always felt terribly sorry for that nun, she only wanted to kiss a baby. But I ignored her apologies. I lifted the baby out on to my hip and with the other hand pushed the pram and ran away home, down the road away from all churches.

I was getting myself into a lot of trouble with my 'in-laws' (isn't that a fearsome title?). The police sergeant of the town had asked me if I could care for an eleven-year-old girl for a long weekend. The girl's mother was being sent down to Hobart to gaol for drunkenness and other 'womanly' crimes and the sergeant couldn't get the child accommodated over the holiday period.

I put the child in the bath and her hair came up shining like golden fairy floss. For me, with my black hair, I thought it was the most desirable feature a girl could have. The child stank and Velvet soap seemed to be the shot. And she didn't mind these ministrations. She loved the bathroom, she loved my two kids, and loved the toys and books and a bed of her own. Two of my women friends helped me to get a supply of clothes for her. And I got her into school. She had somehow fallen through the net because the convent school thought she was at the State school, and the State school thought she was at the convent school. When my mother-in-law eventually heard about this child in my home she was 'disgusted' and demanded that the police send her away. The young girl cried, I cried, the kids cried, but I never heard of her again, and thereafter I was constantly being given lectures on keeping myself 'nice'.

Thinking back, I don't believe these things worried me for long. I was too busy. I was into everything. I was a member of the local drama group playing leading roles; secretary of the Red Cross Ball ('Raven-haired Pat in elegant gown and shoulder-length gloves' as the local paper reported, without noting that both the gown and the arms-length gloves were made by me, the gloves from fly-net and the dress from cheap curtain material dyed blue in the wood-fire copper).

I was president of the Mothers' Club and attended and addressed the State conference in Hobart. I had children's birthday parties, all home-made cooking of course, and fun – except for one day when five-year-old twins grabbed the big pavlova cake and dived underneath the low divan and we couldn't get them to come out but heard a noise, not so much of eating sounds but more like snuffling food down like pigs in mud. By the time they surfaced they were throwing up all over my polished wood floors.

The energy of youth is a thing we never forget and the surge of it remains in your memory. We, he and I, and his aged father, made a long concrete path down to the front gate one day, and on the next we built a huge concrete verandah and the four steps leading up to it. The old man looked after the crude concrete mixer, I ran the wheelbarrow of heavy, wet mixture down to where the third party looked after the task of spreading the concrete – and that was hard, measuring and getting it boxed in evenly while I ran back the barrow for more mixture. The following day, young though I was, my legs were so sore I could scarcely move them.

I put a sealed bottle under the steps and in this I placed a penny coin, a half-penny, a threepence and sixpence, along with a note giving names and ages of the family – and now there is nothing to say a mother and her two children ever lived and laughed there. A fire-brigade building is now on the site but I reckon that no fireman will ever work so hard as did an old man, a young woman, and a soldier who had been away at war for six years.

It was the last great task I did for that house that had given me the pleasure of designing it and the delights of the children laughing in it. Like most things that have dragged on too long, the end came suddenly, and badly.

As my writing of features for national magazines progressed, I was being asked more and more often whether I could get illustrations to go with these stories. Well, mostly I was in places that hadn't been photographed. I had the good fortune – once again good fortune was my companion in life – to be in Devonport, the next town to Ulverstone on the north coast of the island, and went into the chemist shop. During the course of conversation the chemist said, 'You're the writer of all these great features, aren't you?' He said, 'It's a wonder you don't illustrate them, they're such exciting stories that it would be great to let people on the mainland and elsewhere know what the remarkable stories you tell have to show.' 'Well,' I said, 'my mother was great with a Box Brownie.' He promptly asked me why I wasn't illustrating *Hear The Train Blow* with my mother's snapshots and I answered, feeling quite silly, that I had never thought of it. As a hobby, this chemist had been photographing birds since he was young and had a rare collection, much of which had taken hours and days to set up his cameras for one rare shot. Without thinking I asked 'Will you teach me?' He asked 'Have you got a camera?' and I said 'No', so he said I should buy a good one – I would need a good one to cover the good stories I would write.

I returned to his shop a week later and asked 'How much would I need to buy a good camera?' He promptly said he had been thinking about it all through the week and had decided I had to make up my mind to either have a Box Brownie, which would make me a reasonable amateur photographer as my Mother had been, or to get the very best on the market. The 'very best' turned out to be a Linhof Technica, which used cut film 4 inches by 5 inches a sheet. This camera cost over £500 in the early 1950s, and he said 'It's that or the Box Brownie', so I agreed that was it.

The chemist said he would buy it in through his shop, and I could pay it off. I said, 'No, I never book anything unless I can pay it at the time of delivery.' I told him I would have the money within a month, and I did. I wrote till my hands nearly fell off, and I wrote a letter to the wonderful editor, Otto Olsen in Sydney, and told him what I was doing. He paid me for the features I sent and gave me an advance on the next five features. And the day I got that letter from him, I got on the train at Ulverstone as soon as the children went to school, went to Devonport and the chemist had the camera waiting for me. It was a very exciting time, and he was able to take an ingenue such as me and teach me to become proficient in the art of photography. As well, he insisted that I must learn to develop and print my own films.

This became one of the great joys of my life. I could never have imagined such pleasure in work as developing and printing my own photographs brought me.

Because of the type of film that went with the camera, the already cut sheet of film had to be loaded in complete darkness. The merest gleam of light would ruin this film, so to load it meant always finding somewhere that was totally and entirely dark. An added difficulty was that I could only take a certain number of loaded films away with me because of their sheer weight and size. Each sheet of cut film arrived in its own covering and had to be loaded, not into the camera, but into a sheath which took some time and care. The two sheaths were pulled out, one for the front and one for the back, loaded with film, and then the totally blacked-out sheet was pushed across it, the other side was loaded the same way. Invariably you would see your best shots when you were well down on loaded film, and would then have to work like an angel to make sure every shot counted, although, paying as much as one did for the film, one always tried for the best shot anyway. I tried to get by with as little weight as possible: twenty of these laden sheath holders which, of course, meant I was carrying forty shots, then extra boxes of the cut film in case I ran out, and then the great camera itself.

My mentor in Devonport taught me that lots of attachments were not necessary and, if I shot well, I would need only one more attachment to this camera and that would be a very good flash unit. In those days, a flash was a heavy thing, it had its own big battery and, of course, one carried extra batteries. The flash was 6 inches in diameter and then there was the flash bulb. These flash bulbs, for some reason, were more likely to flash if you licked the top of the globe – I've no idea why, but it was a habit we all had in those days, giving a flick of the tongue on the top of the globe.

I decided early on I would never take a tripod with me, not only because of the additional weight but because my shots were invariably taken 'on the run' and I really didn't want studio-type shots – I wanted people as I saw them.

My friend the chemist sold me a pigskin camera shoulder-bag for all the attachments, globes, etc. and with that and the great amount of equipment that was necessary I set off. This camera turned out beautiful work and I loved it. It was one of the great pleasures of my life to go out with all this weight on me and see what I and the camera could do together.

Down to the Sea in Ships

THERE WAS A SMALL WHARF at Ulverstone at the mouth of the River Leven, but there was little cargo to be got now, so was it fortuitous? remarkable? or just plain lucky that the children and I happened to walk that way on our daily visit to the beach. 'There's a ship!' the kids cried and the three of us ran. It was the *Willwatch*, a tiny, old wooden tub that could scarcely keep afloat even at a wharf, and yet I learned it spent its days in the dangerous waters of Bass Strait. There were hundreds of birds strung from the rigging and I called to the Captain, 'What are they?' and he said, 'Mutton birds, from the Bass Strait islands.' I had never heard of them. He told me they were one of the most plentiful birds in the world, and that they travelled annually from the southern hemisphere to the northern but always returned to the Bass Strait islands to lay and hatch their eggs. 'Tasmanians have lived on their flesh for a century' he said. 'It's a romantic and exciting story' and he leapt over the side of the ship and began to walk off to Paddy Bourke's hotel. 'How do I get there?' I shouted at his back. 'A little plane once a week, but if you have any sense you'll go by boat and learn the whole story.' So I did. The children went to stay with my Mother for the school holidays, and eventually I wrote two books: *There Was a Ship* and *Moonbird People* about the islands, people and the birds. It was, in a round-about way, the beginning of my life at sea for six years.

A woman can sense the presence of another woman having been in her domain (perhaps the same is true of a man?) and when I returned to Ulverstone after this trip the vague odour (emanation?) of another's body was in the house. A woman's body. Without hesitation or thought I went to his wardrobe, to the top pocket of his suit, and my fingers brought out a packet of condoms. Condoms! There is something unlifelike, unjoyful about rubber. I could never willingly accept them – he had always made me use the 'devices'. Now they were merely an assurance that intuition had not failed me.

I waited until he came back from wherever he had been and he returned with a young man, who he said was living in the house with him. And I'm sorry I did what I did in front of the younger man. I never knew his name, never saw him again, which isn't surprising because I forgot the most basic of all civilised behaviour and waved the coat and the condoms and shouted and generally went berserk. The children's father, also not surprisingly, was furious with me. He shouted, stamped his foot (twice) – and that took a bit of sting out of the proceedings because I'd never seen anyone stamp their foot although I had seen it written of in books. The young man said he would leave but my children's father said no, that it was I who should leave, but on saying that he himself stumped out, leaving me with the young man who said he was very sorry, didn't say what for but he was inoffensive and he did appear to be sorry, for whatever. I told him I'd be back when I picked up the children who had stopped off to play with the local doctor's kids.

'There's a lot of talk' my doctor friend said. 'What about?' 'You've been on a ship!' he laughed, and kept chuckling. 'A pretty, young wife going off alone with all that temptation around her!' I thought of that most unglamorous ship and wondered what sort of temptation that could possibly offer.

At that moment I decided to leave forever. And I never looked back – physically, emotionally or intellectually. Hans, my beautiful Dutch friend, had already gone and two other 'war brides' had left to go back to the mainland, one to return to her parents' farm in Queensland, the other to Sydney. As for me, I had never given deep or serious thought to leaving, just day-dreamed about it up till this day. I now set the kids to gathering up their toys and books and I packed two suitcases.

He returned and was furious to see his friend had gone (I didn't tell him his young friend had given me a hug and wished me good luck). For the fiery woman I could be I was very still now, silent. I attempted to move but he grabbed me and held me by the shoulders, shaking me against the wall and shouting 'Remember you are a married woman! Behave like one!' He didn't speak again but kept up the shuddering of the upper part of my body against the wall and I said nothing, I just kept thinking 'When he stops all this I must be very careful.' Eventually I sensed the violent exercise was tiring him and I sidled out of his grip. I fed the kids and put them to bed and read them to sleep. There was no further discussion that night. I slept in the guest bedroom with the door locked and there was a lot of beating on the door and threats, even an offer to 'forgive' me 'if you stop all this writing nonsense'.

By 7 am the children and I were off up the road to the railway station, my boy carrying one suitcase and in his other hand a big bundle of children's books and his meccano set, me carrying my portable sewing machine in one hand (they were heavy things in those days) and the big suitcase in the other, with Cathy clinging to its handle while she gathered in her other arm an amazing bundle of dolls as well as her favourite, Diddeley-Witzy. This was a doll as tall as herself that my Mum had knitted for her and to this day we still wonder about the origin of her/his name. At the time, when asked why she created this name, her reply was always 'Because he's a diddeley-witzy, of course!'. In later years she could remember every bit and piece she had gathered into a bundle to carry that day. It reminded me of Kathleen and I, as railway children forever moving to a new station, hiding every shard and tatter of our old life into every nook and cranny we could find in the rail truck that would transport us to a new home.

I didn't then, and never have had, any doubts that I could support myself and my family and I think that was, and is, a prerequisite for a future life if a mother of dependent children is without a partner's monetary assistance.

Friends took us in until I could get furniture for a place I had rented 'up the mountain' (Mount Wellington) – a charming stone house with a startlingly beautiful panorama and a garden. Although the charm of it dulled for me with the first snow fall, which froze me to the bone, the kids built snowmen and put woolly caps on their heads and loved it all. On occasions, when the snow blocked the mountain road, the school children were billeted with city folk, and this made me uneasy not to have my brood with me. We were a tight little family, and remain so.

There were lots of reasons for my leaving, but it is a poor thing who would kiss and tell everything. My children's father (I never referred to him in any other way, it was always 'my children's father') never discussed our relationship. My attempts to talk about it had brought the regular reply 'Don't be stupid.' I can say that he frightened me more than anything or anybody could have done when he said, in answer to my comment 'We ought to do something, go somewhere. We can't just sit here and mark time', and he replied 'What else is there to do until you die but mark time?' I tried to forget those words he had said, but they had gone too deep to get rid of them. It seemed like digging a grave before time.

He told people I was frigid. No lover has ever said that to me. Au contraire! Ah well, time told, didn't it!

Does anyone know the trigger finger that finally percusses the gun? Which moment from among the many horrid moments between an ill-matched pair releases the deepest feeling of finality? I know the day, the scene, the apprehension, and what came out of my mouth – which I will always regret for it must have hurt him, although I never really knew what did move him in life. He was always berating me for something – my actions, interests, friends, clothes, relations, children, food, interior decorating of the house, my piano, my violin, my not keeping the children quiet (why? I wondered), the list was always open-ended. His only love and interest was his vegetable garden, which neither the children nor I were permitted to touch. One day I watched through the window as he came towards the house, a broken onion stem in his hand (dear God! Could anything have been so banal?) and my head, my heart and my truth came into concert and spoke: 'When I watch you,' I said before he could berate the child who had broken the onion stem, 'I weep for poor Richard the Third having to bear that terrible hump on his back for life. I know the feeling but I don't know how to tear the hump off my own back any more than did poor Richard.'

In a sense, the marriage didn't 'break up'. It had never been a marriage. All there had been were two people who met briefly during a war, away from home and their own separate kind of people, she too young among the hysterical excitement of the times, he too prematurely old, worn out by a long war.

I was doing so well as a freelance writer that magazines began asking me to accept assignments, which meant I had all expenses paid as well as the fee for the feature. One of these assignments came my way through the Tasmanian Government Transport Commission. I was to 'cruise on a glamorous little passenger ship around the islands circling Tasmania'. Of course I'd go! Knowing that most of my work was done in tough, rough, sometimes dangerous areas, the Public Relations Officer added, 'Give you a chance to wear your glad rags!' So I began to sew. I made two dresses, one of a thin black and white striped cotton, and the other a silky pale green (perhaps for evening wear? I thought).

Sometimes, in retrospect, I permit myself to feel pleased, even proud of my spur-of-the-moment decisions and actions. This was one such. I minced along in my slim-fitting, black and white dress, knowing it looked good on me, and wearing my three-inch-heel platform shoes. I walked along the Hobart waterfront for the first time and there was so much to see I nearly missed the boat. In fact, I passed it a couple of times before recognising the 'glamorous little passenger ship'. It was a wooden vessel, three-hundred feet long, two-masted, and the crew loading stores looked like clones from *The Term of His Natural Life*. The name *Naracoopa* was painted on the bow and stern so I knew this was my vessel – and I fell in love immediately, and loved her until she was lost many years later. She was my home, my pride and my saviour for almost six years. She was grubby, grimy, sails patched, rigging in some disrepair, but she was mine. And then I met the Captain, forty years older than me, and fell into step with him too. His cap was a bit rakish, his eyes actually did twinkle, and he looked at me teetering on high heels and said 'The owners didn't tell you what the *Naracoopa* is?' 'I don't care' I said, and I didn't. I knew that what I saw was what I wanted. I may not have known exactly what it was I wanted, but I knew intuitively that I would find it here on this ship. It was this seventy-six-year-old man that made it possible for me to live the most free, happy, contented life a woman could have. And it all happened by chance.

As a cruise the voyage was a disaster. The ship was far too small to handle sixteen passengers plus the crew of seven, the steward was far too grubby to have been permitted to serve meals, the cook was often drunk – and so were the passengers as there was a Lilliputian bar on board over which the malodorous steward presided. The old Captain, who knew Tasmanian waters better than any man alive, was aware of the lack of quality of his crew so he spent most of his time, night and day, in the wheelhouse, trusting none but the engineer who, like all ships' engineers I met, was totally reliable. Two days out from Hobart the motors coughed and stopped. The engineer called up on the voice pipe to the bridge: 'The cylinder head's cracked Captain'. The Captain said 'Nothing can be done?' The engineer began to explain why nothing could be done but the dear old man up top interrupted, 'I'm an old steam man, I don't understand these motors.' He went out on deck and reversed the flag at the stern and began hauling it up and down the aft flagpole, the signal of distress. There was nothing in sight, yet within two hours a fishing boat bobbed over, took our message, and sent news to Hobart via their own radio. When the shipping manager arrived by the lighthouse boat, he spent less than five minutes below on our drifting ship. Then, 'Alright ladies and gentlemen, I'll have a tow arranged and here before nightfall. If anyone wants to leave you can come with me, otherwise I'll be at the wharf in two days from now to meet you when the tugs bring you safely into the port of Hobart.' And over the side he went, into the borrowed lighthouse boat, and as the motor leapt into action he called to me, hanging over the ship's rail, 'You ought to get a great story now, Patsy Adam-Smith!' And there was nothing about him at that time to warn me that he and I would spend six tumultuous years together.

When the rescue boat arrived the tug mothering us relieved us of our immortality and reminded us of the morrow. The magical moments of the timeless day had gone. The ship was little and smelt horrible and the passengers were always 'looking for something to do'. I escaped up top-side and knocked on the wheelhouse door and asked Jack, the Captain, if I could join him. The tow rope was very long, its great length weighted down beneath the water with mighty anchors to prevent its 'whipping'. So far away from us was the tug that it was out of sight and we sailed silently, sail-less, in a waveless ocean in a windless world. Later in the night, far ahead, a thousand feet above the sea the lighthouse on top of the peak of Tasman

Island sent out its warning. No other light showed. The whole world, it seemed, was water.

Without thinking, I said to the old man 'I can work hard physically for twelve hours without a break, I'm quick and reliable, I can take orders but I won't take nonsense.' (I am told he later repeated this speech of mine to the whole waterfront.) And the old man said 'Sure, I'd take you on.'

Shortly after that deplorable voyage on the *Naracoopa* I travelled to Launceston in a car with the Commissioner for Transport in Tasmania and the Manager of the Transport Commission Shipping Service. 'And how did you enjoy your trip?' the Commissioner asked me. I had had time to think about the things that were wrong – from the passenger side – and how they could be righted, and told him. Before we reached Launceston I had been offered a job on the ship, with the same pay as the seamen, which was far more than I could earn on shore – and as I had grave family responsibilities this was important. A cabin would be built on deck for me as a radio shack (as it was called on board ship), if I would give a guarantee to stay twelve months, all providing the Captain was in agreement. 'Oh, he likes me' I said truthfully. The old man and I had got along well.

I have often been asked 'But how did you get started? How did you first get on a ship?' More women are interested in the *going* to sea than the actual life and work and the sea itself. The majority are prevented and get no further than daydreaming about it through a haze of romantic paperback literature. From the time the first logs were paddled across rivers, seamen have been used to women on vessels. The fact is that seamen have never objected to a woman sailing if she knew and performed her duties and had ordinary common sense.

I knew the *Naracoopa* was a beautiful little ship. She was only sixteen years old, not at all old for a wooden vessel. She had been built expressly for the island trade. There's a saying among Straitsmen that the little wooden island trader that hasn't scraped the bottom has never been properly worked. These craftsmen-builders knew this and they built accordingly.

While the radio shack was being built on the *Naracoopa* I decided it would be a good idea to get some experience on small ships. It was school holidays and the children were on the farm with my parents when I flew to the Furneaux group of islands and met Les Jackson, 'Wallaby' to his friends for his feats in 'jumping' the shoals that surrounded the isolated islands. I had been told the Jackson family on Flinders Island might be able to give me a job, and that was how it came about that the first ship I worked on was the *Sheerwater*, a scruffy, eighty-ton wooden ketch. There were three little ships tied up at Whitemark jetty on Flinders Island and I was told they all belonged to the Jackson family. 'Wallaby Jackson would take you on board' the proprietress of the only hotel on the island told me. Wallaby came from one of the old island families. His grandfather, father, mother and sister had worked small ships including the *Sheerwater*, *Margaret Twaits* and *Prion*. With no questions asked Wallaby said 'Yes, I'll take you on board', and we set off through the notorious Vansittart Shoals and the Potboil that surround the forty-two islands and its wreck-strewn waters.

On the *Sheerwater* the Manning Regulations demanded only one man be certificated, the Captain. The rest of the crew were the flotsam and jetsam of the land who sailed just for a job. There were men who were willing to work for a handout when we made port, men who were brought to us by probation officers, and many more came direct from gaol knowing nowhere else they would be employed.

I slept well in my hammock-like bed, I ate like I hadn't eaten since I was a child. Since I came on the ship I hadn't had time or the solitude to remember things that time doesn't always heal, no matter how the sanctimonious tell you it will. Most of the voyages on the *Sheerwater* were of only a few days duration. One day, after I had been at sea for six months around the islands, the ship returned to Tasmania and we tied up at Town

Pier in Launceston. Rene, a girlfriend, came to tell me she had found 'just the job' for me, teaching piano and violin in a girls' school. I told her, because the crew were within earshot, to 'stick it up her jumper'. This delighted the crew. Not only had I refused what they considered a 'very posh job''and had preferred to remain at sea, but I had also used a crude expression in doing so. They thought it was something I'd learnt from them.

I had been on board the *Sheerwater* several times but when we tied up I rarely went out on deck or made a spectacle of myself in the port. But one day I heard a woman's voice calling from the wharf 'Gel! Gel! Come out here, gel!' – a most refined accent. Pete, one of the crew, came into the saloon and said 'There's an old tart out there, very posh, wants to see you.' I knew by her voice she was no 'old tart'. As I hesitated, she called, 'Gel! Do you want a bath?' I leapt over the coaming and rushed on to the deck. 'I'd kill for a bath' I said to the elderly woman on the wharf. 'Well, hop in' she said, and I hopped into her car. Violet was Mrs Hay, and she belonged to the well-known Kelly family. (Kelly was one of the legendary eleven men who played and won the euchre game at Broken Hill for the shares in one of the richest mines discovered in Australia.)

And why was this very comfortably-placed lady in such a harsh, hard labouring area as the Furneaux Islands? She owned an island property and it was up for sale and she, in her seventies, was there to see it was prepared well for the auction.

I wallowed in the bath until the water went cold. I ran more. I never knew how utterly gorgeous was hot water. 'Feel like a gin and tonic?' she called. Did I ever! And so began a long friendship until Violet's death.

I never had trouble with the wives. They sometimes came down along the wharf to have a quick look at me but seemingly realised I was no threat. But if I were a wife of an engineer I'd watch out for him. All engineers are in love. And I don't think they tell their wives about it! They all adore their 'donks' engines, to the exclusion of everything else. There are no half-way engineers – they are either dedicated or on shore. They get their pleasure in watching the ship's engine, the pistons thumping up and down in harmony, and knowing the exactitude and precision of this big heart-beat will take this ship over still waters that landlubbers have never known and amid storms no landlubber would risk.

We rarely berthed at Whitemark, the 'capital' of Flinders Island. The rise and fall of the tide at this port was such that when the tide went out the ship lay on her keel with the result that the cargo could not be off-loaded until the ship again rose up with the incoming tide to the level of the wharf.

One day, while waiting for the tide to come in, I put the rope ladder over the side, climbed down and walked out quite a distance on the sea floor without getting the uppers of my shoes wet. From there I took a photograph of three ships lying on their sides: the *Sheerwater*, *Margaret Twaits* and *Prion*. At one time or another Les Jackson's family had owned each of them and by now I had sailed on all three of these wooden vessels, but most often on the *Sheerwater*.

At last it was time to join the *Naracoopa*. Like all men on small ships, I was a jack of all trades and the old Captain of the *Naracoopa* taught me a great deal about ships and the sea. It became my task to man the telegraph when going in or out of port or in tricky waters. The telegraph was a simple thing, a manner of sending messages down to the engineer below. There was 'Slow Ahead', 'Half Ahead', 'Full Ahead' and the same in the other direction for going astern. And the last signal of any voyage was 'Finished with Engines', the best signal of all. Like all other seamen we had an unmarked signal 'Give Her all She's Got!'. The Captain also encouraged me to study on shore and get a radio officer's certificate, which meant I could man the radio morning and night and any other time when necessary. The rest of my tasks were much the same as that of the crew – loading, unloading, tallying timber as it came on board, loading the sheep or cattle, and cooking if the cook was 'on the turps', as Mick, the engineer, explained it to me.

Little ships become figures of fun in big ports precisely because of the funny, off-the-beaten-track landfalls they must make, and take to the people there everything they need to turn their isolation into home. The Tasmanian Government had bought the *Naracoopa* to provide for these people, cut off from other forms of transport provided by the State. Few of the places we visited had access by road; for some we were the only link with the world.

To get to the east coast of Tasmania we had the choice of two routes: 'the long way round', going south past Cape Raoul and round Tasman Island, or 'through the ditch', the canal at Dunalley. This canal route was not only shorter but it was through smooth, sheltered waters. 'Round the Raoul' was never smooth and was mostly rough to very rough. 'Taking her round the Raoul' was synonymous with 'having the guts rolled out of you' in *Naracoopa* language. But the canal had its moments also.

The first time I went 'through the ditch' I nearly said 'Jeez!' like Pete, the deck hand. The actual cut is through only half a mile of land, a narrow isthmus over which the old-timers used to drag their small boats. Near the Hobart side entrance there is a bridge for road traffic to cross. As the ship neared the canal, old Jack pulled the whistle cord and the mournful hoots went whoop-whooping across to the bridgeman who wound the bridge open by hand. I thought there must be a mistake. Was that tiny gap all the space we had? The closer we got to it the smaller it looked and the larger our ship seemed to become. Old Jack called down from the flying bridge (Monkey Island to us) 'Full Ahead' and it was rung through on the telegraph. Speed wouldn't get us through that strongly timbered opening, I was thinking. Then Jack called, 'Half Ahead' then 'Slow Ahead'. Ah, that's better. He must be going to turn her round and head back to the nice big paddock of sea behind us. 'What's happening?' I asked a seaman who was scurrying by. 'Terrible strong tides come through such a narrow cutting,' he said. 'Big bay on either side. They sweep through like fury.'

I looked over the side. The water was charging along, carrying us with it at a speed faster than our motors could ever have taken us, closer and closer to the shrinking gap. The boys on the focsle were hanging motorcar tyres tied on to ropes over the bow as fenders and were standing by to adjust them if necessary. They'll be needed for sure. The mate was standing by to let the anchor go if need be, the wheel behind me in the wheelhouse now being 'ghost driven' by the wheel above on the flying bridge which was swinging first one way then the other as old Jack, alone on the wheel, fought the surging tide.

And then we were into the gap. 'Full Ahead' Jack yelled, his voice strained and panting. The tide was now running against us from the bay on the other side of the cut and he was countering it. Even as we slid through the gap I still didn't believe we could make it. Crowds of tourists, on their way to and from the ruins of the convict settlement of Port Arthur, hung over the gate on either side of the bridge opening but as we came closer they began to run and were well back as we reached the bridge. Only the bridgeman remained. He smiled through the wheelhouse window at me, but I was too startled to return the greeting. Up on the focsle the boys were hauling in the fenders. We were through. Pete came back to tell me. 'There's six inches of clearance when we go through the bridge,' he said. 'Jeez!'

Going to sea on small ships did not mean one was tied to the job as are 'land lubbers'. Crews signed on and off in their home port when they so chose and, as well, we were often 'on the beach' when the ship was held up in port for any or many reasons. Once a year, 'she' went up on the slips in Hobart for annual overhaul and the whole crew signed off. Once the *Naracoopa* was held up for four months during a refit, and sometimes because of odd repairs. For many months she lay in the docks because she was under arrest. The very thought of a ship being arrested excited me and I attended all the court hearings.

The AMV *Naracoopa* was unique in her day: she was the last of the ships in Australian waters to be arrested in the time-honoured way of having her crime nailed to the mast – her being a wooden ship.

The owners were accused of taking the ship to sea in a dangerous condition. What had happened was this: we never, at any time, had loaded beyond the plimsoll line, but often a very heavy load was on deck and this cracked a beam and a disgruntled seaman reported it to the harbour master and he sent a man down with hammer and nails and the accusatory document, and so our ship was arrested, banned from going to sea.

Three men sat in judgment on the lovely ship, none of them, we believed, having qualified to so adjudicate, none of them having been small-ship men and therefore ignorant of the various seas around the coast, and only one of them having been at sea and that on a ship during the war. Some ludicrous things occurred during the hearing – one of the three had difficulty in learning the nautical terms such as focsle. To read the word on paper is one thing, but to speak it is another. Seamen pronounce it 'folk-sul' (the focsle is merely the front part or bow of the ship).

Each day of the hearing I sat with old men in the court, each day lunched with them, and every day I was enchanted. These expert witnesses, called by the ship's owner (the Tasmanian government) were, every one of them, old men who knew wooden ships, knew how they handled, sailed, responded to heavy seas, knew the difference between heavy seas and the dangerous currents in the Straits, knew how to load their cargo, what stresses their ship could take. They sat stonily staring at the three, expensively-suited men sitting in judgment, but outside the court they laughed at the three of them. Their stories were the stuff of life as it is led on the sea – and no landsman can know of it.

In a long break during the hearing the children and I drove north to Launceston and there, on the banks of the River Tamar, the man who built the *Naracoopa* and many of the now-old wooden ships spent a day with us walking around the areas where he had built 'our' ship, showing us the impression on the long-dried mud where the cradle had been shaped, the remnants of timbers he had gone into the forests to choose for the keel that had once been a single tall tree and was now shaped to be her backbone, the stem rising from that shielding and joining her side planks like a breastbone, the planks (strakes, as seamen call them), from the garboard strake to the sheer strake on the gunwale (or 'gun-ul' as seamen say), and the ribs, the keelson, the sister keelsons, butts and stringers.

'The ship must *work* for the same reason that a tall building must *sway* in the wind so that the strain will not cause it to snap,' he told us. 'The harder the sea attacks, the more the ship works, groaning and moaning as her timbers take up the stress and strain.

'The sea can't sink a good ship. Only the land can do that,' this fresh-faced old man assured me.

Back at the court, the ship's own witnesses were at last called. One witness, 'the professor of stresses and strains' as the boys called the in-truth professor, demonstrated with a box of matches that the crack in the beam had been caused by the cargo on deck, not by any weakness in the ship itself.

The ship, already repaired, was, after a long period of time, released and we set sail in rage at the long period of being out of work, and we never mentioned it again.

Not that the lay-off periods worried me financially. I had my portable sewing machine on board and was paid for repairs to the ship's upholstery, sheets, covers etc., and once – a real bonanza – the making of black-out curtains for the wheelhouse with three layers of material. (We were to get the latest equipment, including radar, but of course it didn't work for our rock-hopping, dog-barking type of navigation, so the curtains ended up as decoration.) I made shirts for the crew – never asking where they got the bolt of material – and, as well, I cleaned out all the storerooms, scrubbed and then with the victualler, restocked the 'hard' stores for six months. It was a nine-to-five job and I found it aggravating to hear the five o'clock bell warning the workers to leave. In my life I had been used to working 'until I dropped' as the saying goes – and I learnt that a fixed timetable did not suit my inner clock, and it never has.

With all these long 'holidays' I also learned that growing children don't care to be smothered by their loved ones. They want to be fed, watered, sympathised with, advised (only to a degree!), sometimes chastised if for good reason – and loved. It is the loving that counts, the bonding.

I cannot praise a fugitive and cloistered virtue, unexercised and unbreathed, that never sallies out and sees her adversary, but slinks out of the race, where that immortal garland is to be run for, not without dust and heat.

Milton

In November 1993 the Australian National Maritime Association at the maritime technology conference quoted these words which appeared in my book *There Was a Ship*. These words of encouragement had been sent to me by the artist Russell Drysdale, who was aware of the social disapprobation I might be suffering in my determination to become a seafarer. Thirty years after I had left the sea, the executive officer of the association presented a paper titled 'Women at Sea, a Background Paper' which included records of my journeys at sea. The records seem to show I was the first woman in Australia to sign Articles on a merchant ship in Australian waters.

John Steinbeck wrote in *Travels with Charlie* 'When the virus of restlessness begins to take possession of a wayward man and the road away from here seems broad and straight and sweet, the victim must first find himself a good and sufficient reason for going.' If it is necessary for a man to present a good reason for heeding the urge to be somewhere else, then it is certain that a woman must invent an even more foxy excuse.

If wanderlust has set its seal on you – like in the sign of an anchor coming up – you may be sure, man or woman, it has also been tattooed into your reflexes. It is a hereditary disease in our family. If my Mother were to hear a train whistle on a cold night when all the house slept, the banshee wail crept up and over her and passed on into nowhere just at the moment she was catching her breath. I saw it happen often: the stare, without focus, that to an outsider seems vacant, the slight lift of the head, as though she were listening for some faint, eerie melody. She told me she had once found her Father in this attitude, never realising that she herself behaved in the same way. They were living deep in a forested valley in Gippsland, Victoria. It was late at night and frosty; high above them on the hills the cloppity-clop of a horse's hooves picking their way on the flinty stone track died away in the distance. 'I think I'll have to go to Queensland to try to get some shearing' my Grandfather said. And go he did, all to keep his family in food and shelter while the struggling cow cockies around him were fending for their families by staying at home.

All this made me aware it was no use wasting my Mother's time with excuses for my going anywhere. 'Off again?' was the extreme of her curiosity about my sudden departures.

When I went to sea I was still in my late twenties, had two children, and belonged to the Country Women's Association, the Mother's Club, the Red Cross – the lot. In 1954 to go to sea on a merchant ship, where I would be the only woman in a crew of men would not only shock the residents of a small (two-pub) town, but the rest of Australia. I struck it lucky; although my years at sea were sailed in the most dangerous waters of Australia it could not be said that they were boring – or domestic. Now I'm able to say 'Wouldn't I have been a fool not to go to sea, to miss a chance in a million?' I was the first Australian woman to be articled on a coastal trading ship, to be taken on as an equal by men, to have a freedom few women ever achieve, and to be judged by one standard, the criterion by which everyone is judged on small ships: the ability to work hard and pull your weight and shut up about it.

I was obviously not living, as one society columnist of the day gaily reported, as 'Raven-haired Pat, away from the madding crowd, soaking up the sun on a sea-going cruise.' (The crew didn't see that; they rarely saw a newspaper, thank God.)

Two brothers were engineers on the *Naracoopa*. When I told them I had all my expensive photographic gear in Hobart but had no printing machinery, they immediately saw this as an exciting challenge. Before I knew it there were bits and pieces spread around the small area of the engine room. They made a developing and printing machine as good as any such, and perfectly adequate for all my needs. They used a Glaxo baby food tin as a lantern case. The weight to move the machine up and down was an eighteen-inch solid steel cylinder, three inches in diameter (which came from God knows where and I didn't ask). By removing the back of my Linhof camera when I needed to print, they made slides for me to slip the major part of the Linhof on to this frame and there I had the best lens money could buy and a bellows that extended to twelve inches long, so all my problems were solved. They erected it in my kitchen on shore and I had great difficulty stopping the children playing with it because they could push it up and down and it seemed to be more fun than the meccano sets of the day. The camera and its accoutrements I carried everywhere. Even beneath the waters east of Bass Strait when our boat sank off Babel Island.

When I was a child I had learned morse code from my Mother, the old station mistress, but I couldn't fathom the plugs on the ship's ancient radio. It was a gargantuan museum piece that had originally been on an early aeroplane. I counted thirty knobs, dials and buttons on the wretched thing (modern sets have two), but within three months I had mastered it, had my radio operator's ticket after coaching from Hobart Radio ashore. 'VLQD' I would call up in the periods when the shore station took messages. 'VLQD' was our ship's radio code, Victor Love Queenie Dog. Like your army number you never forget your ship's call sign.

I 'stood by' for fourteen hours the day the *Willwatch* sunk. I'd turned on my radio to 'warm up' at 6.45 am and heard Mac calling. I roused the Captain and he and the crew crowded round the door of my cabin, which doubled as the radio shack. Mac was our friend, we'd often sheltered with him when storms drove us to run. But now we knew he was gone. I'd written down every call he made including the last. 'This is it – cheerio. See you later,' and we never heard his voice again. He and his crew of four disappeared with all the other ships that have been lost in Bass Strait including, in time, the *Sheerwater* and the *Naracoopa*.

I sailed with five different captains, only one of them really bad, but another got drunk and ran us aground and that drove us all into a Marine Court of Enquiry – which we saw merely as a nuisance because it caused us to miss the tide at the narrow bridge and thus made us sail south 'round the Raoul'. I only knew of one poor Captain. He was with us for one trip only but it was eerie: he had never had deep, wild water beneath him, he was a river man and very young. He lost his nerve, or never had it, and ran to an isolated bay, anchored and wouldn't move. Our mate, a very old man, refused to take authority and he too shut himself in his cabin. Soon the cook was also shuttered in his cabin (not that that was so very unusual, the crew knew he kept a fair 'cupboard' beneath his bunk).

As a radio officer I had no authority to initiate a message or instigate action, though I still had to work the radio on the regular schedules. As the third day dawned the engineer suggested we attempt to make contact with the general manager. I waited until 11 am, a time when traffic was very quiet as we wanted to keep our dilemma as private as possible. Things moved quickly – we had been due into port the previous night, thus we would now be three days overdue and by giving our position Hobart Radio would know there was something amiss. I was to stand by and await a call. It came. 'Is the ship at anchor?' 'Yes.' 'Where?' I named the bay. 'Can you see open water?' 'Yes.' 'Is it calm?' 'Yes.' Again I was told to stand by. I still have a copy of the next signal, sent at 5.56 pm to the Captain. 'Your cargo is to be discharged immediately on arrival Stop You are expected to be here to commence on Saturday Stop Advise position with definite indication your intention Signed Baird' (he was the State Transport Commissioner). But by now the young Captain was not speaking or moving. He just lay on his bunk. He wouldn't answer. He was terrified of this fierce coast. Eventually the manager of the State Transport Service, Captain Alastair Maddock came to our rescue and took over the vessel. He had a master's ticket but little sea experience and the crew were sceptical and hostile. They changed their opinions when they learnt Alastair was as strong as an ox. As a young officer in 1943 in New Guinea he had fought the American heavyweight boxing champion. (He didn't win, instead he had his nose broken in the tenth round and that left him with a rather attractive 'skew-wise' nose, as the deck hands said.) He turned our little ship into a business; where we had always run at a loss, now he turned it into a profit. We worked harder and for longer periods than ever before and almost doubled our wages. For me it was marvellous, all fear left me, I could now afford schooling for my children, a car, a house of our own, a housekeeper when needed, and regular visits for all of us to the mainland.

A country bank manager must have had great foresight and recognised a 'goer' when he saw Mum. The bank staked her, she first bought into a share farm, Mum supplying the herd and the owner the land. She moved from farm to better farm (seven altogether), building up her reputation with bank managers – a far cry from the depression days when she 'put it on the slate'. Now she had a lovely property in one of the richest spots in luxurious Gippsland, with a many-roomed homestead, 'The Gables', on a hillside. It had verandahs, gables, and looked down on gardens and paddocks sprinkled with daisies and daffodils, a herd of good jersey cattle and an expensive sire in the bull paddock, barns, cowsheds and a horse to haul the sled carrying milk out to the roadway for pick-up to be taken to the butter factory. The kids adored their visits there and Mum loved having them stay.

For much of the time, my daughter was at sea with me. We had two berths in the radio shack and Cathy had brought her usual uncountable mass of toys and dolls, and the crew added to that and petted and spoiled her. She fished over the side of the ship with the cook, was carried ashore from work boats to play on the sand. One day I heard the mate bellow, 'God almighty! No wonder the loading's going so slow, there's two of the crew building sand castles for her!' And so the siren was sounded and Alex and Pete reluctantly went back to labour.

My son, being older, was enrolled in St Virgil's College in Hobart and I showed the Brothers how to pick up my radio messages on shortwave and thus relay them to Michael. The Brothers got quite a kick out of all this and sometimes they would be down at the wharf waiting with Michael when we arrived in port – and the Captain always asked them on board for a drink. The greatest coup was for two of them to come up the coast by bus to Swansea and sail down to Hobart with us. 'We thought it would give the boy a longer time with his mother' was their excuse. Eventually I had to tell them that their kindness must stop, that Michael must not be given privileges the other boys in the college did not have.

The few of us who stuck the sea-going life for any length of time had different reasons for staying. I stayed because the money was good, or so I told myself at first. In time I knew I stayed for a different reason. As the months went by and I saw men who had been used to manual labour giving in, I developed a sort of stubborn pride that I was still hanging on. But there came a time when I must ring 'Finished with Engines' to my own motors and step over the side for the last time. I debated long and alone. I knew I had to make a break before I got to the point of no return.

My last trip would be to the Furneaux Islands and out to Babel Island to load the season's mutton birds in their casks, and to take the birders off the islands and return them to Lady Barron Island. It was school vacation and my children would be with me, so that when I left the ship the way of life that would then end would be a bond between us, not a barrier.

Seamen have a bond, they might hate one another's guts but even that is a bond. They have shared labour, laughs, hardship, cheating in a way that is unique, and they feel the loneliness when they go ashore. Even I have some of this though I have been away from the sea for so long.

Once, in Florentino's restaurant in Melbourne, a Greek waiter put the plate down in front of me with special care and attention. I scarcely noticed. Next he said 'I do hope Madame will remember this pleasant meal.' I looked up into the face of Hero, one of the Greeks who were in our crew the night the *Mutton Duck* sunk off Babel Island. He lowered an eyelid – much too subtly for it to be mistaken for a wink – and I told him I would 'greatly enjoy my meal'. And he almost ruined our meal bursting his boiler to make everything perfect for us – to the bemusement of my friends.

Another day, one of our crew went by me in the street in Melbourne and gave a most discreet wink. He'd passed by before I could say 'Good-day, it warms my heart to see you again.'

Alastair

INEVITABLY ALASTAIR AND I FELL in love; inevitable, not because we worked in such close proximity but because we were so similar in vigour, spirit, toughness, roistering good humour and furious, almost murderous tempers that always ended in cuddles and laughter. We both had that nicety of knowing how to keep the lid on the boiling kettle, and when to let the steam blow and the whole shooting match to begin. We never fought in public, but many's the time we barely made it to privacy and battle began as the door banged shut behind us.

On the Richter scale we would have hit twelve – full typhoon force. Once he grabbed me from the front and ripped the buttons, twelve of them, off my new overcoat in one mighty wrench, not in sexual passion but with bottled-up fury because of something that happened – I can no longer remember, but I do remember those beautiful buttons shooting off as if from a cannon. And our laughter when we got over the shouting.

Once I deserted him on the top of Mount Wellington because he wanted to stay up there in the snow and I wanted to go down and took the car. We never discussed that one again. He had got home near freezing. But neither of us held spite. We both had marital partners who, perhaps understandably, were cross with us although they didn't know any more about us than did any other citizen. And there were some wondrous, exotic guesses being bandied around.

My most beautiful, tempestuous, furious, and gentle lover warned me about 'people' but I said, 'It's nothing to do with anyone but us.' Of course I was foolish, I truly didn't know what a vicious creature the Public can be. But I soon learned.

Alastair and I shared such years that I cannot regret one hour of our wonderful growing-up together, for that is what our time was. Neither of us had known lovemaking of a real kind, neither of us had had a partner that matched in all ways: mercantile, travel, hard-labour, love, and sexual romping like children discovering it for the first time – as we were.

My children had had such a testing time that when they eventually met him they took to Alastair as if he had been at their birth. He, like me, was young. He was a great picnicker. 'Hey! The sun's out! Get the billy and bread and I'll get the car out!' We drove from one end of the island State to the other. The kids followed Alastair everywhere. He was interesting, interested, entertaining and firm, never harsh or unfair. They blossomed.

Alastair's marriage was broken, so was mine, and for each of us work was paramount. And so was money. We both had children to keep. We were both toilers, both had a brain and the want to exercise it, and we separately and together wanted to charter a ship on our own. We ran the *Naracoopa* for eight months straight, two crews, one off, one on, but we two worked unbroken time. And, dear God, how hard we worked.

We brought down timber (wired in great packs) from the east coast. The crew, including the engineer and sometimes the cook, would work up to forty-eight hours without a break (except for meals) to enable us to make the turn-around. My work on these trips was not physically hard: I had to tally the timber on board and was answerable to the timber mill and the ship. But as the hours wore on, particularly at night, my feet began to go numb and have no feeling at all as I stood at the wheelhouse window, making sure each pack was swung in-board and not taken back out for some reason. I had to note the numbers of every pack. Sometimes they would hover, swinging in the air for long periods when the men in the hold were rearranging cargo, and just before sun-up, when the energy had 'leaked out of our finger tips' it was tricky to remember if you had entered the number. You couldn't ask the men – in their state any little hiccup by this time would have caused near-mutiny. By now the calves of my legs and my thighs would be 'dead' and I'd try to use the high 'mate's' stool, but one could never take short cuts on a ship.

We proved we could work hard, and everyone knew it. But it nearly killed the three of us who went the whole distance. We were shaken, jittery and thin. Apart from our splendid engineer, there was no one else to talk to and he, like us, was exhausted.

When the last pack of timber was chained on the deck and the cargo was all aboard, it was 'all lines gone' and we'd head south, Full Speed Ahead, and as often as not I took the wheel as the sun came up and gave the men a rest for two or more hours.

We bought a house overlooking D'Entrecasteaux Channel and when we'd return from our sea-going, we'd spend nights flounder and flathead spearing, sometimes wading, other times in our flat-bottomed boat. We found secluded Randalls Bay and holidayed there many times, driving down all packed in the little 1940s black, square Ford with the row boat tied on top and our tents on top of that, a big water container strapped on the back and the four of us so squeezed in with gear and food that Smoky, our cocker spaniel, usually sprawled over the shoulders of the children. Smoky always went out with Alastair and the kids in the boat when they went fishing, but he always leapt over the side and swam ashore to relieve himself before paddling back out again. This lovely hideaway was never invaded because when any car pulled up the kids raced to assure the newcomers there was no drinking water and no toilets. We had this bay to ourselves for as long as we lived in the midst of the then vast apple orchards of Tasmania, along a bush track twenty-five miles from Hobart.

I was always glad that my two children had seen both Alastair and I at work at sea so that by the time the two of us were bonded the children knew our background, friends and workload, and each had become a part of this affection – and love.

We had never thought of parting – we were too busy. We were not only working the *Naracoopa* but Alastair was sent to New Zealand by the Tasmanian Government for many months to supervise the buying of three ferries that would not be needed any longer once the new bridge was built at Auckland. We had a grand time there. Each weekend, from mid-Friday to mid-Monday, we were guests on great yachts with men and women who delighted us with their way of life. In New Zealand I wrote a dozen stories for the magazines of the day. We were feted – Alastair and I had never known such times.

The yacht I most liked to be invited to sail on was owned and skippered by a now-elderly New Zealander who had won his wealth from the kauri forests: he had pioneered the building of quite big dams to enable the logs to float down the rivers where they were dammed until the whole big wooden structure was tripped, the waters crashed through the dams and logs floated many miles to ports – just as Canadian lumberjacks had done for a century. I was taken to visit his old Maori friends, and once he arranged for me to stay for three days with guide Betty at her home in Rotorua where she cooked our vegetables by dipping them into the boiling waters bubbling up from the geysers. I can't remember much of this visit. She was a stalwart drinker. I went down to the South Island with deer hunters, a painful cold place, walking across snow and ice and camping well, but it was still too cold for my desert-bred blood. I wrote some of my best features for leading Australian magazines at this time.

When my time to go back to Tasmania came I was happy to leave as I was returning to bring my children home from college. Alastair had to stay but would follow in two months time. We two lovers parted with no thought of the hatred that was about to end our idyll.

Shortly after we parted the children's father wrote to me, in a peremptory way, that he was going to use as evidence for the divorce that I had been 'guilty' of adultery. This was the 1950s when divorce, adultery, all things that should be private matters, were the province of the open courts; indeed, police were sent out to investigate such allegations. No adult in those days, particularly a female adult, was unaware of the penalty of copulation outside of marriage: it was a crime and police could investigate. That the *man* had been living with a woman was of less concern. Private investigators were said to 'sniff the chamber pot under the bed' to learn who had been in a room – at night. (One wonders if, in those inhibited days, few knew 'it' could be done in daytime?)

Alastair returned to our home from New Zealand. He had delighted in 'Ahava', the house and property my Mother and Father had bought on Phillip Island. Mum had given the house sign to Alastair to put on our house because he had so much liked the transcription, 'a place of peace'. Now our 'Ahava' was the lovely home among the Lady in the Snow apple trees.

And then, one night our bedroom window was smashed in. I was in shock when the man stuck his head in and formally stated that he was a private investigator who had been paid by 'the lady's husband (who is with me) to find evidence and sue for divorce'. By now the children had wakened and run up to my room. Afraid they would cut their feet on the glass I leapt out, dressed in my long, winter nightdress, and gathered them up on to the bed just as Alastair's car came into our grounds and the two men ran away. I heard their car start up as Alastair came running up the hall to our bedroom. He held the children tightly to him, calming them as I told him what had happened. He, Alastair, was savage. I remember being very calm because of his rage. 'But it's our home!' he said. I remember that, I remember he said it again and again. 'People can't sneak into a person's home and perve on citizens.' He was rigid with indignation. 'What sort of person would do this? What sort of man would peep through windows? How can the law condone it?' I realised he was in a state not so much of shock as of disgust. 'It's not right!'

While I made cocoa and settled the children he hurtled off in his car. 'The dirty brutes' he was saying. 'What a grubby mind.' And hours later when he returned he said, 'They've dirtied "Ahava".'

I didn't think anything of that at the time, what with mopping up the last of the glass and getting the children to sleep. Alastair came back with a policeman who took notes and drew diagrams of the room but left, saying, 'I don't think they'll trouble you again Captain, it's the evidence they were after.'

And then, one night Alastair said, 'When are we going to get married?' And I said, 'No.' 'You mean you won't?' We sat for a while throwing the words around a little. I knew he wanted us to be married but I knew I didn't. I said, 'We're getting along very well as we are, why spoil it?' He said no more, never mentioned it again. But that was the beginning of the end, and the end was bitter, destructive and costly while we fought for our possessions and the estate we had built up. All the threads that had held us together had suddenly gone, in the way threads do snap rather than unravel.

I didn't notice for some time that the house sign was no longer on our wall. Alastair had taken it down. Not until we parted was it returned to its rightful place.

There was still work to be finalised in New Zealand but Alastair went back alone. Christmas was coming closer and I expected him home. I phoned his apartment in Auckland. When he answered I knew there was someone with him and my common sense told me it must be a woman. 'When will you be home for Christmas?' 'You take the children to Victoria for Christmas' he said. There was a popular song at the time and I heard it running through my ears: 'Put your sweet lips a little closer to the phone, Just pretend that we're together, all alone ...Tell the man to turn the jukebox way down low, And tell the girl there with you she'll have to go.'

We three went to Melbourne and stayed with Phyllis, my army mate, but I was bowled over in a way that startled me because I could usually fight my way out of anything.

After a public debacle, noted for its bitterness and hate and financial arguments, we met again only once. He had married for the third time (not including his six unwed years with me). I no longer lived in Tasmania but was there on a promotion tour for one of my books when he sent a courier to ask if we could meet. My schedules were too tight. Then he phoned, but I was still unable to meet. I didn't know if I wanted us to meet again. I learned he was now in the prestigious government post he had always wanted, and I was happy for him. At 3 am the hotel desk duty clerk phoned my room and asked if I would take a call. We talked of the halcyon days and he asked for news of my children. 'They remember you with love and warmth.' 'Tell them I still love them, always will,' he said. I asked if his present wife had children and he said yes, and I asked if he was happy in his marriage and again, he said yes. And then, God knows how it happened, he was in my room. He had driven through the night from the east coast and was in my hotel when he phoned me. And he wept. And I wept, but we both knew we now had other lives to live and the meeting hadn't been planned for anything more than Auld Lang Syne. It was a cup of kindness and a grip of the hands across many miles, many labours, many kisses. 'How we worked!' he said. 'How we played, but how we fought!' I said.

That night, when I saw him for the last time, he surprised me by asking 'Why didn't you marry me?' I laughed, I thought of it as a joke, after all this time it had fallen very lightly on my ears. But he said, 'I never thought it was funny, the only thing that seemed funny to me was that you didn't marry me after all the turmoil was over.'

'We paid enough for it' I said.

And troubles never come in singles. I was being pestered by my children's father who wanted the divorce finalised quickly so he could remarry immediately. I'd never thought of divorce. The vows I had made were meant by me to be irrevocable. I never thought of them, they *just were*. I had sworn an oath, a vow, in front of a man of God or of goodness, and 'in the presence of' my friends and relatives. How could I then say no, I did not promise those things. I *had* promised, I wished now I hadn't, but the deed was done. I had lost any faith I had some time past, and because of that religion had nothing to do with my obstinacy: I had promised everyone I knew at that time that I would do this thing and so how could I go back on that? I still cannot believe I could break the only oath I made in my life.

So I said no, I wouldn't take part in a divorce and no, I wouldn't agree to give up my share of the house in Ulverstone that my money and my parents' money had been used for, and no, I would not have anyone else play my piano. And he got a lawyer and this man told me I had no choice: 'Your children' he said. I was told in the court I would not be allowed to keep my children. 'Their grandparents [his parents] are now in residence in the house you claim in part and they will bring up the children. The court will decide what access you may or may not have.' That was an evil thing to say. Those two old people were doddery, they could not look after themselves. But I was terrified because, for the first time in my life, I was aware that there was someone who could rob me of my strength and dignity and in doing that steal my children from me. Did I not leave the marital home? Yes, but . . . Did you or did you not? And so it went on.

Those were the worst days of my life. And when they had nearly crushed me they said he had come down to Hobart 'with his solicitor' and we could 'come to terms'! I had been told to get a solicitor, and he told me to sign. 'What? Sign what?' 'That you will forego any claim to the house and land and any monies you claim are yours.' And? 'In return, you may keep your children.' I only wanted the children and told them so, but I also shouted that I could provide all things for the children, including greater love and greater financial security, than could this man who was selling them. _Selling_ That was stupid of me. It reflected on the solicitors who, unknown to me, had of course made a deal. They both now shouted at me – all this was going on while we four were out on Murray Street in Hobart. They were indignant, they would 'not allow such scurrilous things to be said of men of the law . . . ' My solicitor apologised profusely 'for my client'.

And we started again. They exchanged manilla folders, I signed that of the man whereby I would not claim my rights to the house etc. and he signed mine saying he would not claim the children – and that stated precisely what I had been told: in other words, he did sell his children. And I was unsure that such an act was legal. So the rolling of the eyes and apologies from one lawyer to another about this dreadful woman client began again, and my children's father entered the remarkable exhibition and began grimacing at me – still outside in the street – at which his own solicitor came down in high dudgeon and abused him, telling him to neither speak nor 'poke faces' at me or he, the solicitor, would retire from the case.

It would be nice for me to be able to say I conducted myself well. I certainly didn't 'poke faces' but I knew nothing, had never before spoken to a solicitor except for one brief discussion on this matter. I only wanted the children – and I knew their father didn't care. He would get the house and land and the money my parents had put into the house. His lawyer said he would 'wish to have access', the father said 'Certainly' and got his military bearing underway, and it was all over. And despite that earlier protestation that he must have the children, he never from that day onward came to see them or asked for them to be brought to him, or learned if they were alive or dead.

I went back to sea. The crew knew all about it. The newspapers had loved it. A woman on a ship! Running the radio! On an all-male ship! The deck hands loved it. They were all for me, and offered to 'snotter' anyone who stood in my way. The Captain and the engineer took a truck up to my old home in Ulverstone and we got my piano and learned that although the old couple were living in my house, their son was living in a hotel in Brisbane, not in Tasmania. So I learned a lot about the law being a cruel ass, but mostly I learned what a precarious position a woman was in and the foul usage of the law against her. I was furious. I had mixed happily with men all my life and never had cause to learn what a shameful thing had been done to keep women 'in their place'. I'd always thought people used those words as a joke. I hadn't known until now that there were laws that certainly would keep women 'in their place'. But no matter what anger and frustration was in me I had to grin and bear it and get on with my work. That was a great thing about the sea – being a tough mistress it kept us too busy to waste time in tears and recriminations.

The
Sins of the
Flesh

I WAS THIRTY-TWO YEARS of age when I first used The Word. I had a happy home life, I had resolved the terrors of childhood, financially I was as comfortable as anyone bringing up two children can be. I had a pleasant home, great friends and social life, was a successful writer and, as well, I had a permanent professional position with some modicum of clout. I thought it was now time I exorcised the terror that remained from childhood. I walked down to the railway line, and going from sleeper to sleeper I tried to say ————, ————, but for the first two days I only got The Word as far as the front of my forehead, it was nowhere near my tongue. I tried it at home, but that was worse; there I couldn't even get The Word into my head.

Of course, I had heard The Word but not near so often as one would hear it nowadays, but I had certainly heard it and winced each time I did. But that was a long way from *saying* it. The day I got a whisper of it out, or thought I heard a whisper, I spun round and ran back along the side of the rail track and hid in a shed. *Hid in a shed*. I, a grown woman with two children. The day I actually said The Word aloud – not *very* loud but at least audible, I trembled, I actually shook, and the roar and the rush to my head made me giddy and I stumbled around until I eventually found my way home. I persevered, but it took time and didn't come easily until one day I made up my mind and practised, and when the postman blew his whistle I flew out to the gate and said 'The stupid bastard has come early'. I don't think I noted any reaction from the postie, but I know that when I got inside I felt wonderful: the sky hadn't fallen in, the earth hadn't trembled, I hadn't dropped dead. And in time I added The Word to my vocabulary that had never been 'nice'.

A strange aura hangs around the term 'bastard', and it is almost as remarkable today as it was before the 1960s, the years when the supposed sexual freedom began. Children of unmarried mothers do not usually attract unpleasant attention today, yet a discussion of bastardry *pre-dating* this freedom does retain the stigmata it had back in time immemorial.

The lexicon relating to bastardry is interesting. The *Oxford Dictionary* gives us a splendid history of The Word: bastard – illegitimate, one begotten and born out of wedlock, 'a natural child' (which begs the question 'when is a child unnatural?'). Of King Henry VIII it is said that he 'sent to bastardry his daughter Mary in favour of the Lady Elizabeth'. And there was 'the bastardisation of the children of Edward IV'. The dictionary continues: 'to declare or stigmatise as a bastard', and 'an illegitimate child by the civil or canon laws is legitimised by the subsequent marriage of his parents'.

I've not discussed bastardry with any other bastard, the subject never interested me as much as it has interested others around me. It has always seemed to me that a bastard might be much more free to develop as one wishes instead of being moulded into what you see and what is expected of you by a 'legitimate' beginning. Lawrence of Arabia was 'crucified', as has been written, for being a bastard. But if he had not become the friend and adviser to King Feisal and had remained quietly in a backwater, he had a much better chance for a quiet life of anonymity – a sort of marking-time until death, a slow death that I imagine the great majority of bastards do choose rather than to go in fighting under almost unbeatable odds.

In my childhood there were orphanages bulging with babies

brought there direct from the maternity hospitals. Institutions were organised and oiled to run smoothly: in Grattan Street, near the Women's Hospital in Melbourne, pregnant single girls could be housed safely out of sight until their nine months were up and then they would trundle across the road, give birth, sign the adoption order, or have the child placed in an asylum. She could go home as slim and single as she had been before and sometimes none but she knew. And the child? And the seventy-year-old child? What if she or he needs their original birth certificate?

I had phoned and asked for my original birth certificate to be sent to me. All I wanted it for was to enable me to get dual citizenship as I was considering living in Ireland for some time for study and, as an author, I could live tax free under this duality.

They replied 'Dear Patricia'. Their condescension offended me. I receive many hundreds of letters annually from men and women I've never met, but like me they take no liberties until the ground rules are laid down. I hadn't known that, since 1984, I was a genuine freak set apart from others, unable to be given my original birth certificate without having to walk on coals. The new laws mean that I am officially recorded by the jack-booted title of 'an adopted person'. My birth record is not part of the normal population, I am separated from the friends and people I have loved for seventy years.

Does this sobriquet apply to both of those whose seed and womb caused me to be born? And if so, are they listed somewhere in government files? And what are their titles? Are they listed as am I under a group separate from normal average humans? If I am recorded as 'an adopted person', 'illegitimate', are they too listed, exposed, as – what? 'illegitimate parents'? The document the authorities use call them 'birth parents'.

I learned all this after reading eleven pages in startled shock. I had served my country for three years in wartime and my birth certificate was never questioned. But this was different. Hell!

Half the army, navy and air force would have done a bolt had they been confronted with this document. 'Before information or documents are given to applicants, they must attend an interview with an approved counsellor' I am informed. Struth! I have to be interviewed! What sort of hoons are they, I'm thinking.

I'd like not to go, but I can't resist. It is so Dickensian. 'There is an application fee of $75 of which payment is required at registration.' I haven't been upset about these things since I was a little girl.

Only once was I annoyed by a young woman whose mother was a poor dumb cow of a woman who would have been an embarrassment to any family (well, after that outburst a reader may anticipate that I was rather cross about something). The daughter had said to me, 'I've been lucky to have a *real* mother, haven't I?' To compare my vital, feisty, hugging, loving, whacking, snapping, cuddly mother with this poor thing of a woman unleashed my disdain and I've never been sorry for it. She never put mettle into her daughter as my mother put mettle into me, nor the courage, the lifeblood that she sent coursing through me to enable me to live to the fullness of my capacity. Before Mum's death I told her of this encounter. She was shocked and angry with me: 'That was cruel. I never thought you had cruelty in you! That girl couldn't help having a poor sort of mother.'

It came 'out of the bag' in *Hear The Train Blow* and my large family of aunts went rigid. When the book was published they all (minus Mum who would have made seven if she'd been invited) gathered at my Aunt Anastasia's house and had their photograph taken in her front garden. My cousin Stephen told me much later that they had got a solicitor, but as far as he knew none of them had either seen or read the book. They'd merely heard that I'd written a book about the family so they assumed it would be very bad news. 'No one would have known,' I have been told. 'You know, people would never guess.' I didn't let any cat out of any bag. If there was a cat it had been bagged by society and tradition and dropped over a wharfside for the contents to drown, as had unwanted kittens for centuries.

I do not believe I am illegitimate, however, I believe that my 'natural' father and 'natural' mother were. Being born into bastardry today appears on the surface to occasion little remark and perhaps little or no disgrace. But to be born a bastard in the 1920s was to be a bleak outcast and few mentioned it though all showed it, either by over-acting in an attempt to show how very broadminded they were, or by suggesting 'you just want to forget about it and no one will know'.

It is not possible to tell today's generation this story and expect them to understand, and yet only two generations have gone by since a father took his shotgun off the rack over the back door and said to his daughter, 'Start walking. Down the paddock.' The eighteen-year-old girl began to walk and the father followed. But quietly, sidling from tree to tree, the mother followed him and when he raised his gun she called his name, 'John!' And so I, the foetus, lived to tell the story. Kathleen, my foster sister, had learned this story from my Grandmother, the woman who had saved me yet hated me for being what I was – before I was born.

'How wonderful! Are you really and truly a love child?' has been said to me. Love child! 'Jesus wept!' as the saying goes – or did He too, weep? I have never read of His mother's marriage, although in a European cathedral I once saw an ostentatious gold ring on the Virgin's hand while she gazed in adoration at the little boy on her lap.

And when I was growing up, what would I have done had I found myself 'in the family way', 'up the duff', 'cooking a scone in the oven'? I have always known what I would do. I would go to the sea. As a fifteen-year-old I had been down to the sea for a few days with an aunt and cousins. None of us could swim (we have a snapshot of the water mark on our bathing costumes to prove it), but I just wanted to sit on a tor at Black Rock and watch the water gently moving. The previous night I had heard through the bedroom wall the adults reading aloud from the newspaper of a baby found dead and wrapped in newspaper on a doorstep. If that girl had been me, I thought, I would go with the tide out to where no one would disturb me and my baby and the water would be lapping us to dreams. The babe would be in me, we'd be together. I could *never* have had a child out of marriage, *never* expose a child to the second-class status it was given in that period, *never*.

In those pre-pill times many, perhaps most, unmarried women 'gave their child away' and it would be a fool who would criticise them for it, and a cruel, ignorant, arrogant fool at that. Had they kept the child they would have been branded, both the mother and the child, and often the child would grow carrying the stigma like a visible neon light. And where would they live? Women didn't live away from the parental home until after the Second World War. Before that, the pattern was that one left one's father's home to go to one's husband's home. So, who would employ them? If she kept the child, there were no child-minding centres, no kindergartens in those days, no government handouts, no refuge centres. An adopted child – therefore a *real* child of a family, if the adoption was not mentioned – was almost as free as any other child, but an illegitimate child had little hope, social, economic or even religious.

Sometimes I look at the parents of friends and I think 'Hell! How would it be having *them* for parents?' No thanks, I'm lucky. I got fixed up with someone I could relate with, even grow to look alike and think alike and love, so I have to believe miracles really do occur.

It took a long time before I could utter The Word but once having it inscribed on my tongue I became most proficient. During the filming of my book, *The Anzacs*, I likened a man to a 'rotten, stinking, mongrel, dingo, bastard' and thought nothing of it – even if it sure did bowl the crew over!

And spare me, do, the smarmy titles. If you call me a love child I will call you a bastard.

The 'sins of the flesh' were mighty in those days if the priests, and doubtless every other preacher of religion in every pulpit, were to be believed. 'Eternal Damnation!' was one of the things you contracted from this particular sin, followed by 'Hell-fire Eternal!' and exhortations to follow the example of the Virgin Mary who was the only 'pure' woman on earth. Over this I got *what for* from Mum when I asked how could Mary have a baby if Joseph wasn't the father? 'By jingoes,' Dad said later, 'you'd better watch your P's and Q's before you say anything like that again to your mother.' By then it was all too late. I was about to lose faith for all time.

It can hardly be said that I delved deeply into theological works. I had no conventional piety. But I can say that I had, without knowing it, a great intellectual ardour untrammelled by 'the great believers'. My belief regarding religion, the hereafter (or not) remained my own. It is not a thing one must make public. As for Sin (writ large with capital letter), the bed seemed to be the cardinal sin when I was growing up. 'The Church' did not rail against the conditions of the poor, yet no priest in the country towns could have missed the sight of the holes in the soles of the altar boys' shoes when they knelt. The congregation could more clearly see this and one Sunday I and my sister saw a boy, well-known in our town, in mental torture throughout the whole hour of the mass when a piece of cardboard that had been cut to hide the hole in his shoe escaped and slapped around like a flounder fish whenever he moved.

Marion Tuohy had a friend, a milk-truck driver. In those days milk was left in big cans at the farmers' gates and brought into each town's factory for churning into butter. The young lads of our village discovered a relationship existed between the milk-truck driver and the 'toffee-nosed' Marion, whose father had a small grocery store which placed her in a superior position to almost everyone in our poor town.

Bert, the milk-truck driver, was married with children. Marion was a virgin about to be married. Well, of course, she was a virgin. What else would a good Catholic girl be if not a virgin? And if we wanted final proof it was that we had been given details of her white wedding dress. Well! There you are! No one would get married in a white wedding dress or even announce the wedding to people if they were in sin, would they? (And there was really only one sin for girls in those days.) We never doubted it. At least, not until the night before the wedding when the boys of the town were threatened with a belting by Bert, the milk-truck driver, when he found them on the back of his milk-truck looking through the cab window while he and Marion were stretched out on the front seat of the cabin – a very comfortable, long, undivided leather seat, as anyone who was around in the 1930s will remember.

Looking back, the odd thing is that the adults never appeared to 'get wind of it', but the story spread round all of us young ones, even to the details of Laurie Beatty's shoe which was lost forever when he tripped jumping off the tray of the truck, and of Ben Baxter 'getting a toe up the arse' when the mad-as-a-bull Bert caught up with him.

And there, next morning, Marion stood, a madonna in white, a virgin lifting her white veil, the symbol of purity. I was on the inside edge of the pew, near the aisle, Mum beside me. The organ roared out in triumph, the final vows and blessings had been given, and here she was, coming down from the altar. We all knew one another in that small town, and women were leaning over to kiss the bride as she was led down the aisle by her husband. I don't recall having any sensation except disbelief that such a thing was happening until Mum leant past me and, with the back of her hand, wiped her lips clean, ready to kiss the blessed bride. 'Don't!' I growled, not a screech, because I was too shocked. But Mum had got past me and kissed her. I wanted to scream out: 'No, Mum! You're too good for her. You shouldn't kiss her! She should kneel to you!'

I think it was Mum wiping her lips clean to kiss Marion that shot the light away from me. And it wasn't Marion's act that shocked me, but her lie.

I've never regretted having spent my childhood a 'Catholic', even if only in a very intermittent way. On the contrary, it was one of the great motivators of my life. From our relatively few forays to mass (in comparison to other Catholics who lived in built-up areas) I gained an abiding love for classical music as opposed to the cowboy and popular songs of my home and era. Where else could a bush child from a poor family listen to Haydn and Bach for a full hour, learn the ancient Gregorian chants, listen to the Te Deum, the Agnus Dei, thrill to the men's deep voices when they rolled out, like golden syrup, 'Kyrie Eleison', with the sopranos interrupting the last note with the entry of their 'Christe Eleison', and at Easter to take part in the Stabat Mater on Good Friday, that drama that excels most operas because you are crowded into the centre of the unfolding drama and turning your head and body to keep in step with the odyssey.

This wealth was the legacy left me by a priest who probably coached me because it prevented him being bored out of his chasuble in the dreary bush town. I learned liturgical Latin, not only for something to fill the vacuum of my days when I was fifteen years' old and already two years out of school, but because I loved it. And the priest began to teach me Latin 'proper'.

As well as the music, there were joyous, emotive, stirring, pretty things for a girl-child of the Australian bush, starved for anything that represented an attempt at beauty in those days. Mum bought for me a little, cheap, blue glass lamp with a candle inside to light at night when I knelt to pray, and there were pretty, glass rosary beads and 'holy' pictures. At New Year, the Saint Columba calendar arrived with reputable reproductions of great paintings for each month. When that was all you had, it was beautiful.

Because it was the only language I had heard spoken, other than that of my own country, Latin flowed like the honey the wild bees made. Black Viney, who came to us often, used to climb the trees and, with a little axe, cut out the 'sugar-bag' and the honey would run up our bare arms as we'd eat it with our fingers, and our black hair blew into it and the odour was like a sensuous lesson in antiquity and mystery. I could never forget the Latin, Viney, or the honey of the wild bees; they were exotic, even if they had originated ten thousand miles apart.

Very few of my years were spent as either a Catholic, or as a Christian, for that matter. Mum had been so often and so long away from a church in her remote bush childhood and bush roamings that she could have been a *nothing*, as she once wailed about me: 'She is growing up a nothing!' Dad was informed. 'Oh well,' said gentle Dad, 'I don't think she'll go far wrong.' Mum's reply to any words of wisdom from Dad was always a loud explosion of air that could have come from any or all orifices of her body. She would *boil*. 'Savages! That's all! Savages! How could she learn anything in this godforsaken mulga but the behaviour of savages!' And as likely as not, she would add, 'I'll apply for a transfer'. And she would, and all of us, kids, cats, cockatoos, parrots, Chu Chu (our Major Mitchell), cow, horse and dogs would be 'off on the wallaby again', without taking a moment to wonder if there would be a church within a bull's roar of us – and mostly there wasn't.

But I went through all the hysteria that many young children were swept into through the undoubtedly well-meaning pounding into our yet-undeveloped brains of the fear of eternal fire awaiting us if we sinned. My earliest fear was of this fire. 'Beginning at your toe-nails and slowly creeping . . . there will be no remission, no forgiveness, you will burn in hell-fire everlasting . . . '

My sister was a part of the nightmare that came every night from what seems to be my fourth year. If I was four years of age, my sister was eleven, and remembers it well: 'I used to put my head under the blankets so I couldn't hear you,' she laughingly says now. Each night I seemed to be awake, as opposed to waking up, I had flattened myself out with my back pressing on the wall above the single wooden plank that served for a mantelpiece above our fireplace. I was walking across the mantelpiece in my long nightgown, the flames were flaring up to catch me from the fireplace below. My feet were slipping, I had my hand out, reaching for Kathleen's hand, but she was always ahead of me, I was always reaching for her hand, but couldn't catch it, crossing the mantelpiece, above the leaping fire. And I was whimpering and could hear faraway sounds of – I didn't know what – and then I was beside Mum's bed, screaming, and she would reach out to tuck me under the blankets beside her warm, plump body. 'It's alright. It's alright.' Night after night, until I was quite a big girl, until I could control it, until much later when I faced it for the evil thing it was. And it never came back. But then, I didn't believe any more either.

The Sweetest Thing

IT IS SAID THAT THE 'fifties, the 1950s that is, was the dreariest decade in living memory. The smell of war was still palpable, reminding us of things we had to forget if we wanted to live, the economy had not got back on its feet, wages were still low, and an acceptance of drabness was etched on many faces. But not on mine. The 'fifties were the best times I knew and there was no grey time for me, not even low wages. If that decade had not swept me away my life would have been so very different I cannot envisage it, even to the point where I sometimes think I could not have survived it. Each decade of my seventy-odd years has been so good that the loyalty, tragedy, tears, shame, laughter, love, deceit, ecstasy, pain and the whole damned comedy/tragedy of life has made me glad my Grandfather lowered his rifle and left me my life. The old bugger!

As for sin, in the 1950s it was spelt with capital letters and read BED, although you could hardly call the odd places lovers had to resort to in those days BED. 'He's gone to move a cow' was a common joke, intimating that the area a cow had been lying on was at least warm and dry for the lovers. As were school shelter-sheds after night fell.

'Bed' was the cardinal sin when I was growing up. I eventually worked out in my mind that a bed wasn't the same thing as what I knew as a bed. 'Don't you go to bed with anyone, ever!' was an astounding warning to a young girl who knew, in that life of big families, that there was always someone going to bed with someone. Once there were five of us in the bed Kathleen and I shared all our young lives. It was an emergency – cousins and their parents tumbling off a train unexpectedly at 4 am – but it was a thing that any family from that era would remember. Until Kathleen married I had never slept in a bed alone.

The 1960s were the best times one could have chosen to make a break. The coming of 'the pill' opened up opportunities for women that we had not had since Eve plucked the apple and was damned as a temptress for giving it to Adam – the 'original sin'. None comment that Adam accepted the apple with alacrity, gobbled it down, and looked to Eve for more.

For most women the period before the 'sixties was the period of the missionary position. Until then I had put up with sex like many other women did, it was no joy just dull thumps and grunts until you were released. Deep in their psyche men had been brought up to believe we women were temptresses who led them to sex, and in one sense this ricocheted on them. I am sure many of us girls were so obstinately 'pure' only because we were determined that boys wouldn't be able to say 'she asked for it'. The men were, in a way, as badly off as were the women, and we must admit that. Now women can say 'No, I'm not afraid of sex, I just don't like you.' I am sorry AIDS has put a check on young girls today – I wish they could have the freedom that the pill gave to us women in the 1960s.

In the 1960s and 1970s the solid citizens of Australian towns were disgusted, and then alarmed, at the 'filthy' language young people were beginning to use. 'Four-letter words' were being hinted at. 'The most disgusting thing that has ever swept over our country' a most respected leader said. 'Four-letter words will be the downfall of the nation.' The four-letter words, fuck and cunt, are words in common use today, and I don't believe they have killed anyone. 'It's not a four-letter word that is obscene' I wrote. 'It's a three-letter word.' War.

*   *   *

Some women manage life without a lover. I don't. I never try to manage without one except when I'm so engrossed in writing a book that no man in his right senses would stay with me – or has. And I wouldn't want him, wouldn't want the sort of lover who would want to live with me at such a time. He would be an awful fool. This has caused many a donnybrook, tantrum, even hurt, on both sides, but that's how I am. It's nothing to boast about but at least I'm honest about it. I know I'm hard to live with when I'm writing.

I've loved my lovers with great sweetness, great fights, fun, gusto, laughter, danger, tough living, and sometimes living off the fat of the land in high places. Some are still friends although we may seldom see one another. But when we meet, whether it is in the southern hemisphere or the northern part of the globe, it is as sweet a thing as it was when we were declaring undying love to one another, even if dancing to a different tempo.

One should never ask questions of an old lover who has been absent for many years from your life. It is the time you had together that was the sweetest thing, the needy, warm loving arms, the kisses, the sentences cut short by one another – 'No! That was on the ferry going to Amsterdam!' Another man, another place: 'I remember you climbing up the rope ladder from the pilot boat that brought the mail, and you out from Hobart when we were on our way back to Denmark from Antarctica, and you laughing as the roll of the ship swung you from side to side ...' And I interrupt: 'The decorum when I got on deck and was formally greeted by the crew, until you opened a door and said "Quick!" And we ran off like naughty schoolchildren up to your cabin.' 'And didn't come out until the mate came knocking on the door. "The pilot is ready, captain, he's waiting to return." And we appeared, sombre, serious on deck and shook hands formally and you quietly said, in English, "Until next year", and I said in Danish, uncaring if the crew heard, "Jag elsker dag". And I climbed back down the swinging rope ladder and never looked back as the harbour master's boat bucketed about all the way home to Hobart and you went north to Denmark.'

But oh how we mourned each time the mooring lines were hauled aboard, with you on the ship and me on the shore, and sometimes a whole hemisphere about to divide us. Whether you sailed to the Antarctic or to the Arctic it made no difference, we mourned just the same even though the separation was for a shorter time down south in my realm. There was always a large number of people to see the polar ships depart each southern summer, and you were angry once with me and by the time I'd got back up to my eyrie on the high hill in Hobart there was a radio ham on my front doorstep with a message he had picked up as you sailed out past the Iron Pot. 'I couldn't see you. Don't hide in a crowd again.' And I never did stand 'with the crowd' again but always sought a spot distant from the mob so I could be seen by you until the ship disappeared.

Back in the early 'fifties when I was first at sea I got to know the Arctic and Antarctic polar region men and the thrill of their adventures enthralled me. The first Antarctic ship I knew well was the *Norsel* (the Little Seal), a small Norwegian sealing ship turned into a polar vessel. Her captain, Torsten Torgerson from Tromso, up in the Arctic Circle, had been to sea since he was twelve years of age. When we met he was thirty-four – my own age. We became warm friends and remain so. We were the closest, dearest of friends but never lovers – we were too wise for that.

Thirty years after our first meeting I was on an Arctic voyage which was to call into Tromso, in the far north of Norway. As I spoke no Norwegian I asked the ship's radio operator to try to find Torsten and ask if we could meet. 'Be tactful. I do not know the wife', I warned. Within an hour the ship's 'sparks' phoned my cabin. 'He's retired, but away helping a ship in trouble today. His wife says I'm not to let you go past Tromso without seeing him or her life won't be worth living.' Well, I knew the message wouldn't be quite like that, but it was very warm.

And there they were waiting for me on the wharf at Tromso. Torsten stood there beside his Norwegian wife who was smiling with delight 'Australie!' she said, the extent of her English. I pushed through the other passengers and ran into their arms. The grandmother was waiting at their tiny house to begin cooking delights. A big low table was set with the finest needlework cloth, and I remembered one summer night in Hobart how Torsten had told me he had studied for years to pass his master's ticket. 'Me at one end of the table with my work and study, every night. Yes Patsy, every night I was home from the zee, and she, my wife, sewing at the other end of table to sell we was so poor.' And so often apart. 'We people at Tromso are much with great aloneness.' My daughter and his daughter of the same age had written to one another.

He remembered our first meeting. I was a full-time sailor by then and this night, as we were sailing up the Derwent River to our home port of Hobart, the Captain said he couldn't recognise our berth. I signalled, but couldn't understand the reply, except that our usual berth was not free. It was the apple season and the big overseas ships had come in and the port was jam-packed with ships.

I was at the telegraph, not understanding the signal, and the Captain heard our victualler on the long pier calling 'Go alongside! Antarctic!' We were to tie up to the *Norsel* which was making its first run down to Antarctica. The small crew were on deck, delightedly tying us up to their side, pleased to be in the company of a ship like theirs, small and workmanlike and game for anything the sea sent. I had not yet been cleared to leave my post at the telegraph, and from there I could see and be seen by the crew of the *Norsel*. I had my children on board with me as it was Christmas holiday time, and they scampered to the ship's side, trying to talk to the very foreign men. 'Are you the Captain's wife?' the Norwegian Captain called to me. 'Certainly not!' I didn't care much at all for our particular captain of that time, and didn't care who knew it.

'What do you do now?' he called out to me, still at the telegraph. 'Is Christmas. For your children?' I told him I owned a house in this port, up on the slopes of Mount Wellington, and had made decorations ready to put up when we reached home, and we had a plum pudding I'd made on the ship. We were ready and had a turkey cooked for our own small celebration. By this time I had received the order 'Finished with Engines', and now rung it down with the double swing of the bell to denote to the engineer that we were indeed now free. The engineer acknowledged it and I too was then relieved of any duties.

By now both the children had been lifted across to the Norwegian ship and were being feted by the men with games and toys. 'You come' said Torsten, the Captain, and I stepped across the railing of the deck and he steadied me as I jumped down to his deck, and he said, 'Is our Christmas Night!' 'Is ours too' I said.

Few in that little city could have had such a Christmas Eve. Before they left their northern port, the men's wives and children had filled big, ship's laundry bags with gifts for Christmas as well as a vast amount of decorations and lights that lit the upper deck as well as the men's decks below. Cathy was still very young and soon dozed off and a young steward was sent off to fix up the Captain's bunk for her. When I followed I could hardly see her for the gifts each man had crept in and showered on her sleepy little figure. 'Goodnights, goodnights' she was murmuring, trying very hard to stay awake and be polite.

I had no compunction in accepting their hospitality, instead, I knew the coming on board of little children had brought a softness to their evening. Photographs of wives and pale-haired children were taken from pockets and shown to me while each of us tried to make ourselves understood. From where I was seated I couldn't see Michael but could hear him often imitating the men's 'Skol!'. And then the box of hymn books the wives had sent for this occasion were opened up and the whole crew sang – including my son, whose voice I heard singing clearly, although he knew not one word of Norwegian. My God. He's been drinking, I thought. 'Skol!' between hymns. 'Skol!' It was certainly time to go home. Boxes of food were packed for us, aquavit, puddings, sweets, boxes of Anton Berg chocolate, sides of smoked salmon and foods I'd not known before. Our ship's agent had brought my car to the pier as was usual when we reached port, and now it was stuffed full of booty, the children wrapped in rugs and curled up on the front seat beside me, and off we went, climbing up the side of Mount Wellington in the sharp, clean air of beautiful mountain nights.

Old Captain Hans Christian Pedersen liked me, as an old man likes a laughing young woman. Vilhelm Pedersen had done his time at sea as a boy under Hans Christian, who was one of the pioneer Antarctic and Arctic ship's captains. In one Antarctic year Vilhelm and Hans Christian both had their ships tied up in the port of Hobart, only a few berths away from each other. We must visit for aquavit. 'Com!' shouted Hans Christian down the phone. We wandered along the summer waterfront. 'Com!' Hans Christian bellowed from the deck at our tardiness, the sun of a Tasmanian January seducing our footsteps. 'Are stuck?' 'No, not stuck' we shouted, 'just going slow.' 'Com!' The laughter along the waterside at this square-bodied man anxious to throw his arms around his friends pleased all.

Once inside his cabin it was 'Skol!' followed with a beer, an aquavit followed the beer and an aquavit followed that, and so on; talk, laughter, frequent translating – and when that was too slow and the words too fast my hands were held by the great old man. To be in their company was to be in a rare world where both had seen death, both lived within a toughness no landsman would be expected to accept.

Both these men had been at sea since they were thirteen years of age. The older man looked on Vilhelm as he would a son, and Vilhelm looked at Hans Christian as he would a father. 'Ah, Vilhelm! You good?' 'Yah Captain, I keep very well.' Man, mate, master, they had climbed the ranks to the top. 'There is many man' Hans Christian said that day in his cabin, 'but only one captain, eh Vilhelm?' 'Yah! You are Captain here' Vilhelm said, 'but you come to my ship you ask permit of me for you to come aboard. Eh?' There was ship's talk and icy wastelands' talk. 'You bring back ice for your whisky?' Hans Christian shouted, laughing. Yes, Vilhelm had done that.

That season, as usual, he had done two trips down and back from Hobart to Antarctica. On the second voyage, in narrow waters among the ice, the ship's bow had swung and jammed into a berg, 'a blutty big growler'. In the attempt to free their ship a huge lump of ice broke off and lay over the bow and there it had stayed until the ship sailed back into Hobart two weeks later. It caused great interest in a town that had seen Antarctic ships coming and going since early last century, but never before had the ships brought ice back to Hobart. And that was not the only novelty: that trip Vilhelm had brought back Emperor penguins to take to the zoo in Denmark.

Vilhelm mothered these birds with the help of one of the young hands until they reached their new home. They had come from the perpetual ice of the south up to Hobart in summer. For as long as the ship was tied up in Hobart crowds came down twice a day to see Vilhelm let the big birds with golden crests out on deck and there he and the lad hosed them down for half an hour, fed them, then hosed them again before herding them back into the forward hold. There was much beak-snapping and pretence of attacks, and things were lively – it all made for a good side-show. But Vilhelm got them safely to his homeland and sent me a photo of the local mayor and brass band welcoming the first penguins to come to that part of the northern hemisphere. 'They were still trying to bite me, even at the last! After all I did do for them!'

I was amazed to witness the free manner in which the ladies of Hobart boarded the Antarctic ships – it always reminded me of the stories of the lovely bronze girls who swam out to entertain the crews of the sailing ships that stood off-shore from the Pacific islands. One season, Vilhelm and I, accompanied by the ship's first mate, came on board for a drink after a formal official dinner ashore, and as we walked along the lower deck I heard giggling, murmuring, sighs, thumps – but neither Danes commented. It was January, warm, and the cabin doors were open. The reason why I didn't at first understand what was going on was that I had seen the small cabins in daylight and knew they were each fitted out with four bunks and, because of the need to utilise every bit of space in these ships, there were kit-bags and God knows what crammed in, leaving scarcely space for the voyagers to put a foot down. Would a woman . . . ? In evening clothes . . . ? But 'love' conquers all, we are told – including the gentlewomen of Hobart who organised the annual welcome for the expedition. They were now giving them a good send-off. But eight in a cabin? Phew!

I never understood women. Men are more likely to be honest, some brutally forthright, straight to the point. I didn't approve of this mass love-fest, so I tried to mind my own business. But drinking with the mate and Vilhelm I felt I'd lost something of the easy companionship we'd had, and this could be replaced with another thing entirely if I was not careful. I left, and they said 'Why?' When they saw me off the ship into a taxi they were upset, afraid they had lost my friendship. Next day we lunched together and things were back in place with us and the mate was telling his funny stories while he twisted his red beard round his fingers to keep the great bushy mass from 'swallowing in my mouth' as he put it. Hans Christian would have understood: 'The richer they is they more blutty ranty [bloody randy] they is'.

All that I understood was that no matter what I did or said I was always open and frank about it and never hid a thing. Life

would have been easier for me had I not done so, but I am as
I am.

Russell Drysdale, Tas to friends, was a delight, a man stalwart
in friendship. When I first cut loose from the oppression of
convention in the 1950s and ran off to the little trading tramps,
Tas had encouraged me. He too loved the small ships. 'Public
opinion' he quoted Dean Inge, 'is vulgar and opinionated,
attacking anyone who is not content to be the average man or
woman.'

'It was a memorable time' Dominic Serventy wrote of the
summer when he and Russell Drysdale and two more of us
camped on Babel, Cat and Storehouse Islands in Bass Strait.
Three of us had come to assist Dom to catch and band short-
tailed shearwaters (mutton birds) and gannets on these uninhabited islands. Dom had been coming annually for many years
and I had known him when I worked on the ships and we had
transported him to these isolated places.

'Patsy, this is Tas,' Dom introduced me to the big artist. For
the rest of our summer we lived hard, often dirty, with little
water to drink and less to wash in, sustained mostly by 'tea and
tin', as Tas called it. He would merrily wave the tin-opener,
calling 'Who'll cook tonight?'

We slept in sleeping bags on the earthen floor of deserted
huts, or out on the rookeries to observe the birds. We worked
long and hard. It could have been awful. Yet when the sun was
dappling the sea surrounding us with daytime moonbeams, Tas
would suddenly stop work and shout 'Down with the cathedrals!
Out with the monks!' and he and Dom would go hurtling off
across the burrow-riddled rookery playing Cromwell. 'Monaster-
ies! Abbeys! Away with them!' Running down the stony peak
of lovely Babel with his long crooklike stick, Tas would shriek
'Begone!' and Dom sooled him on. 'Patsy! You're Ludlow in
Ireland! Remember Connemara!' Across the white sand of the

beach to the rotted remains of a long derelict shed. Whack! Whack! 'It is the Lord's work!'

Nights were spent in what Dom called 'disputatious friendship'. We argued about everything under the sun until we fell asleep for the few hours Dom permitted before we were off again. Tas would grumble and mooch along like a wombat until suddenly, 'There goes a monk! After him!' and he'd be away again, laughing.

He filled his pockets with pebbles he was constantly picking up, feathers, grasses; he'd sift sand between his fingers, staring at it as though it were the first day of creation and this the result. He didn't ask one to pose for him, instead you'd look up from where you were resting and he'd be making a rough sketch of you. Once, when he saw me hold a bird aloft so it could get the lift of wind necessary for it to become airborne, he asked me to repeat the action in daylight and he sketched that.

Gannets are big birds, quick as a snake, with razor-sharp bills, and they make a dangerous foe. When one snapped too narrowly at Tas's arm, he abruptly snapped back:

I once knew a gannet outrageous
Whose temper was something contagious
When bit on the head
His adversary said
You'd make a damned saint litigious.

One night Dom, Tas and I went off to band a few adult mutton birds. These can only be found at night when they come back to the burrows to feed their young. For every step we took I believe we fell over twice with our legs knee-deep in burrows. Tas dropped the torch, I dropped my protective gloves and scrabbled round in what we knew was snake-riddled sand and Dom was impatiently rattling his Monel bands like a Mother Superior with the convent keys.

It was all insanity, what with Tas finding the torch and

sending imaginary morse code to Persons of Importance, and me wanting the light shone in my retrieved gloves In Case Anything Has Crawled Inside. Soon we were all laughing and I was squealing every time I grabbed a bird and it nipped into my wrist and arm, and Tas was throwing the beam of the torch to the sky like a searchlight – 'Down! Planes! Are they ours?'

Then suddenly we realised there was a stranger standing with us. A fisherman anchored off the island had seen lights flashing and 'unearthly noise' and come ashore to investigate. He'd had bad luck, lost a whole catch of crayfish ('went bad in still waters') and if he couldn't fill up before he ran out of fuel he wouldn't be able to meet his payments on the boat. He would be finished. I said I'd come with him the following day and help him pull pots. That night, in lantern light, Tas carved a cuttlefish. He elongated tiki-like hair flowing down the side of the pumice material, carved in maritime symbols and things of the sea. 'Take this to him when you go,' Tas gave it to me. 'He must throw it into the sea when he casts his cray pots.'

I should have liked to have kept it. I looked at it all the time we were rowing out to the fishing boat. So beautiful a thing to sacrifice to a wanton, capricious sea. But the fisherman cast it into the water when he shot his pots. That evening, when we went back near the continental shelf we all had to lend a hand when he hauled in his pots. They were laden, all of them, with big crays.

Men do things to pleasure a woman, and to please. Abraham, a negro cab driver at Oxford, Mississippi, where I travelled every second year to be with William Faulkner aficionados, always thought of ways to make me laugh. Years ago, on my first trip, when James Cleaver was making his run to gain entrance to southern universities, Abraham met me at the airport. I got into his cab. 'Yassum?' he queried, asking for my destination. He met me again when I travelled there recently. 'Yassum?' he said. I told him I thought he no longer spoke in that way. 'Ah don't,' he replied. 'Ah just did it to make youall smile again.'

Men are a joy to work with, real mates. I like them all but am sorry for some who have an inability to ride with the blessed waves of change: men of my age, who were boys in the hard, manhood-destroying years of the depression, and were swept up in the following war. Men who missed out when opportunity came for women and men to understand one another.

Post-war changes have polarised many men of this age group. Intellectually they know, and accept, the changes in relationships between the sexes, but emotionally they are stuck in the 'keep-em barefoot and pregnant' past. They get only half a woman, and they, of all men, deserve the whole article. It was easier for women who grew through the same era. My generation of women had so much further to leap to fulfilment and had to make such a stupendous effort that we just up and flew.

In many ways we left men of our age group behind us, earthbound. I like men. They have been good to me. Mostly. The same as women have been. I find there is little difference between the two except for that little that makes all the difference. Men have no monopoly on the joyous cry 'Vive la différence!'

Things
Turn Up

IN JANUARY 1960 I WAS appointed Adult Education Officer in Hobart and the children and I moved into a city for the first time, to a beautiful big apartment with four bedrooms, a spacious drawing room, a study, large hallways and kitchen with the biggest range I had ever seen. (In those days I was noted as being a fine cook. Ah, how times change.) The children took to city living as if born to it. I began to get more 'mainland' requests for me to write for Sydney-based magazines. Although I had trained the children to be as self-reliant as young teenagers could be, they were at that stage when they could no longer take time off from school. I thought I would have to delay my flight into serious writing for many years but, as always, I was lucky.

A French friend, at a United Nations meeting (you never know where things turn up!), told me of an aunt who had just migrated from Belgium and was very unhappy. 'There is nothing for her to do at my house and she's been used to cooking and minding her grandchildren and bossing young people around. She is unhappy.' I arranged for the lady to come for an interview at 5.30 pm when I would be home from the office, but she got there early and when I arrived I found her on the carpet playing cards with the kids in front of a big fire. I knew then she'd fit in well and she did.

Within a week Madame Meiders was settled into my home. I hoped she would teach the children French and, as she had no word of English, that they might teach her Australian. But she was the one who picked up the language from the children – they felt they'd had enough French at school. Even so, when I was travelling she wrote her weekly letters to me in French and, since I had none of her language and could not understand, particularly when she wrote of things medical, Michael would translate the more arcane sentences on another page for me.

Along with Madame Meiders came darling little dancing Miss Lamprill, fresh from Tahiti where she had been a missionary for many years. She, like Madame Meiders, wanted independence and, as I had a spare room, this little fairy-like lady danced into our lives as well as being a companion to Madame. Miss Lamprill had no missionary rectitude. 'How could anyone living in Tahiti not know all there is about sex?'

My house was always a joyous one. When the ladies retired I struck lucky again and beautiful little Ruby Ho from Hong Kong settled in – for eight years. Later there came a Malaysian girl, and there were always Asian boys cooking in our kitchen and feeding us meals fit for a king.

Adult education was a new concept in those days and I was lucky to be working with, and for, a gentle man, John Thorpe – peerless company in the organisation, as well as socially. When he had taken on this new post, adult education courses consisted of cake decorating, dressmaking, and talks, etc. In a short time we were enrolling hundreds of men and women in courses from photogrammetry, aerial photography, ancient history, physics, speed reading, painting, literature – scores of subjects. To begin a course we had to have ten students and at first we had to go out after them, but within a year we were swamped and many new subjects were being suggested to us.

Apart from lecturers from the University of Hobart we recruited many men and women who had varied talents – such as fly tying. This was a very popular study among the fishermen of the State but when I first had the subject suggested to me I thought it was a 'leg pull'.

For me, Hobart had one drawback only – I became a chronic asthmatic, but even that didn't deter me as I had to spend much time in bed and here I began writing in earnest. *Hear The Train Blow* was launched in Hobart at the headquarters of Adult Education. I had often been rushed to hospital with sirens screaming and I had made use of my rehabilitation periods. As well, the Adult Education Board gave me leave during the slack periods and this enabled me to investigate many outlets of folklore. Kylie Tennant had encouraged me to write *Hear The Train Blow*. I had read her books, of course, and once, during my time at sea, I had read the newspapers after we had tied up in port and found she would be at a conference in Hobart that night. 'Quick!' I said to the agent who always brought my car to the wharf, 'I've got to get up the mountain!' and off I went up Mount Wellington to the chalet where the conference was being held. I rushed in: 'Where is she?' 'Have you an invitation?' 'No.' Upstairs I ran and into the conference room. 'Kylie Tennant!' 'Patsy Adam-Smith!' We'd never met but each knew each other as well as if we'd grown up together.

Forgetful of the people who were there to gain knowledge – and were paying for it – we two immediately left and went to Kylie's room, talking for hours. From then on I often visited her in Sydney.

Staying at her home and listening to the wisdom of Roddy, who himself could use a pen and had given her the freedom to write and travel, was good for me. I've never mixed with authors – never been in a position to do so – but this was different. Kylie and I were friends first, writers by habit, and the force of family pressures each of us were under and didn't speak about bound us even tighter. She knew my writing. 'I like lively writing' she said. 'We owe it to our readers.' She wanted me to put my feature articles into books – 'You've got to write books!' And from that encouragement I began work on *Hear The Train Blow*.

Then I became interested in Hobart's splendid Georgian

architecture, and the artist, Max Angus, and I published several books on this subject.

While living in Hobart I read my own stories and gave talks on the ABC radio. Later I was one of three women on a weekly panel on TVT6 Hobart where we discussed problems of the time.

Later I had a folklore session of my own on this station, and during this time I discovered something that had puzzled me since first coming to the island State: when little boys were being troublesome, here they were called 'nointers'. 'He's a real nointer.' It was a word not known on the mainland, yet it was widely used on the north-west coast of the State. And so I asked for help in pinning it down. Many letters came in to say the writer – and sometimes their mum and grandma – always used the word, but none knew the origin. Until an old man from the Midlands phoned in (and three others wrote in). The story was total 'folk' as any lore recorded anywhere could be. In the 1800s there was this great big man in the Midlands (of Tasmania) who bet that he could eat a whole sheep in one meal. A local woman offered to cook the sheep and make mince pies to make it easier for him to handle. Seemingly, the meat from the carcase yielded ninety pies, and the big man ate them all – and from then on he was named 'Ninety' or, in Tasmania-speak, 'Nointy'. And so legends are born and little boys 'stacking on a turn' (including mine) became 'nointers'.

I had been collecting folklore long before I knew its title. My parents, grandparents and great-grandparents had handed stories down to me as a child and I had believed that all the forests were peopled with spirits and lonely, lost souls. As I grew older I began to read what could broadly be called 'folk stories' from a book, actually from the only book I owned as a child: *The Children's Treasure House* which my parents got for me by saving coupons from the Melbourne *Sun* newspaper.

In an area where you come upon place-names such as Bust Me Gall, and Break Me Neck, and Black Charlie's Opening, you knew you had a story, and Tasmania had all of these and many more.

I once met a hermit, the only hermit I ever knew (apart from Denny King across on the south-west coast), but Mr Stanley Gurney denied he was a hermit. 'I did not retire from the world as a hermit chooses to do, the world receded from the horizon of my being. That is not the same thing as being a hermit.' To get to this aged man's residence – a tumble-down old shop, where once a boom town of 1500 miners had 'dished' for osmiridium – I had to get help. I borrowed a four-wheel drive vehicle and someone to come with me – as it was, we bogged countless times and at one stage had to build a 'bridge' that fell down under us and later on, when the old gentleman was stewing tea for us, we went out into the perpetual mist of that area and saw our vehicle disappearing down into the ground. 'Yes', said Mr Gurney in his charming, modulated voice, 'The old well.'

During the day I had walked for four hours round the small ghost town and had met two 'hobby' miners, Charlie Cooper and Wally Constable which, as Mr Gurney said 'now made a population of five souls'. Darkness falls swiftly here. It was 6 pm and already dark in the forested gullies between the mountain ranges. We sloshed along in the mud to Wally Constable's 'cottage' and he lit a huge fire and fed us, in the meantime going outside and banging loudly with an iron spoon on the bottom of a frying pan. Charlie heard the signal and splashed over. But the only vehicle – other than the disappearing one – had a wheel missing. So they jacked up the sinking vehicle enough to get off one of its wheels, fitted it on to Wally Constable's vehicle, and slowly we began to creep back along the Adamsfield Track. Charlie walked ahead with a lantern until Wally 'got the feel' of the slabs of wood that made the track beneath us. The two men came with us all the way with picks and shovels.

And yes, I did return – five years later as the old gentleman had invited me. 'I had food for thought for many months after our conversations' he told me. 'I have been looking forward to your next visit and the subjects we would discuss.'

I was ordered to a warm, dry climate and nothing could have been better, not only for my health but for my writing.

The first time I travelled right around Australia I travelled with the poet, Roland Robinson – a gorgeous travelling companion as long as he stayed with his poetry and his bush craft. In any other field he was, um, difficult. We fought so badly that on our way home across the Nullarbor after two months together I couldn't bear him any longer and I told him to pull up and throw my camel-skin bag out. When he said no I opened the door, so he pulled up and I got out and sat on the roadside and waited four hours before another car came by. I didn't have to do anything to 'thumb' a ride. Thirty-odd years ago things were very different out in the bush to what they are today. A pleasant group was driving across 'the long stretch' and they not only picked me up but shared their food and took me all the way to Adelaide – where Roland was waiting for me, sitting on the steps of the Adelaide General Post Office. 'How long have you been here?' I asked. He looked at his watch, 'Sixteen hours'. Then he said, 'Where have you been all this time?' He was irrepressible.

He accused me of punching him. 'When?' 'Up at Geraldton.' 'Two months ago, for God's sake!' He had jumped out of the Volkswagon we were driving down from Geraldton at about 50 miles per hour. The wild flowers were out, miles and miles of them as far as the eye could see – and in the ecstasy of it all he jumped. Luckily he somersaulted and rolled, and by the time I'd stopped the car and run over to him he was rolling over and over, intoxicated with the joy and colour. 'We'll make love!' he shouted, but I was still too startled to even tell him to go to hell.

Roland could woo a bird down from a tree with his voice and

fluid, sensuous verse. We had met in Hobart in my Adult
Education Office; I had fixed for him to do a series of poetry
readings around Tasmania and he later wrote in one of his books
that I had seen a loose strand of wool in his tie, had reached
across my desk and snipped it off and tied it round my little
finger. He also wrote of a night on my rug in front of the fire
when the two most lovable and erudite men I had invited for
dinner had gone home. I think it might be the only part of his
book worth reading.

Roland dedicated a poem to me:

For Patsy,

Exhausted, this migratory bird
carried far southwards off its course,
lost to the consistent streaming flight
of its companion's polar force,

Swift that, emerging from cold rains
passed on between two skies of stars,
failing towards the deep, to find
branches to cling to: shrouds and spars

Spirit or derelict, mere hunched sweep
of wings that fold within the fire
of elemental storms that burns
blood, flesh and sinew in desire

Identifies me, and I hold
to frozen ropes of those cross-trees;
a hunched sweep of mere pinions, bone,
spent on the dark Antarctic seas.

from Roland.

Max Harris took us to lunch. Gwen Harwood had that day taken the mickey out of the *Bulletin* by using the device of sending a message down the first letter of every line. Hers read: 'Goodbye Bulletin. Fuck all editors.' As soon as it was discovered the magazine was recalled from all newsagents, but Max had grabbed some and had a copy each 'for you two intrepid and beautiful travellers'.

The 'intrepid and beautiful travellers' fell out again that very night. We were invited to a 'literary' function up a mountain and Roland was encircled by buxom girls and he ignored me. So I called loudly, 'Could I have the key of our room, please?' He asked why did I want the key. I replied, 'To get my contraceptives, I'm going out.' And while everyone else went string-lipped and silent, the two of us burst out laughing and ran out the door and went to the river bank where he told poetry and wooed.

As the children grew up I became more independent and was able to travel more freely. My children have never been surprised at my loose-footedness. How could they be? It would be a case of 'the pot calling the kettle black'. Cathy has been a courageous traveller and has been to scores of foreign places, including some not visited by me. She once chased a man in Iran and hit him on the head when he attempted to steal her friend's handbag. She also got caught up in Afghanistan in the bloody sport of riding for the body of a goat! Michael has taken his wife and family to live in Canada for a year, and they have had a long string of moves, although he has settled in Australia again – for the moment.

When I was free to travel I found the heat of the northern area of Australia, from Cairns across to Broome, was splendid for my lung trouble. For many years I left the south and spent four months of each year in the north, mostly in the Kimberley. I first went to the Kimberley in the days before the roads were sealed. Sometimes I travelled with stockmen, sometimes I holidayed with the nuns who cared for the lepers at the leper colony at Derby, and sometimes I lived on properties as a locum caretaker with a man who taught me much about the outback – Gerry Ash, a well-known head stockman on some of the greatest properties in the Kimberley. I'd been told to 'try and find' Gerry. 'You ought to look him up,' they said. 'We reckon he's the greatest ringer in all the Kimberley.'

Together with his friend, Whip, an Aboriginal woman who was one of the best cooks in the camp musters, we looked after four different homesteads and properties over a period of ten years for the owners or managers who needed a holiday. This was great for me because there was no white woman there to make me feel obliged to stay in the household with her. Many's the time I heard a shout from outside, 'Hey, Pat! You couldn't hop in the truck and go and get (such-and-such), would you?' Another time, it would be, 'Hey, Pat! Hop on one of the horses for us, we haven't enough boys.' So off I'd go. Nowadays, of course, the horses are not used in this manner and riders only help to bring in the cattle which are rounded up by helicopter. But even rounding up cattle in an open-sided helicopter, or riding in the bull-buggies as they catch the wild bulls in the bush, was exciting.

Back in the days when there was magic in the land, there was no place in Australia like the Kimberley. The times when you sensed men in the land but didn't see them, when they were like the rocks, dark and deep, living within the soil, attuned to all things as though the sky and the men and grass and animals were not separate but each a part of the other. These are the times men make poetry on the land.

At Christmas 1984 Gerry, Whip and I were caring for a very run-down property. The few stockmen and the mechanic had been kept on while others were 'turned out to grass' because they had no special skills and wouldn't be wanted until the Wet was over. The Wet is the northern season, roughly from December to March, which is the monsoon period and the heat in these areas of no air-conditioning is truly indescribable. The men who are left behind on the properties go 'on benders' no matter how the boss keeps his eye on them. This time we were about 80 km from the nearest small town and they would still get into the town and go on such a bender there was no way you could get them back, other than throw them on the back of a lorry and drive them back. Once, the police lent us their hose to wash the men down before we set off. It was a hard life.

On Christmas Eve I phoned my Mother about 10 pm. I was sweating to such a degree that the phone piece slipped out of my hand. I excused myself to my Mother and she said, 'You ought to put the phone down, dear, and have a cool shower'. I'd already had six showers that day; it was just a matter of standing in my cotton dress and knickers and letting the water pour down until I could cope again.

When I finished my telephone call, Gerry suggested it might be as well if we got in the truck and drove to a waterhole and sat in it. We set off with a little tucker and my blow-up mattress, which was always a cause of much ribbing from the folk up there. I took a photo the following morning of my waterhole and I thought, 'we got it all for free and people down south, whether it is hot or cold, could never be in such an idyllic spot'. Further up the river, Gerry in his waterhole called out, 'I'll light a fire and make you a cuppa in a minute, Pat', and I thought 'I could live like this forever'. But the legendary days were ending and it's a very different life there now.

There were stories galore. Living in such isolation, hardship, unbearable climate in all but the Dry season, has developed a different personality from those who have had life easy. In the early days when I went there I travelled with a group that had only one white man, the head stockman, among twenty men. I once asked Gerry why they didn't come and corroboree for us as I could see them dancing in the distant firelight. Gerry said he wasn't against having corroborees, it was just that by daybreak they must be ready mounted and off after the cattle. But he called them and asked if they'd like to have a corroboree, so in their own good time they did dance for us, and it was not at all like the stage because the wildness and the wandering in and out of these natural performers was so superior to the confines of our European-style stages. The artists didn't announce themselves so much as infiltrate our consciousness. The dancers were still going at midnight and I could have watched forever. I later learnt that it wasn't polite to show too much interest in the dancing. Because of the long hours worked on camp muster or droving, the few hours of darkness are needed for sleep.

One time we were locum caretakers at a big, very well-known property with a decent homestead. This property had a 30 km beach frontage and the homestead was a stone's throw from the Ninety Mile beach. Just when I was beginning to think it was the most marvellous area I'd ever been in, Cyclone Chloe swept in over us. The three men left on the property leapt to their feet as soon as they saw the storm blowing in from the Indian Ocean, and as the black wall came towards us they shouted to me, 'Batten the house down'. I yelled out 'Where are you going?' and they said to tie down the windmills – and there were over forty on the property. They lowered the big radio pole to the ground and secured it, then they went off in trucks in various directions to secure whatever they could. The battens were well made and easily fixed on the windows, and the homestead also had a partially-underground room. However, I wasn't putting my trust in that as there was still a watermark to show where the water had risen in there during the last cyclone. Our two-way radio went off the air immediately, and we then went for two weeks without contact with the outside world. We were without refrigeration. The 'hands' were complaining about lack of fresh meat so Gerry set off at sunset 'after a killer'. He is, of course, a superb shot. He 'dressed' the beast as it is called and we loaded the still quivering meat on to the flat-backed truck and set off for the homestead several miles away. But the old truck 'gave up the ghost' or, in southern parlance, the motor broke down. No lights, nowhere to sit (I'd been riding on the step and was now frightened to get on to the ground for this was snaky country,) and all the coo-ee-ing in the world wouldn't reach the homestead. Hours later Gerry got the motor moving and it slowly groaned home. The owners were away on the east coast of Australia. We'd been due to leave that day to go to Port Hedland to stock up on food and supplies, so it was very much a case of living on 'hard tack' – canned and dried food – until we were able to get out to the road.

I learnt that cattle are apt to panic and bolt into the sea at such times, but I doubted whether any would do so during this cyclone. What I had never expected was the vast amount of magnificent seashells that were washed up on the beach. I walked there one day after the cyclone passed and tried not to crush any of them but it was no use, there was no space in between the shells to put my feet. As fast as I picked up one shell I picked up another two, some quite rare.

We had an ordinary radio set in the homestead and we had batteries so we could hear what was going on in the outside world, although no one could call us. The heat was terrible but the humidity was worse. Water rolled down our faces, our clothes clung to our bodies.

We had just got things tidy when the cyclone swung back again and the whole performance was gone through once more. When it had exhausted itself we set off in the old truck down the coast to get supplies. There was still plenty of water around and we were late getting to Port Hedland so stayed overnight and drove back the next day with the truck laden. The heat and humidity was still intense. Once we stopped and walked into a river fully clothed, and another time we took it in turns to stand under a flowing bore – we just pulled the plug out of the top and the lovely cool water came out like a fountain. But as soon as we stepped away from the bore the clothes dried on us and we sweated again.

As soon as we got back to the property, although there were still miles to travel to the homestead, Gerry 'felt' there was something amiss. When we got even closer I realised it was strange that no one had come to meet us, seeing these men have an ear for the distant sound of any vehicle in that silent land. We got to the homestead and began unloading, and 'the old soldier' who did odd jobs came up. 'He's gone', he said, 'they took him.' He had been drinking, but not much more than usual. 'Took who?' asked Gerry. 'Teddy. The cops came and got him and took him up to Broome.'

There had been an Aboriginal, a very handy man, who lived on the property and he stayed there throughout the Wet. He'd come to the kitchen to collect his meals and that was all I knew of him except that I had been told by the stockmen that he was banned from Broome. I had asked 'the old soldier' about Teddy and he had said 'Oh Gawd, he can't go back to Broome, you know, he blew a girl up'. 'He what?' I had said. 'He blew a girl up, a nice girl she was too. He's blown up lots of girls. The Blacks won't let him back into Broome, they're on the warpath after him. That's why he stays here and works all the time.' Gerry had been cross and I realised there was something that I wasn't being told. Blowing up a girl? Oh, yes, I see. Not with dynamite!

Gerry asked 'Who alerted the cops to take him out?' (off the property). And then it all came out. There had been an argument and 'the old soldier' had phoned Broome and said Teddy had gone mad with the drink and was swinging along the roof guttering with his hands and had pulled down part of the water spout. In the midst of his telling, Gerry said, as cold as I'd ever heard a man speak, 'And you rang the cops?' He turned and went up to the kitchen and I found him there when I came in. 'You never call the cops on a man' Gerry said to me. 'You never do that.'

A quaint thing had occurred with Teddy some weeks before and though Gerry had been angry about it I thought it was

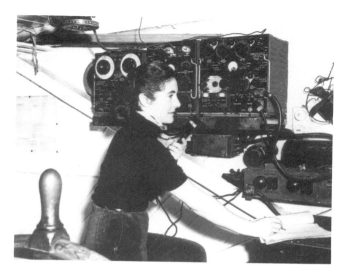

I went to sea in 1954 and became the first woman to receive signed articles in Australian waters. As well as my ordinary duties on board the *Naracoopa*, on which I served for six years, I had to stand by and man the ship's radio three times a day.

The majesty, power and cruelty of the ocean is always there for a small ship's crew to see. My radio shack on the *Naracoopa* was to the bottom right of this picture.

Michael on the *Naracoopa*. Term-time was spent at school in Hobart but holidays meant going to sea.

Dear lovely ALAStair I. Love you so much that I will give you a present.

Cathy doted on the *Naracoopa*'s captain, Alastair Maddock, from the time he took over the ship in 1956. This was her birthday card to him a year later.

The crew of the *Naracoopa*, 1956. Clockwise from me are Bill and Wally, who had both owned fishing boats before signing on; the captain, Alastair Maddock; our splendid engineer, Mick; the bosun and the cook. The other crew members were, like many of our seamen, men who moved from ship to ship, the gypsies of the seaways.

We would anchor off Tasman Island and row to the rocks to the left of the crevasse in the centre of this photograph. From here we climbed into a basket and were pulled up to the landing via a cable. A trolley, operated by a winch and a horse, hauled us 1000 feet to the top of the island, where a horse-drawn sled took our cargo to the lighthouse.

Sometimes the Tasman Island's lighthouse keeper's wife and children would come to meet us.

Our engineer played his bagpipes for Alastair's 32nd birthday – a rare break from the toil.

Alastair – the 'Big Fellow' as the crew called him – on 'Monkey Island', the exposed deck above the wheelhouse. He took station here when we were in narrow or dangerous waters, calling instructions to the 'man' on the telegraph below in the wheelhouse (the engineer below had an identical telegraph face).

Loading cattle was always fun – for the onlookers.

'Inevitably Alastair and I fell in love.'
In 1957 we all holidayed in Victoria
with my parents.

Michael took this photograph of
Alastair and me at Randalls Bay,
Tasmania, in 1957.

Camping at Randalls Bay, Tasmania, 1958.

Alastair on Mum's farm teaching Michael to drive the tractor (Cathy, ever the dedicated reader, sits behind on the trailer).

Alastair and I were happy. We fitted well together. New Year's Eve, 1959.

Captain Vilhelm Pedersen, Arctic
and Antarctic mariner, 1960.

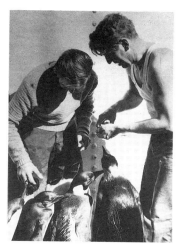

Vilhelm ('Bill') Pedersen (right)
feeding the Emperor penguins he
carried from the Antarctic to his
homeland, Denmark.

Lovely Ruby Ho from Hong Kong
came to live with the children and
me – and stayed eight years.

Mr Stanley Gurney of Adamsfield,
Tasmania – the only hermit I ever
knew, although he denied the
description.

Before Lake Pedder in Tasmania's south-west was flooded, a group of friends went to bid farewell to this enchanted, doomed piece of earth. Here, artist Max Angus prepares to take up his brushes.

We flew into Lake Pedder and walked out. We were a weary lot at night and ate huge meals before turning in early. Clockwise from left: me, Tricia Giles (obscured), Max Angus, Frank Bolt, Geoffrey Tyson (standing), an unknown bushwalker, Olegas Truchanas, another unknown bushwalker and Leslie Greener.

Roland Robinson at Mataranka in 1960, on our trip around Australia.

I have many good friends in the Kimberley but none better than head stockman Gerry Ash.

Since the 1960s I have travelled to the Kimberley annually. In that time I have worked on four large properties to relieve owners in need of a holiday. Now the Kimberley is simply my home in the winter months.

In 1961 I went on a long trip with Kimberley cattlemen, musterers and the women who cooked for them.

Publishers helped me from my first days of writing. Here the poet Ian Mudie launches my book *Moonbird People* in 1965.

Peerless company – on uninhabited Babel Island in Bass Strait with Tas Drysdale (to my far right), Dom Serventy (to my right) and a bird catcher in 1967.

At the age of 75 Dad brought this tree down to size to fit the kitchen stove using only maul, wedges and a cross-cut saw. But by his mid-eighties he knew he was done for.

My parents, Birdie and Albert, on their golden wedding anniversary in 1969.

Kathleen and I help Mum and Dad celebrate their diamond wedding anniversary in 1979.

Our family parties are always great fun as everyone, young and old, joins in.
Mum and Dad's diamond wedding anniversary, 1979.

My travels have taken me to ninety-
seven countries. On my first trip to
Japan in the 1950s I went on to
Hong Kong and into the New
Territories. These Hakau people
were photographed near the
Chinese border.

On the Isle of Irishman in 1972,
collecting material for *Heart of
Exile*.

In 1982 my publisher's Christmas gift was a cartoon by the designer Tom Kurema. It showed me wearing a digger's hat (*The Anzacs*), driving a railway engine (*Folklore of the Australian Railwaymen*) and accompanied by a sheep (*The Shearers*).

In 1986 I worked with the BBC on the documentary 'Australia Will Be There'. This meant climbing the Kokoda trail, assisted by this man, Luther.

Edward Dunlop spent much of his last ten years at my home and we travelled overseas three times to old haunts. In 1987 we were on the infamous Burma–Thailand Railway with Blue Butterworth, Edward's former batman.

Birdie's children: Albert and John Atkins, Kathleen Bradley and me.

E.E. Dunlop – 'Weary', as some call him – was, to me, Edward and a good mate. Here we are pictured at a breakfast in 1993; Clive James is to my left.

hilarious. In the terrible heat we were all sleeping out, the workmen down in their quarters, us on our cyclone wire stretchers at the homestead but outdoors under the huge shelter that was open on all sides.

One goes to sleep quickly in those latitudes, partly from the hard work of the day and partly from the climate. Before I went to sleep I heard Gerry, over in the far side of the shelter, using the last of his radio batteries trying to find out the cricket scores of the match being played in England. The next I knew was that I was totally awake and totally still, totally alert. I couldn't hear anything, the radio was turned off, I didn't want to turn over towards Gerry in case my movement might provoke danger. I slowly opened my eyes and there it all was beside me. I let out an almighty yell and Gerry leapt up running, calling 'What's the matter Pat?' On the other side of my bed there was Teddy, with all his blankets – and a grubby malodorous lot they were – and he in full dress of shirt and trousers. He had settled himself down on the concrete floor beside my bunk. 'What the hell do you think you're doing?' Gerry yelled and grabbed him. 'By cripes, you'll get it for this.' I lay still under my sheet, unsure of what was happening, and the next I heard was Gerry calling to me, 'It's all right, Pat, don't get upset, the stupid bastard, if you'll pardon the expression, is only mad. Nothing else wrong with him.'

I waited a few seconds, heard them begin to go off across the concrete with Gerry shouting threats all the way, and was then free to turn over and see what was happening. There was the funniest sight: Teddy was afraid of the dark. I knew that but didn't know he needed to have someone near him every night, and this night 'the old soldier' had locked him out of his room in the quarters and Teddy was too afraid to stay alone and had merely come to me thinking to get a little human company. What I saw when I turned over was Gerry, a very big man, displaying a back view of a huge pink torso and buttocks in the moonlight, as naked as the day he was born, and Teddy staggering alongside him weighed down by his massive bundle of old coats, wheat bags, blankets, and a wool bale of straw. All the while Gerry, annoyed at his sleep being disturbed, was hitting him over the ears with his ten-gallon hat and Teddy was complaining that he 'never knew nothing about no woman sleeping there' and anyway, 'she's old'.

Another night, still in the monsoon period and so we were therefore sleeping out of doors, I was again wakened but this time in total terror. It was a scream from the jungle around us. 'Gerry!' I bawled out across the shelter; I could see him already off his bunk. 'What is it?' 'God knows' said Gerry, and he had been in this wilderness for a lifetime. The screaming continued but all the time it was moving and seemed a little further away. Sometimes it was almost silent, then next would come the most blood-curdling screech and this continued until, little by little, it faded. Gerry called 'Where did you see those little kittens today Pat?' and I knew immediately – the big snake, the python that had crossed in front of me the previous day. Later I'd come on a batch of tiny wild kittens in a thick bush. I had put out my hand to entice them but the game little things had hissed and spat at me and I had left them. 'The old soldier' told me his version: 'The python grabs them by the back so they can't use their teeth or claws on his lips and he slowly digests them with . . . ' I didn't wait to hear the end.

This is the land of the baobabs (some call them 'bottle trees') with elephant-hide, bulbous, and grotesque; of great grasslands that wave twelve-feet high in the Wet, where brumbies scatter into the scrub when they hear a car, and wild cattle threaten to charge as you drive over their fenceless runs. For mile on mile the ranges melt from pale lavender to violet, from pink to the scarlet of congealed blood, rufous, harsh, barbaric and beautiful. When night comes it turns lustrous deep purple and exotic.

In the Kimberley you sleep out under the stars if you're travelling. My camp was in a circle of baobab trees, fat and leafless. Dust hid the setting sun and the colours of sunset passing through it lay in bars of colour. There was nothing to indicate the cause of this low-lying blanket, a vivid fog from horizon to sky, but the air told me I was not alone on the broad bronze plain. All sound was blotted out by the talking of flocks of rose-breasted galahs overhead, flying to the water at the bore near by. Numberless finches, budgerigars and cockatoos settled on the trees around the bore, decorating the bare limbs like clusters of green, yellow, pink and white flowers.

The birds chattered and squabbled and pushed each other off their perches on the droll baobab branches until dusk. I could hear nothing from that distant blanket of dust, but an excitement was there. It filled the air around me. Suddenly a little donkey ran by, right beside my camp fire. A bell round his neck went clok-clok-clok. He brayed in ludicrous delight and scampered on to the bore.

Then, there in the dusk and the dust and the last of the setting sun was a string of horses with a stockman taking them to water. The donkey was among friends. I ran to a big rock near the baobabs and climbed it. Sticking out of the top of the dust layer were the big ten-gallon stockmen's hats and horses' heads, and the horns of cattle tossing and dodging as stockmen rode the herd to settle it down for the night. Suddenly it was dark – it's always sudden in the Kimberley – and with the darkness the birds abruptly stopped screeching and only then could I hear the complaining of five hundred head of cattle as they were brought into a tight circle.

I travelled 'soft' by outback standards: I had a sleeping bag. Now, with the fire smouldering low I was comfortable, happy, but the excitement was still there. There were noises everywhere. Somewhere out there the dark was full of moving animals. I was never too sure whether animals would tread on a prostrate sleeper in the dark and still can't believe they never do. There were noises everywhere. Clok-clok went a bell – surely scores of bells? I didn't think of hobbles. The tinkling disappeared and came again. Then the tread of high-heeled boots and concertina leggings on the dirt track to the bore, past my head. A voice said 'This bin good country. I bin walkem fifty mile. Plenty tucker. Bin catchem wallaby, emu, goanna, turkey. Plenty beef. You no starve here.' The scrunch of footfalls faded away. The cattle were lowing, quietly now.

And then it began. Gently, softly at first, the stockmen began to 'sing' the cattle, make them content and aware of the presence of men. If one beast became uncertain and panicked, the whole herd could have stampeded within seconds and no man could have stopped it. So, the stockmen 'sing the cattle'.

The words eluded me, the melody too, but inside my head the rhythm was pounding through from the ground beneath me. And the darkness was part of the words, and the ugly freak trees, and the men who had walked by my camp, and the area itself. You knew then that these were Aboriginal stockmen singing their tribal lullabies and 'rubbish' songs. As they rode around the closely packed herd their voices faded in the distance and then grew louder as they neared me. First they were high and clear, then the same rhythm was repeated in the middle register, then came a deep ᴄhrobbing in the chest. It went on all night, broken sometimes by an elusive whistling, an occasional lowing from a beast. At midnight the watch changed and an older songster took over, but the wild, primitive, disturbing rhythms were the same.

The moon came up, the bloated baobab trees were things of fantasy, great rocks crouched all around, and when the singers passed between me and the moon their tall hats were silhouetted black across the golden ball. And on and on went the song. Sometimes I dozed, hating every minute of sleep that blotted out this thing that might never happen to me again.

Then they were gone. It was daylight. Where five hundred cattle, and men, donkeys and horses had been was flat, red, plain, scorching already, but empty. Even the birds had vanished.

Later that day I caught up with the mob. Out on the unfenced plain the red cattle moved over the red land. They were jittery too, for they could smell the meatworks awaiting them at Wyndham. The drovers felt the meatworks too. The Aborigines said 'We bin leave cattle quick all alonga meatwork.' They delivered them to their destination the next day and immediately rode away. The cattle had shared the long, dusty, dry journey over the lonely weeks with them. The stockmen said 'Them meatwork plenty rubbish.' For the cowed cattle, being cooped up in the slaughter yards was a travesty for the untamed creatures that toss their horns, bellow and break away in a rush and thunder of hooves, until they learn to settle when stockmen sing them.

Never again did I camp apart if there was a cattle camp near by, and always it seemed as magical as it had on that first night.

It wasn't easy living for months in this way and it wasn't always pleasant – sometimes it was most unpleasant. One evening, when we were caretaking another homestead, some bull catchers turned up after Gerry had left for an overnight trip for supplies. They moved into the homestead and began drinking, four of them, ten-gallon hats and all. Gerry's friend Whip was staying with me and she was immediately alarmed. 'No good them,' she said. 'Them been steal, fight, take thing. We been get out Pat.' But I had no car. The owner had taken the four-wheel drive, the property mechanic had gone on leave and taken his truck with him, and the only other Aboriginal workman had hiked to the road for a lift into Broome.

Suddenly they besieged the dining quarters which were built well away from the men's living quarters, and also away from the homestead. They were foraging for alcohol and I knew there wasn't any and there would be trouble once they learned that. We two women went up to our quarters in the homestead where there was a telephone. The only number I could remember was the Melbourne home of my friend, Sue Ebury, who was my editor at that time. (Over the years we had telephoned each other so often that I could never forget her number.)

It was a Saturday and her husband, Lord Francis Ebury, answered and quickly said, 'I'll get Sue.' And from then on a strange conversation took place. She later told me that right from the beginning she sensed there was something dangerous going on which I could not handle. 'Where are you, dear?' asked Sue. 'Yes,' I said. 'You're still on the station in Kimberley?' (She had received letters from me.) 'You all right?' 'No.' 'In trouble?' 'Yes.' 'Can't talk about it?' 'No.' 'Where is Gerry?' 'Two days away.' She asked if Whip was with me. 'Yes.' She asked, 'Who else?' 'Five.' She then asked me what could she do? Call the police? 'No.' The bull catchers might cut the line. 'You *know*,' I said. 'You just want someone to know you are there' Sue said. 'Yes.' Sue then said something to the effect that she would phone me in three hours' time and if I didn't answer she would 'take action'. The bull catchers were getting nastier and they took the phone, but Sue had already hung up.

Whip was so frightened she clung to me, pasted her body down mine, and I pulled her outside with me and we walked towards the river. 'We swim underneath the river,' Whip said. 'They no get us there.' 'Where?' 'In river.' God help us, I couldn't even float, let alone swim. Whip kept reassuring me, 'You no drown Pat.'

Then I heard, a fraction after Whip, the beat of a beaten-up motor, coughing and spluttering. It was the station mechanic returning for spare parts. We ran to him and told him the situation. He didn't hesitate and said, 'Let's get out.' He got my gear and we roared off in the poor old ute.

Nor was it the end of that day. The first hotelier at Derby looked at me and said, 'You know better Patsy.' And he looked at Whip and said, 'You do too, Whip.' His was a white hotel. The mechanic had left, so we carted my gear down to the only other hotel in that town in those days. 'Two singles, or separates?' 'I stay with you Pat', Whip insisted. 'Two single beds.' And so it was, in one room. We were too tired and dirty to go for a meal, so we showered (Whip was a fanatic for showers), and after I had phoned Sue and told her the story we two run-aways fell asleep.

In twenty-four hours Gerry had learned of the 'dirty trick'. He was truly sad. 'It used to be one of the greatest stations,' he said, 'but it's like many now, beaten – times change.'

When I first went into the Daly River country in the 1960s the Daly was still 75 miles from a telephone, crocodiles still barked at the door of the few houses stretched along the river bank, and every snake in the area was poisonous, including the deadly taipan and death adder. Thirty years ago I made an unsuccessful attempt to get a four-wheel drive vehicle out along the track, and even now it is no more than a dirt road, 170 miles from Darwin. In the floods of the early 1960s the settlers were all washed out and rescued by startlingly crude methods; some spent a night in trees. This flood inundated 100 000 square miles of land.

Charlie Dargie and Squizzy Taylor went out to the Daly in the late 1920s. When I met them, they were the last two survivors of a rambunctious, legend-making, end-of-an-era mob that had disappeared. Dargie lived 10 miles from Squizzy and 5 miles from the Lavaters who lived on the grounds of the Maluk Maluk tribe.

The first settlement in the area dates back to the 1880s when a copper mine was opened up. Later the Jesuits built a mission, but both the mine and the mission went into recess for different reasons. The Brinkens, the Aboriginal tribe on the area next to the Maluk Maluks, turned up one night at the copper mine and murdered the five white miners. In return, the scattered white settlers wiped out most of the Brinkens at what is now known as Blackfellow Creek. The Jesuits were flooded out three times, and as all good Jesuits do, they retired from a fruitless area to gather their strength elsewhere.

Feeling between the few surviving Aborigines and the white settlers of the area have been strained. The Aborigines were strong and fierce; the white men were battlers. Men with the guts that were necessary to settle an area such as the Daly had neither the training nor the time to appreciate the ethnic idiosyncrasies of the natives when they were battling for their very lives as well as their livelihood. This wasn't milk-and-water living. This was the real blood-and-guts we admire in other races but deny to our own because it is dangerously unfashionable to walk the tightrope of a middle line on the colour question. We laud those who built the great cattle stations, the 'cattle kings', but never ask them where are the schools, the houses, the wages, the amenities for the Aborigines who live and work on their properties. Yet, God help the battler who has hung on and actually lives on his land in the 'colour belt' – it's more than can be said of the absentee landlord and his family who live in the comfort of the cities, a safe distance from the problems of colour, and thus safe from criticism of his treatment of Aborigines because he does not involve himself with them.

As for Charlie Dargie – he'd never understand, or care, why the coffee-shop folk-singers would ban words such as 'Three whites, two chows, four bucks and a gin'. He was not one of the landed gentry who drove their herds across the continent and about whom books have been written and who were said never to travel without a book in their pack, be it to read or to write in. Charlie couldn't, and wouldn't, want to go down in history as one who spent his time reading and writing. I once heard a bloke say to Charlie, 'You oughta write all this into a book', and Charlie said, 'Aw Jesus, they'da gaoled me.'

It is certainly a sad commentary on our national outlook that, while we extol our pioneering gentry who could afford to take up the best land and who, in these northern latitudes, worked whole tribes of Aborigines for no more than scant food and not even that during the Wet, we rarely mention the gallant, unlettered toiler who set out to 'give it a go' without money, property or family to back his sortie into the wilderness. And – this is the important thing – they lived with the blacks and formed some sort of alliance with them. Of course, it isn't the sort of alliance the city committee member understands, but it is a tolerance based on what they know they and the Aborigines can work with as a basis of co-existence, demanded by the place and time.

'This climate breeds good kids,' Charlie said to me as a coffee-coloured youngster toddled by. 'My grandkid.' So Charlie had children? 'Yairs. I adopted two.' He pointed to a half-caste girl down by the river and a dark boy by a tractor. 'They're mine, of course.' A pair of stick-thin black legs passed beneath the partitioning wall of the verandah-cum-living room and the kitchen. 'Me cook.' In this way Charlie Dargie has legally guarded his children's, and therefore their mother's, future in a way most of us would wish the hundreds of other white men who passed along north of Capricorn had done.

Charlie Dargie is all man, the type of man you'd expect a real song to be written about:

Now come all you sports that want a bit of fun,
Roll up your swag and pack up your gun,
Throw in some sugar, some flour and tea
And don't forget a gallon of Vic. O.P.
Crank up your lizzie and come along with me
And I'll show you such sights as you never did see,
Down on the Daly River O!
Chorus
There was Wallaby George and Charlie Dargie
Old Skinny Davis and Jimmy Panquee,
Big-mouthed Charlie and Old Paree,
The Tipperary Pong and Jim Wilkie,
And wherever you may roam you will find yourself at home,
For they're noted for their hospitality.
You'll wake in the morning and your heart's filled with glee
By a little nude maid with a pannikin of tea;
She'll give you such a welcome you won't want to go
Away from the Daly River O!

Now I saw a nigger sitting up an old gum-tree
The crows had picked his eyes out so he couldn't see.
Never, oh never a word said he –
For he was as dead as dead could be
He was just about ripe, you could smell him for miles
And his bum was sticking out like a horse with the piles,
When Dargie threw a gibber and hit him in the guts
And the nigger went 'Whoof!' and we all went bush
Down the Daly River O!

(Then out with the chorus again, pre-breakfast rum swishing away in the tin pannikin as it is swung in time to the music.) Charlie Dargie told me the 'big-mouthed Charlie' and 'Jimmy Panquee' were the Chinese who started off at Fletcher Gully gold mine – 'found nothing worthwhile, but kidded everyone they had. You shoulda seen the mining engineers and whatnots that came pouring in to look for gold, and big-mouthed Charlie and Jimmy Panquee smiling like the Chinks they were, and nodding and saying, "Plenty gold, plenty gold".'

Squizzy, holding out his pannikin for more rum, launched into a poem: 'Oh, I've taken my fun where I've found it . . .' – 'that's Kipling's "Ladies" you know" – 'she knifed me one night, when I wished she was white'. He'd asked me earlier if I wanted a drink. I didn't know how I'd go on rum before breakfast so I said no. Near to midday I was dehydrating fast, so I asked what else there was to drink but rum. This request threw Squizzy, who claims his father was at Eton, into a flurry. So courteous was he that each time I stood, he leapt to his feet. After the second time when Charlie had followed suit, Charlie said 'What're we jumping up and down for?' and Squizzy said 'Because the lady's standing up'. Charlie said to me 'Well, you'd better sit down or we'll end up bloody well killing ourselves'. So I didn't stand again but lolled back as they did in the wheatbag-covered deck-chair-type seats. Charlie reclined like a Roman at a feast, with one foot cocked up on the other knee, and Squizzy jiggled round displaying his chest. I couldn't take my eyes off it; it was like the back of a crocodile, as dark in colour and horny, and down below where his navel whorled there were occasional noises that threatened to geyser out in a boiling spurt when he told me, 'I drink anything, spirits of salts, anything.' 'Surely not spirits of salts?' 'Yes, certainly a few drops in a glass of water, tastes dreadful but settles the nerves.'

A seed buyer had risked his axles and come to talk business with Charlie, but he would have to wait until Charlie was ready. He said, 'I once came out here and Squizzy had been on the Worcestershire sauce. You were a mess that day, Squizz.'

'Oh' agreed Squizzy, 'I'll drink anything. But I prefer rum.' This last was a hint to the seed buyer that if he had anything in his car, now was the time to produce it. 'I've some whiskey' the innocent announced, 'I carry it in case of accident. I only mention it because perhaps your guest may prefer it to rum.' (By now, the 'guest' would have settled for spirits of salts, anything.)

The whiskey was produced and the seed merchant tried to hang on to the bottle, but Charlie threw the cork away. 'We don't keep corks here', he said. Squizzy was in a private dither. There didn't appear to be a spare pannikin. Then, 'A glass!' Squizzy cried, as though he had invented a new vessel. He stirred around in a tin trunk and magically came up with a glass, unwashed since something like Condies Crystals was last mixed in it. But that was soon fixed: Squizzy had long fingers, particularly the index finger which reached to the bottom of the glass where his black nail scraped off the brown sediment before the whiskey was poured in, neat.

'There's been plenty seen the possibilities of The Daly' Charlie claimed. 'It was the battling they didn't see. We used to have a licence to work the blacks. One day a policeman came down the river like a packet of salts. "Where's your licence to work niggers?" he says to me and I says, "You can kick me arse, I've got a licence." And I did too. I'd be a goner if I hadn't.'

'You know what that track you were on this morning is called? The Pumpkin Road. That's because we once carted truckloads of pumpkins over it, trying to make a go of things. A city scientist fellow came out here once and tried to tell us what to grow, strutting round he was. If you'da stuck a feather on his bum he'da looked like a peacock, but every time he told us what to grow we said "we tried that". We tried everything. When the crop was good, the market was bad; when the crop was ripening, the wallabies came in and ate it to the ground; when we put up fences, the floods washed them 20 miles away; and last year when we had a bumper crop and had 7000 bales of hay and down south the animals were starving for want of food, no one could pay the freight out. So it just rotted.'

Charlie later made good with Townsville lucerne seed. So well did he do that he may be remembered for it up in that area. I wish history were the stuff of life and that Charlie could be recorded as the man who came to some sort of terms with living in a plural society. But this isn't the way history works. We'll record the exotic, for it is facile, simple, romantic – and with it the half-truths that are sticky with sentimentality. These things will come to be traditional beliefs, a sort of folklore, the limbo-like life of white and black Australians thrown together today will not, I am convinced, ever be recorded.

I envy those experts who see a solution for every problem. I hope they are right, even though each has a vastly different idea of the solution. In fact, in no other field of endeavour have so many people, each unquestionably sincere in their approach, been so bitterly divided as to what should be done. As Bill Harney once said, 'The poor old Abo is being pushed and pulled one way and another by the lot of them.' The critical analysis and judgement of the exploitation of the Australian Aboriginal was made long ago. Nothing new that comes to light will alter the finding. The future alone can be altered.

My travels in the outback gave me material for *No Tribesman* and, later, *Outback Heroes*. When *No Tribesman* was published,

Lord Casey (then the Governor-General) wrote to me: 'You have presented them (the Aborigines) to us ... as people we can relate to, the good and the bad, men and women any of us could meet and know, if we were as enterprising as you obviously are ... It is one of the best books about Aborigines I've read.' It was not as good as all that – even for those times but I paid my way everywhere I went – no fancy grants, and best of all, I fitted in everywhere I went and made friends, black and white and can still greet those alive today. And mourn those dead in this hard land.

The commendations for *Outback Heroes* came from quite a different quarter. Once, only once, Gerry came down south. He loved the green grass, sparkling cities and 'the posh' style of eating and drinking. 'Struth! They'd never recognise me in the Kimberley!'

When he and I returned to Kimberley I wrote this letter to my daughter, Cathy. We'd flown up to Alice Springs, picked up the old truck, and traversed the Tanami desert.

Alice Downs
Locum caretaking
My dear
It is 42° from 8 am to 11 pm, then temp. drops to 38° until 7 am when it rises suddenly. No air-conditioning, TV, radio, newspapers; nearest town Halls Creek, 60 km away for mail. But all fun.
Had a grand trip up. The old truck crossed the Tanami Desert in great style. Reached Rabbit Flat – and tin shed and bowser (but licensed!) and Bruce the owner shouted 'Gerry Ash! I've just been reading about you! Last night!' His wife had returned from the 9 hours journey to and from Alice Springs and brought him *Outback Heroes*. Gerry said, 'And this lady is the author!' Well! The cavortings, slapping of hand on forehead, exclamations of Jove! Blow me down! Small world! kept up until 3 am when we tottered out of the tin hut to our swags rolled out under the great big stars.
We clocked up over 1000 miles before we got back to Alice Downs

after taking the family being relieved to Kununurra airport then getting back here. I travel with a sopping wet bath towel hung over the truck window to ease the heat and when it dries I dip it in water again, but nothing makes it bearable. Nothing.

Have a lovely Christmas m'dears and I'll see you in the New Year. G sends, 'Courteous good wishes.' Struth!
Love P.

Footloose in Australia, *The Barcoo Salute*, and *The Shearers* all came out of my extensive travels throughout Australia. Apart from my years of taping the reminiscences of railwaymen, soldiers, sailors, airmen and Merchant Navy men, my greatest work was done with shearers. This large body of men, who have been migrating the length and breadth of Australia almost since settlement, provides Australia with our most unique wealth of folklore. To meet and tape these shearers I went to all States, even to areas where sheep no longer run, such as the Kimberley. Once huge flocks of 100 000 and more were shorn here, and great numbers of Aboriginals worked around the shearing floor and their womenfolk drove mobs down dry creek beds to the sheds. Gathering this lore was the most valuable and pleasant labour I have known. The shearers were the most helpful, and the female cooks, shed hands, pressers and sorters were the most generous with stories. And it was fun. Mostly I stayed at country pubs and got a lift to the distant sheds with the agents for the growers.

There was a pub at Longreach, in the heart of Queensland shearing country. A wide upstairs verandah ran the long width of the building and hung over the footpath. The proprietor in the bar told me to 'settle in any room that takes your fancy, love'. His wife said, 'Better take these with you'. Two sheets. I climbed upstairs. All the rooms looked alike so I took one in the middle. They had bare board floors (no, not polished wood), the sheets were the only bedding (and all that was needed in that broiling climate), there was a weak, fly-speckled light-globe away up on the high ceiling which didn't give enough light to enable me to read the firearms notice on the back of the door and, of course, there was only one light switch. It was beside the door, a long way from the bed. The bathroom was at one end of the long passage, and if you wanted to have a bath you had to order ahead because the big boiler outside in the back yard had to 'get up steam'. The rooms had no windows except for a piece of frosted glass in the upper part of the door that led directly on to the front verandah. The single pane of glass had lost much of its frosting, both from age and the scratching of etched initials.

That first night I scarcely got into my room when a great thumping and stumping and dragging sound began. It went on for about ten minutes and then stopped. I had been told I was the only 'guest' in the huge, old hotel. I was in my dim room on my rock-hard iron bed when I realised I had to get up and tramp over to the door to turn off the light. I got the feeling I was being observed. Yes, I looked at the glass pane above the door and, sure enough, there was an eye. We observed one another for some time, quite unfairly because I could see nothing but the eye could see all of me. I had to get off the bed with the sheet wrapped around me, trot over to the door and turn off the globe, and fumble for a door key until I realised there wouldn't be one. As the door to the verandah was locked it would be silly to make a fuss, so I returned to bed and went to sleep.

At breakfast in the morning, in the kitchen of course, I mentioned the eye to the proprietor. Quite unruffled, he said, 'Oh, that silly old bugger. He doesn't come into town often. I told him to take any room. He'd only be having a squiz to see who's in the pub so he could have a yarn with them.' As for the thumping noise – 'that'd be him dragging his mattress and gear out on to the verandah. He never can stand being shut inside.'

My dog, Tigger, was sent to me as a gift by shearers after I wrote *The Shearers*. She's a Jack Russell, a gutsy little dog who has accompanied me on many a long, sometimes lonely journey. Up north she rides on the flat-top tray of trucks, giving the Kimberley cattle gyp. She takes on anything. She can be the 'dear little dog' (as friends call her), but when she gets out in the bush she's a hoyden. She has journeyed by helicopter on cattle mustering, and on down to the Great Sandy Desert of Kimberley where she once visited for three months when I had to go overseas. 'Oh, she's got no morals at all,' said the stockman when I returned, 'she'll sleep with anyone, Pat.' Tigger had simply gone to the man who picked the cosiest position to throw down his bedding roll for the night and Tigger snuggled down with him. 'When daylight comes she sticks her head out the bottom of the swag, looks around, treks off over the desert for a quickie, and back to the bed roll until she smells the breakfast cooking. When she's through that and the boys are heading off for the trucks or horses, she's waiting for them. She rides on the pommel of the saddle or, if things are dickie, is shoved inside the front of a stockman's shirt. Talk about a dog's life!'

Research for *The Shearers* took me to all States: inland to places such as Marble Bar, Leonora, Quilpie, Derby, Barcaldine, Bourke, Broken Hill, Port Hedland and Albany which were all jumping-off places to head to the shearing sheds further out. Hay, Hell and Booligal, Old Man Plain, One Tree Plain, and the great rivers, the Paroo, Barcoo ('where churches are few'), Lachlan, Murrumbidgee and the Billabong Creek where Granddad Adams sheared and Grandma caught one of the monstrous cod on the great Boonoke Station. This is one hell of a great country and God alone knows why we're so timid in saying so.

The
Road to Samarkand

IN RETROSPECT, MY TRAVELLING DAYS were like gipsy caravans moving sometimes languorously through fields of flowers and sometimes in whirlwinds which could sweep me off at any time to any land where I cared to go. Poor people rarely have the opportunity to travel like that. There was one thing that favoured me: I was, and still am, a chronic asthmatic and it seemed to me that as I got no pay for my long periods away from work when I was in hospital I may as well have long periods away when I was well and could earn money by travelling.

I have travelled to ninety-seven countries, and only in more recent years could I truly afford to do this. In those earlier days I just made up my mind that I *had* to see and be part of an event, or *had* to stand on a rare spot on earth, and I would fix the date, make plans and organise my household, arrange with a bank for money to be held to keep things running at home, get a passport, and then begin to scrape up the money for my ticket. My first long journey was to Japan in the 1950s. I had to go.

I was bitter about Japan, bitter in all ways and of all things Japanese. It wasn't just the loss of the four boys whose childhood and young adulthood was part of mine. No, it wasn't because two of those boys had been murdered when they were prisoners on Ambon Island. And it wasn't because the other two boys had died in Japanese POW camps. What I was bitter about I never knew. I never analysed it. I only knew I was bitter and I had to get rid of it.

I booked a berth in a six-berth cabin aft in a Dutch passenger ship. It was the cheapest berth on the cheapest ship afloat, and after booking I began to work on getting the money to pay for it. It wasn't just the cost of the trip, but there was the cost of keeping my home establishment going in Hobart. The children were at two different schools, one primary, one secondary, each school miles apart from the other, but each school uniform having white shirts – which meant ten white shirts to be laundered each week, apart from the myriad other clothing that children had now begun to need. It was a far cry from the 'play clothes' we had known as children. No more hand-me-downs or clothes with patches: now children were beginning their march for freedom. Up until now I had made all my children's clothes and my own. (Incidentally, if you've never tried getting the fly right in a pair of boy's trousers before the days of zips you've never known total frustration. Those bloody button holes!) Clothes were so very expensive in the shops and now I had less money than ever.

With only two weeks before the ship was to sail, a friend, Margo Roe, then Senior Lecturer in History at Hobart University, turned up with a great big bag of materials she had 'always intended to make into dresses'. I sewed and sewed, and by the time I was to leave I could pack quite a few reasonable outfits, as well as a surprise dress for Cathy who was to spend a three-week holiday with Mum in Victoria.

Our ship lay for two weeks in Hong Kong harbour and I lived on shore at the newly built Mandarin Hotel, as a guest of the management. All I did to earn this was to write a letter to the Hong Kong Tourist Bureau asking for information and any help it could give me. I enclosed with my short letter copies of two recent feature articles that had been published in *Walkabout*, a well known Australian magazine in the 1950s and 1960s. As a result, I was offered a week's accommodation in the Mandarin

Hotel which was then the finest hotel in the world. Also I was to have a car and chauffeur.

It was the period when the colony was going through one of its worst water shortages. There had been no reporting of this in Australian papers. I wrote of the sights on the long waterfront where a cyclone had wrecked the always-poor shelters of the destitute and sunk much of the maritime shipping. Every second day there were queues of people stretching over a mile as they waited to get water from the one water stand that operated on that day. Mothers left children in the queue for hours, returning when their turn at the water was near. Little kids sat nitting one another's hair, cracking the nits between their fingernails as they waited. A very old lady tottered back down the line humping on her back a plastic bag filled with water. Police told me it was difficult for people to find anything to cart water in. 'They are poor. Look at the sampans. The small belongings in there are all they ever own.'

I came upon a middle-aged man holding on to the only post left standing of his on-shore living hut. He smiled and gave the international shrug 'that's life'. He couldn't leave the site as someone worse off than he would take the post, the one thing he now owned. It was a dismal, sad sight.

Although I had free accommodation, car and driver for the week, I did need money so I wired Otto Olsen, editor of the magazine *People* (not to be confused with the later sex journal of that name). More swiftly than I could have imagined, he wired 'How much do you need? Can supply immediately.'

I made that driver work for his money. It was all wonderfully strange to me. Suzanne, a young New Zealand girl who was travelling on the ship, accompanied me most days, going back to the ship to sleep at nights. We two went to the New Territories – not the tourist area it is now, but then a fiercely held place where tourists were not welcome. The people abhorred cameras, believing the image would steal their soul. Suzanne held her camera up to photograph a narrow alley way and a tall woman swooped on her, grabbed the camera and belted it about the young girl's head and when that didn't smash it she shattered it on the side of the wall. My big Linhof Technica was well closed up and not likely to be recognised as a camera, but we retired smartly.

That was a strange day: because Suzanne was upset over the camera incident we went back to Hong Kong and she went to the ship to rest. I went up the steps of the Mandarin Hotel and the huge Sikhs who manned the door swung them back and smilingly asked had madame had a nice day? Actually, madame was going to finish with a surprisingly nice day. The hotel social hostess was waiting for me. She had been instructed to ask a table of 'interesting' women to lunch and would I come? 'It is for the young Duchess of Kent whose husband, a soldier, is doing his military time on the island. Will you come?' Why not? 'No frills. She is very sensible.' And she was, as were her companions. And the big meal stood me in good stead until the free breakfast next morning.

When I left Hobart, Madame Meiders had been in the house, as well as Ruby Ho (Ho Ting Ngor) who lived with us for eight years while studying at the University of Hobart. Ruby had written to her mother that I would be in Hong Kong and the mother replied that she would greet me if I cared to call. When I had left Hobart to join the ship to Hong Kong, Madame and my children came in the car to see me off but Ruby had come on the back of a motor bike, with her Australian boyfriend revving up and passing us at intervals and beeping his horn while Ruby waved a big bunch of flowers non-stop, as if we were all off to a wedding.

The meeting at Ruby's home in Hong Kong was arranged by phone by the hotel hostess. 'She will not speak English,' the Chinese hotel hostess said. 'Of course, she speaks it fluently if she wishes, as she owns much land on the waterfront, but she greatly respects her position and scorns the English language.'

Mrs Ho greeted me regally. I tried several times to start a

conversation, and Ruby's sister translated for the mother who said or did nothing with any visible sign – until I said, 'Please tell your mother Ruby has learned to cook.' The girl didn't acknowledge my request so I said once again, 'Ruby can cook quite well and is very proud of doing this.' At last the girl decided she must deliver the message. The terrifying lady didn't meet any eye, but somehow a muscle moved ever so slightly away as if she were alone.

I left Hong Kong for Japan when the week was up. Japan was still smarting, still beaten. Rebuilding was going on, done by armies of women in total black, even to the rags over their heads. I didn't get from Japan what I wanted: Peace. Instead I saw the ex-soldiers begging on the streets, their pathetic little army caps held out in parchment-thin hands. There is no glory for a loser – particularly in Japan – and I just wanted to get away home. I was bewildered and sad.

Nor was I overjoyed with the behaviour of the Australians on board the ship. When the ship tied up at Yokohama the little sin-wagons were lined up ready – and the requisite number of men who had asked for this convenience were also lined up on the rails, ready. Their wives were there to farewell them with 'Now don't you be a naughty boy, dad'. And the next morning back came the 'naughty boys', giving the pretty little Japanese girls a fatherly kiss and their small change (the fee proper having been paid before they left the ship). And the mums on deck were joking and teasing, and Suzanne and I had to believe that these women, through ignorance, stupidity or lack of interest, did not know what it was all about.

But the ship's surgeon did. Suzanne and I dined at the captain's table in First Class by invitation throughout most of that trip, even though we were only able to pay for a berth in a six-berth cabin. 'We'll dance tonight,' said the old surgeon who had been to sea for nearly forty years and knew it all. 'I'll be too busy in a few days to do anything but clean out this lot.' He knew to the day when the disease would present. 'And sometimes it wears a steel helmet,' he said. 'I can't do much about that.'

It wasn't AIDS in those days, merely VD, but it wasn't the act or the disease that seemed to both of us to be so disgusting: it was the pretence that it was alright to be 'naughty' when away from home.

I didn't return to Japan for more than twenty years, and then I flew there on a diplomatic visa.

Dad may have been a quiet man but he had an apt turn of phrase when he did speak. 'Things turn up if you are always ready on the starting block' he would say. Things have turned up often for me and given me the chance to go on or do something more interesting, exciting, even sometimes, unique. Some people prefer a steady, stable life in the one place, some even live in the one house from birth to death. That they live full, contented lives is a mystery to me even when I contemplate two of my oldest, dearest friends who have so lived. Some say it is my roving childhood that made me like this, some say it is my 'blood' (ahem!), but I don't care what the cause is – I just fit happily, or furiously, into movement and change.

In 1969 a great thing 'turned up' for me. I was offered, through the funding of the Myer Foundation Fellowship, the unique and pioneer position in Australia of Manuscripts Field Officer in Victoria. It was a position that had no blueprint until I drew it. I was to travel throughout the State of Victoria and attempt to discover documents historical, rare, or of value to future scholars. If possible, I was to attempt to encourage the owners of these papers to present them (via the back of my government station-wagon and sometimes through the loan of the State Museum's truck), under legal conditions, to the State Library. Here the documents would be protected and be available for bonafide scholars of the future.

When I prepared to settle in Melbourne in 1970 to take up the fellowship I knew no one except the actor, Brian James, whom I had met when he came to Hobart with the play *The*

Odd Couple. I had two concerns about living in Melbourne: How would I get to work? Where would I live? I'd never lived in a city – well, there was Hobart, but even then I was either up on the mountain or living on the outskirts. I wrote to Brian and the reply was immediate: he found me a tiny apartment in the heart of the city from where I could walk to work.

An apartment all to myself! It was too good to be true and, of course, as anyone who has had children will know, that was indeed the case. Within twelve months the children had left Tasmania and were dropping in for a bed, a meal, a yarn, or a button to be sewn on. But I couldn't complain. At first I'd spent my weekends flying back and forth to Tasmania to see the children. One night in Melbourne, out at dinner with Geoffrey Serle and Ian Turner, one of the wives (after listening to me talking about 'the children') asked me their ages. 'Twenty-two and twenty-five' I said, and as the words came out I realised, 'My God! They've grown up. They've gone. They've been bearing up with me. They're nice. They're mothering *me* now.'

It was a moment each parent knows, or should know. But you can't step up to them and comment, you dance around a bit and make yourself unavailable – even for sewing on buttons. Let their lovers do that for a change; let them pick up their own dirty socks.

But it isn't fair, is it? Mother Nature, that dirty old trickster, makes us nurturers, makes us think we adore waiting on our children, loving and caring for them, giving the best of our energy while they grow and thrive. Then suddenly, overnight, we are to disappear, step into a big hole, get out of their lives. And no tears mind you, not even a bow as you quietly, secretly creep out. It says a lot for mothers that we do this, generation on generation.

A party had been arranged for me to be introduced to prominent Victorians as I would be spending the year attempting (and succeeding!) in divesting them of their private papers for deposit in the State Library of Victoria. I was brought into the midst of a group of men and I found myself shaking hands with Edward Dunlop. 'Are you from one of the Western District families?' I was asked by one of the men, referring to the so-called leaders of society and politics from that area. 'No!' said Edward, 'she can't be – she's too good-looking for that!'

Year after year Edward came to my house on Sunday mornings after he had been to church (Presbyterian) and he brought a bottle of wine, swinging it in his hand for the neighbours to see and smile at. He would wave the bottle on high as if it were a trophy.

The night before he died Edward phoned me asking me to do two things for him. I said I'd take responsibility for one but not the other. He then said 'You never bend,' and I said 'But you've admired me for it'. His secretary of many years, who knew him as a *good* secretary knows her employer, called me on the phone and transferred me to Edward's phone. 'He's asking for you and I think he's most terribly ill,' she said. 'His voice, it is going.' And it was. That slow country voice that he could use to become a great teller of stories or ribaldry that would have shocked the many ladies who admired him as a saint.

But he was no saint. He was a very ordinary man who did as many another ordinary man or woman has done, rose to great vision when there was a need for it and few ready to go for it. If EED was a hero, he is in great company because there have been many a man and woman his equal.

I wear his hat, what he called his priest's hat because it was black. His monogram is stamped inside, EED. I'm told the hat looks great on me and I'm glad it keeps me warm. When he died I was asked if I would like a keepsake of my old friend and I said 'only the hat'.

There has never been much time in my life to socialise with the writing world, but the little socialising I've done has been warm and pleasant. The first group I got to know was that affable bunch of men of the Melbourne Bread and Cheese Club, chaired by Johnny Moir. One met a lot of great people at John's home in Bridge Road, Richmond. There was a little booze, a little food, and much laughter. There were always several Fulbright exchange students from the USA, visiting literati and authors from far and wide. I met Katharine Susannah Prichard here, the Aboriginal artist, Albert Namatjira, Professor Morris ('Mossie') Miller, and lovely Olaf Ruhen.

There was good companionship, but I couldn't remember everyone. There was one letter, for instance:

Dear Pat,
To hell with double spacing. It's single space for you – and like it. That's all you deserve after leaning against Moir's doorway one night, with a bloke on a motor bike waiting for you and with a tilt of the head, saying *at* me, 'He could have been interesting, if only I had the time to find out.'

'Hmm,' thought I to myself at the time. 'She'd get a helluva shock if she had.' Still, I must admit men are inclined to kid themselves a bit. Okay, okay, keep calm, MORE than a bit. Does that satisfy you? Just because the poor guy that shared your little wooden hut with you a few nights while you dunked yourself at night in and out of the ocean – just because that poor guy couldn't take a trick with you – you think men are all the same. Me, I knew that all along.

Actually this letter is solely written to talk about myself but best to say how pleased Jack was to get your letter and how he liked your breezy style. Come to think of it, I'm not sure he said breezy. Might have been full blown.

(Sadly, I didn't remember the writer when the letter arrived!)

The reference to the wooden hut was funny, though when the episode occurred I had been furious. I'd been commissioned to do a feature on the mutton birds of the Furneaux Islands and was ferried across to Long Island late at night. I washed in the sea, rolled out my sleeping bag, when in came the photographer. 'Where's your sleeping bag?' I asked. 'One will do us,' he said.

'No it won't,' said I, and without any bravado or hesitation I told him the truth: 'You try anything funny and every fisherman or seaman around these islands will deal with you.' And, as if on cue, up from the shore climbed Jimmy Sholto Douglas and the Aboriginal, Eric Maynard, carrying a mattress from their boat. 'For Mrs Pat,' Jimmy said, in as ominous a tone as his lovely voice could manage. 'Yair,' said Eric to the photographer, 'you heard.'

When John Kinmont Moir died, the Melbourne *Age* carried an obituary: 'Co-founder and President of the Melbourne Bread and Cheese Club and one of the foremost authorities on Australiana.' Moir had donated his large library of Australian literature to the Public Library of Victoria and the Chairman of the Trustees stated that 'Mr Moir was one of the best friends Australian literature ever had.' He certainly was a good friend to me.

Friday night at Moir's house was when everybody turned up, but the great night was Sunday night. Then it was not 'open house' but just an exclusive few would be invited – usually three – and there would be toast and tea in front of the fire. James (Jim) McAuley was there once and we laughed at the Ern Malley furore.

Perhaps the loveliest man to meet in Melbourne was A.A. (Arthur) Phillips. Arthur and I were walking along Toorak Road one day, at the expensive end. 'Do you know' said this now-aged man, 'Here there is everything man could buy and nothing he needs.' Arthur had edited my story 'Hot Eyes' and from the time it was published in *Summer's Tales* he called me 'Hot Eyes' – and I didn't mind at all.

Cyril Pearl and Paddy (his wife) were part of the breezy literary crowd in those days. He it was who wrote about Sydney in *The Girl with the Swansdown Seat*. Years later, I saw him in Dublin in the research room in the magnificent old library and whispered to him, 'This is almost as good as having your own Swansdown Seat' and he, Paddy and I broke the forbidding silence of the ancients with laughter. For a time Cyril was editor of *Australia Magazine*, the first magazine of its type in this country, and he often commissioned me to write for it.

My work as Manuscripts Officer was a natural extension of the folklore work I had started in Tasmania. I had begun tape-recording reminiscences in 1962 with no particular subject in mind. All that motivated me was the painful knowledge that we had already lost so much of the history of our race of people. I was alerted by Mary Gilmore who wrote, 'Ours are ours.' She was referring to the vast influx of migrants who had rushed to Australia since the end of the Second World War, but already I had seen so many of the things of my childhood change – and with the change, expunged as though they had never been. Many of my early tapes (on a great big heavy machine like an old-time portable gramophone) I gave to the interviewees, in the hope that their children would care for them and hand them on to future generations. I soon learned that that was wrong: folklore is apt to leap a generation, sometimes two or more generations, with no member of the family caring where they came from or what their forebears did.

My work in Victoria was meant to be tracking down documents of historical importance, but I often found that the people who had just one document of interest also had vast, unwritten memories which were of just as much importance. I began to work seriously in the field after I was awarded a Literature Board Fellowship in 1972 which allowed me to travel to Ireland. There, in the folk archives, is a great mass of material about Irish emigrants to Australia that would have been lost had it not been for the Guinness company which assisted in financing the work. The discovery stirred me greatly. 'Why don't we, our nation, preserve the documents and words of our people?' From that time on I have climbed many ladders into attics and ceilings, into the scaffolding above shearing sheds, into old hotels, magnificent homes, tiny houses, and boxes under the house. Many times I have had to shower immediately I finished the search, and once I got into a bath fully clothed and soaked myself and undressed there after a long night in a grand old home with dead mice, living mice, and insects for company. Even my hair stank – but if you are going to worry about that you should never take up this kind of work.

One of my close friends is Beverly Dunn, the actress, well known to TV fans in her roles in long-playing drama series and for her work in hundreds of plays. One day she was dusting her library and came on a large bundle of correspondence she had kept over our twenty-five year friendship. 'It may nudge your memory' she said, dumping a big parcel on my table. Cards and letters galore sprang out. Most of the correspondence sprang from my travels in the outback or overseas. Sometimes I couldn't recall the event I had written about: 'Welcome Home! O rolling pin thrower; sleeping lizard racer; seal adulator-ess!' But I could certainly remember the 1972 trip which had prompted the following letter:

Cathy [who had come to Ireland with me] and I went to Sissinghurst in Kent with a loving Australian friend, Sybil Irving. A warm day of gentle breezes and we like three little girls on a picnic. It was a laughing day. We got a train to the wrong station, paid too much for a taxi, and so on . . . There was a test match at Lords, England versus Australia, and I was anxious to know the state of play. Sybil asked the Station Master 'Who is winning?' 'We are,' the Englishman replied. In her most elegant diction Sybil asked, 'Who are WE?'

The book I had come to Ireland to write was *Heart of Exile*, though I had to return often before it was completed. Each day I spent six hours at the National Library studying eleven great tea-chest sized crates of letters and diaries that had been written from Australia to Ireland in the 1840s and 1850s. It was the most exciting book I have written, both the labour and the result.

Ireland beguiles me as it has generations of travellers; it is small enough to give you the feel of its long generations and the poetry. Cathy and I once walked from Cork to Donegal in the balmy Irish summer, with a stopover at Galway University to do a short course of Anglo-Irish literature. She is a trained nurse and worked at various Irish hospitals to earn the money to make the journey with young friends to Iran, Afghanistan and India, driving in through the Khyber Pass.

I learned what a joy it was to travel with a different age group from my own, and had the opportunity, rare for most mothers, to watch my adult child perform so adventurously and well so far from home. A few years later we set off together once again, this time to Sri Lanka. My son, Michael, accompanied me on a trip to China and once again, I counted myself lucky to have the company of my adult child.

Irish talk is lively, amusing, and sometimes chilling. In 1972 when 'The Troubles' broke out again in Northern Ireland one heard many stories. Contraceptives are banned in Ireland, but I liked the story about the huge number of condoms smuggled in by the English pharmaceutical firm, Boots. 'The very best, smooth rubber,' the advertisement said, 'Factory tested' – thus making them a more satisfactory casing for home-made bombs than the Hong Kong balloons which had been used up to that time.

I travelled to Northern Ireland – Belfast – many times for research as three of the seven Irish exiles I was studying (Protestant rebels of 1848) were from Newry over the border. I travelled on Thursdays because there was an excursion ticket on that day. Many businessmen travelled up and back for the day and it was said you were less likely to be searched by the British troops as you crossed the border on that day.

But I learned that was not always the case. My attache case and handbag were grabbed and, when I unwisely tried to hang on, the soldier just tossed the contents of both down the corridor and no one made any effort to help as I crawled around the floor, trying to retrieve my loose cash, pens, note books as well as the loose foolscap pages that had fluttered all over the place. The catch on my attache case was broken and I was unsure what to do. 'You needn't have done that. I would have opened it if you'd asked me.' And that was a mistake. 'Australian! Bloody Australia getting into it now!' Two soldiers began to imitate my Australian accent, laughing. The Irish didn't laugh: they looked out the window, they had seen it all before. But when I got off the train at Belfast one traveller and then another came to me asking if I was 'alright' and whether they could help fix the broken catch.

Another time I missed the return train and had to stay the night, without money. It was my own fault. I always left the Public Records Office giving myself over half an hour to walk to the station, but this day I heard an enormous 'bang' between me and the station. Two 'Pigs' (small armoured vehicles) raced by. I began to run but it was winter and the snow had been pounded into ice so I kept falling over. I got wet through – my overcoat, hem of my dress, gloves, stockings and all – and was trying to get along quicker by going hand-over-hand along the railing when I was grabbed and shoved into a passenger bus that was already over-full. The light was going fast and I couldn't see anything. I couldn't understand a word that was being said – the Northern Ireland workingclass accent is as difficult for us to understand as our accent is to them. No one spoke to me, not even the driver. At intervals another body was pushed in, caught up like me and grabbed 'just in case'. At least, I supposed that was why we had been nabbed. The windows became fogged up and men and women were smoking. I tried not to think of anything but held my attache case hard against my chest with my arms wrapped round it. I was damned if I was going to let my hard-won research be stolen for the sake of the case.

Suddenly, quietly, with little fuss except for the astonishingly fruity cursing you can hear any day in Belfast, everyone except me got off and disappeared in a flash. I sat down on the floor. I didn't know where we were. It was pitch dark outside. The driver roared at me. I moved toward him and he made a push at me. I grabbed the rail near his seat and shouted 'Europa!'. God knows why I remembered the name of that hotel. It was the five-star hotel of Belfast that had been bombed recently and the repairs and alterations were said to have made it the safest place in the city. 'Europa!' I screamed every time the driver kicked and yelled at me. He kept shouting but apart from a lot of 'fecking!' I couldn't understand a word of it. Then, suddenly he braked, the door opened, and he shouted 'Europa!' 'Where?' I yelled while he began to kick me again. 'Where?' He pointed down the deserted, black street and I fell out.

It would look fine for me to say that I stood up to this well, but the truth is I have never been so desolate, cold and terrified as when I heard his bloody bus rumbling off – no lights, I don't know why, perhaps because of the curfew. I began to try to hurry down the street but when I got to the first corner there were still only rows of houses built flat onto the footpath. I banged on a door and no one answered, but I had heard voices before I knocked. I called out very loudly and a woman spoke, as if she had her lips to the keyhole. 'Who are you?' Irish, but softer than most Belfast speakers. I told her I was lost, could she give me directions to the Europa Hotel. Quickly, clearly she did so, then told me to walk on the gutter side of the footpath, not to creep along in the shadows of the houses as I had been doing. And she said not another word. I felt that my lone footsteps on this locked and shuttered street had been observed from the moment I had been pushed out of the bus.

I was only two streets from the Europa. A British soldier at the guard house frisked me lightly, then a British woman soldier did it more thoroughly, and I could go inside. I must have been a grubby sight: wet right through, covered in mud and dirt from my falls when skating along the ice and from squatting on the floor of the unlovely bus. At the reception desk the staff made no comment about my appearance but asked me how would I pay? Pay? Hell, I had only my now-useless day ticket back to

Dublin and my scholarship didn't run to extravagance. Then I remembered an old friend who lived in Dublin. Dr Brendan O'Brien is a descendant of the Irish kings and to give his name was a bit of an over-kill, but I felt better for having such a friend at such a time. The porter took me up to my room and took elaborate care explaining fire drill if an 'alarm' sounded. No one bothered to ask if I had any luggage and I had a feeling that this little adventure of mine was a quite frequent occurrence in this city. Without breakfast, I boarded the train the next day and at Dublin, since I no longer had a current ticket, I made a dash through the gate past the porter. It seemed such a neat exercise I could have been doing it all my life and should never need to buy a railway ticket again.

In all the trips I made to the English-ruled Northern Ireland I had only one other mishap and again, that was entirely my own fault. I took a photograph in Derry. It was not long after Bloody Sunday when thirteen Irish men had been shot during a peace demonstration. The English had painted on their tanks 'British 13, Irish nil'. Feeling on both sides was violent. The photograph I took was of a mock-up of a body hanging by the neck from an archway, the legend around the neck read 'Fuck the Pope'. That endeavour cost me a perfectly good camera and a very hard kick to my spleen, which does demonstrate that when a country is at war, or even in distress, one should not intrude. There is something cruelly indecent in probing or peering at a society wrapped in a tragedy that is four hundred years' old.

And then there is the lighter side of research, such as the day in the Dublin Public Records Office when for hours I had been reading colourless, unyieldingly dull material about a trial. It was a rape charge, and right in the middle of proceedings the judge pulled up the accused and snapped, 'What did you say the young lady had in her hand?' 'Me Parnell, sir' replied the accused. 'Your WHAT?' I nearly rolled off my hard library seat. Parnell, of course, was the Protestant Irish hero who fell in love with the married Catholic woman, Kitty O'Shea, and not only lost his seat in the British parliament but lost all respectability in the community, as did Kitty. And now, what had been 'me John Thomas' to Englishmen had become in Ireland 'me Parnell'.

My folklore work had resulted in my collecting a large amount of material from the old Diggers who had fought in the First World War. I mounted an exhibition about the Anzacs in Melbourne's Public Library which brought in more people on the opening day than had ever attended any of the other exhibitions which had been held there. The vast and complex concept of *The Anzacs* book began to take shape in my mind and, for a number of years, the writing of it took over my life and pushed my other writing projects into the background. As I wrote to Beverly:

18 January 1977: It's three years since I began THE BOOK [*The Anzacs*]. It takes all my waking hours and, as you know, it is 4.30 am regularly except for the loving times when good friends like you startle me out to dinner. I've got to get it to the publisher now. Stuck at it all last Friday night and went to bed 9 am to noon Saturday then at it again until 3.45 Monday morning when it was done, all 661 pages of it. I'm happy about it. Perhaps some other writer could do it as well – but I feel none better. The old men and women have been terrific, not only giving me beautifully rich material but enthusing me with their frankness and desire for the truth to be told.

Took it to Nelsons at midday, Monday – they near collapsed with the size of it. 'Three books in one!' Barney Rivers said – and then lunched me at Lazars until 4 pm. But it will take longer than that to unbind me. I'm tense in every fibre. My walk is jittery and I have pins and needles in finger tips and toes. My stomach is all of a twist, has been for months. But it's done now. The baby has to battle alone now. Do wish me luck in the printing m'dear. I can now say to the surgeon: 'Do your damnedest. I'm ready now.'

The Anzacs hardly needed luck. It ran alone to best-seller lists for over a year, and still sells.

One of the reviews of *The Anzacs* better describes the book than I can now do. Written by John Larkin of the Melbourne *Age*, it was headed 'Real People in a Real War':

Something extraordinary happens as Patsy Adam-Smith pares away the Anzac myths, all that Union Jack and King and Country drivel inflicted on generations of school kids.

You've only read a few chapters before you realise that the reality – the truth Patsy Adam-Smith has lovingly and stylishly stitched into a superb book – is nobler than the myths.

Take Simpson and his donkey. The authorised school version, the municipal sculptor's version, depicts this saintly figure, serene, eyes raised above the petty horizons of mortals. Patsy Adam-Smith's Simpson is no less heroic. But he is also a wild colonial spirit. He swears; he loves a stoush. 'You couldn't see anything for blood and snots flying . . . ' he writes rapturously about a fight at sea. He's fond of his mum and stray dogs; he misspells terribly; he has humped a swag and been skint. He was heroic in Shrapnel Gully. But, above all, he is flawed and real.

Mythology gives us a saint we admired but could not comprehend. Patsy Adam-Smith gives us a bloke we might have known and liked . . . and who was as much a hero as the saint.

And it is this flavour of the book. It is about real people and the real war, the greatest ritual sacrifice of the young by the old, the innocent by the corrupt, in history. It is not about generals, strutting and thinking of posterity, or the chess world of strategy and diplomacy.

No, the hero is a bloke who walked out of a shearing shed, joined up to fight for a cause he did not understand, for a monarch he had never seen, for – God help us – a 'mother' country where he was not born . . . and fought and endured and died with a bravery and stoicism that in these soft days seems unreal. Actually, the hero is hundreds of such men. Patsy Adam-Smith has read nearly 8000 diaries and letters and interviews with many of the survivors, and she skilfully lets them tell the story.

And this is perhaps the book's great power, this first person in the trench. A soldier crouching in the bone-strewn slime of Flanders has no time for affectation; . . . like Simpson, he is real.

They can make you weep, these diaries, when they suddenly run out, or when the author interposes a line like: 'Perhaps now we could walk day by day with him, for there is only a little time to go.' There is often a poetic quality. ' . . . I saw an Australian and a Turk who had run each other through with their bayonets . . . their arms must have encircled each other . . . they had been in that sad embrace for at least a week.' There's she'll-be-right optimism: 'One old chap when he was dying kept saying: "Stop the bleeding boys, and I'll get back home to the missus and kids." '

In one sense it is the technique of the New Journalism, the non-fiction novel: let people tell it their way; leave the omissions, the wrong tenses, the vernacular, for they are the things that make it authentic.

Patsy Adam-Smith writes with polish and clarity; she never departs from her aim of letting the men tell it themselves. She is sympathetic when interposing her own conclusions, but never cowed by the Anzac ghosts she has grown up with. And, apart from its inspired use of photographs and captions, this book is an exquisite piece of engineering and editing; a lesser writer would have been overwhelmed by the weight of research.

And Patsy Adam-Smith deserves a special place – not just for getting it right but for doing so with so much style and so much heart.

In 1977 the Literature Board of the Australia Council, in partnership with the Department of Foreign Affairs, invited me to visit the USSR on the first government-to-government cultural exchange of writers between the two countries. Three Australian writers were invited: Barbara Jefferis, the novelist, David Williamson, the playwright, and me. We each knew we could raise a laugh in a tight corner – and what more do travellers need to know of each other? The exchange had its origins back in the days when Geoffrey Blainey was chairman of the Literature Board and it had now materialised in the form of an invitation from the Writers' Union of the USSR.

Before we set off for the USSR we learned that we were also to go to Japan for three days. I didn't care for that: I'd already been there before. Now we were to take part in a seminar and an exhibition of Australian books. It turned out to be like the curate's egg – good in parts. Ambassador John Menadue did us proud. The books were set up in the embassy and we arrived to lunch with invited writers, publishers, translators and professors of literature. We promenaded through the gardens and I forgot to talk of literature because I was agog with the changes I could see in the country. Affluence, power and confidence had replaced the land I had known more than twenty years before.

Later we answered questions at a seminar, a pretty translator taking notes and reading the whole thing out at the end. David brightened the day for Barbara and me by stating that something was 'ratshit'. The Australians in the audience laughed: how would the translator handle that? She did well: 'Of no value, useless.' A professor who knew David's work inside out bombarded him with questions; another professor got into holts with me (and later took me to dinner) on the strength of *Yoknapatawpha County*-type writing in Australia. That was OK because I had been at the university in Mississippi studying Faulkner. In her own impressive way Barbara handled Australian-fiction-today questions.

She and I deserted our playwright companion the following day when he was to show the film of *The Removalists* at the embassy to Japanese guests. Barbara and I boarded the Bullet, the silver, streaking train and in fifty minutes were 68 miles out in the countryside. 'My God!' David greeted us on our late return. 'I fear I've set Australian–Japanese relations back ten years!' He was sure that the silence which had followed his film showing indicated displeasure, even distaste. 'Not so,' Professor

Mikio Hiramaku told me later when he visited Australia. 'It was the colloquialisms. Few Japanese could follow them.'

Before we left Tokyo we strolled down the Ginza which, on Sundays, has been turned into a mall, and David's height made the day for the Japanese. They pointed at him, laughed, came right up to him and talked of the sight; one lady actually raced over to get her husband from a shop to view the spectacle, and a small boy ran into David's knee before he realised there was a man on the top of it and he yelled 'oooaahh!' as he stretched his neck skywards.

In return I found myself staring at the Japanese. They seemed taller than I remembered them, better looking and more smartly dressed. I had not been back to Japan since 1960. I remembered then seeing armies of women on their hands and knees all through the night beating wooden blocks into the wide pavements, making a new road or a new pathway, with their masters, the men, overseeing their work but, of course, upright! At daybreak you'd hear the clatter-clatter of their wooden clogs as they returned to their homes to do their day's work and be back on the pavements by sundown.

Then we did the long haul across Siberia. Three hours after our arrival at Moscow airport we were taken to dinner by Yuri Nagibin, whom some of us had met when he visited the Adelaide Arts Festival (and we waited in vain to meet his ex-wife, the excitable and exciting poet, Bella Akhmadulina).

We were weary. The flight to Japan, three busy days there, followed by the long flight across Siberia – and, in the case of at least one of us, copious stone bottles of warm sake – had taken its toll. Barbara, cool and gracious as ever, sat as befits a representative of government, and kicked neither of us under the table when first David spilt a whole glass of red wine and then broke the stem off the glass in putting it back on the table and I, not to be outdone, appeared to act with precision in tossing a full glass of lemonade the length of the table. When a monumental lady had mopped that lot up and we had recovered our aplomb, we ate heartily as all the other writer-members in the Writers' Union building were doing: olives, lush and black, rye bread, bowls of caviar, cucumber in sour cream, cold meats and tiny spiced sausages, vodka, neat and copious and wines, red and white. One feels replete and content – when in comes the main course: the other was what would be called 'snacks'. With an 'Ah my country, it is all for thee' feeling, we began again.

Next day we were to meet our hosts. The USSR Writers' Union was housed in the building and grounds used as the Rostov's home in the film of *War and Peace*. The graceful circular driveway sweeps up to the steps where fussy old Mr Rostov had scampered down to ask Audrey Hepburn why she was taking the furniture off the escape carts and putting wounded men there instead.

Inside we met the Deputy Chairman of the Foreign Commission of the Writer's Union, Mr Sheshkin, who sat us down and told us about the Union. It was rather heavy, with a certain feeling from the voice and surroundings that we were to listen and take notes. I am not at my best at such times and refused to lift my pen. We were told that the print run for the average book of poetry was 15 000 and for prose it was 50 000 copies. We did not buy or, indeed, see any of these works in shops and on enquiring we learnt that they were sold out immediately on publication. The Australian Ambassador, Sir James Plimsoll, told me that he went to a shop two hours after opening time to buy a novel he wanted to read on the day it was being published and the work was sold out.

Now, about Russia. There is one hazard to avoid there (I'm damned if I know how you can avoid it but have a go): those mighty, big-bummed, doughty, Brobdignagian keepers of the keys of rooms in Russian pubs. Respect them, do as they shout, for you haven't a Buckley's chance against them. These women were positioned on every floor of the hotel, placed at the vantage point on the corner of the floor so they could see from both angles. They were the caretakers of morality.

Our hosts were generous. They took us in hire-drive cars to galleries, ballet, theatre, the circus. They gave each of us 150 roubles for 'extras': our accommodation, travel etc. was paid for. We had few chores. We addressed an English-speaking audience at the State Library of Foreign Literature, an unnerving experience as we followed Pablo Neruda, Robert Frost, Richard Aldington and other eminent authors of past years. Seated in the front row were the noted English translators, Oxana Krugerskaya and Alla Petroviskaya.

Then we were off on the Red Arrow to Leningrad (as it was called then). I do have to boast (and after all, I've travelled more train-miles than most Australian backsides), the pride of the USSR railway system could not compare with the *dolce far niente* of Queensland's long, slow shunt into yesterday. There were no WCs in the cabins, dirty (even to grey) rags were used to wipe floors, then the samovar and then flapped to frighten one away back to one's own seat. There was no shower on the train, no tea or service of any kind from the time we boarded at Moscow until an hour before we reached Leningrad, when we were given a cup of tea. For much of the time we were entertained by David singing 'My Funny Valentine', a sort of hung-over effect from our last few hours in Moscow when he'd danced with a Russian lady who had held him Moscow-style – very close. She was very tall and that was necessary if one was to dance very close with a man who was 6 foot 7 inches high. Barbara and I were afraid that if we danced with him the buckle of his belt would scratch our foreheads.

It rained in Leningrad as if the Second Flood was due, but even that couldn't hide the legendary beauty of the place. We spent a day at Petrodverets, the most enchanting old Summer Palace, wandering the grounds which had fountains cascading and gilded statuary lining the waterways to the sea. There, across the water, live the Finns, a race superior even to the Russians in putting away their liquor. And this led to yet another *petit embarrassment* for David. We had stopped to have a beer at one of the convenient beer kiosks on the street (why can't we have beer kiosks in Australia like wee tobacco shops, where a thirsty passer-by can have a quick, cold beer?) and the lady dispenser took exception to David, the gentle giant. She shouted (so we learnt from our translator) that it was 'because of Finns like him coming over the border to drink that people say Russians drink too much!' Well, well – as our translator, Anatole, said returning to the car with David. I banged my drinking mug down on the counter, presented the shouting lady with the two-finger salute, and ran like hell in case the gargantuan blonde took after me.

At Petrodverets, Anatole met his match with one of the mighty keepers of the keys. He was attempting to get us into a gallery at the head of a queue and told the big lady we had come from far away, from Australia, and that we were writers. 'So what!' this admirable Amazon shrugged. 'I am a member of the Russian Architects' Union!' I loved her for that.

We had heard that one needs to be a hero to drink in Georgia, but the sunshine and the balmy air of the land undid us and heroes we became. Here we went to the famous Georgian brandy distillery and emptied our glasses into a crystal bowl on the fruit- and biscuit-covered table as we tasted one, two . . . six brandies. And then the toast. Always they toast in the USSR, anything up to a dozen toasts at a meal. We three agreed we were bumble-footed about this but occasionally we hit the right note. The toastmaster, Tamadah, was a tyrant. 'Bottoms up!' he cried in the Georgian equivalent and valiantly we upheld our country's honour in brandy, vodka, Georgian wine, and the local cha-cha (or is it tzcha-tzcha?) that reminded me too terribly of Irish potheen.

Once again we were at the airport in the wee small hours. Uzbekistan was fabulous; its capital, Tashkent, had treasures, but Samarkand . . . well! The markets, both here and in Tashkent, were a joy – very like eastern markets anywhere except that there were no beggars and everything was clean. Our Uzbek guide, Alisher, as gentle as a girl, took my hand and held it out to a stallholder; the man placed a vine leaf on my palm and piled it high with the golden flesh of peeled figs and Alisher fed them to me with his slender fingers. (Note for D. H. Lawrence: you'd have slipped your trolley here. I did.)

David was suddenly accosted by a tribal-costumed, merry-faced lady stallholder. She held up three fingers, struggled for English, and said, 'Three metres?' His height. 'No,' said David, charmed like a little boy at her merry approach, 'two metres', and held up two fingers. The lady scampered back to the other gaily caparisoned women and held up her fingers and waved and greeted David when he next passed.

Having a guide who travelled with us meant that language was no problem, except for the vernacular. While Anatole may have had his problems getting over to us the subtleties of a Russian joke, there were times when we too had our difficulties. In Samarkand a pretty, scholarly lady guided us through the 15th century observatory of Ulugbek. Nearby she showed us the ruins of the 15th century building that the beautiful Bibi-Khanym had had erected to surprise her husband, Tamurlane, on his return from conquering India. The legend was that the architect fell deeply in love with Bibi-Khanym and refused to complete the building unless he was allowed one kiss. Bibi, anxious to see the roof-beam raised, said 'Da, but only on my cheek and through my hand'. The lover approached, Bibi placed her hand upon her cheek and he kissed the palm, but his passion was so strong that his kiss burnt through her hand and branded her cheek. A sort of medieval love-bite resulted which Tamurlane recognised as swiftly as any returning husband would, and the architect fled on wings to Persia. At dinner that night David attempted to relate the story to our interpreter, Anatole. 'There was this Bibi Khanym you see, and this architect got the hots for her . . . ' 'What is "the hots"?' asked our faithful guide.

Later, in Georgia, Datar, our companion who spoke Georgian and French but no English, suddenly learnt, from God knows where, a line that enchanted him. After a lunch in a country restaurant where we sat on low stools and ate a sort of soda loaf, borsch and greens with, as ever in Georgia, much local wine, Datar skipped with glee to David and cried, 'You are drunk as skunt'. We quietly corrected the final consonant, and for the rest of our days in Georgia, Datar told anyone who would hearken that David was 'drunk as skunk'.

Our leaving was warm and sad. As all travellers learn when touching a little of another world, if we exercise sympathy, patience and love, a journey becomes an entrancing field in which, perhaps, even the most erudite may learn something.

The Flowers in the Cannon's Mouth

IN 1978 MY BOOK, *The Anzacs*, was published to great acclaim, but I did not wait to see it launched. Instead I went overseas with First World War veterans to France and Belgium to stand at the eleventh hour of the eleventh day of the eleventh month, sixty years after the end of the war.

This was no political stunt, as was to be done by governments in later years, but a yearning of men to once again walk where they had walked with their friends when they were all young. The men had all paid their own way. On return I wrote of the pilgrimage. Of the seventy men, half were from a later war ('My God', one old man said, 'if you'd told me there'd be another war in my lifetime I'd have said you were raving mad.') The others were the survivors of the most terrible four years endured by modern man.

Otto Nielsen (24th Battalion) was 'outed' at Pozieres where a small plaque told us that more Australians died there than at any other place in the war. 'I ran in the dark through a gap in the wire with some others, and I'd hardly got through when I was hit on the leg.' Otto was a massive man, bent from the hip-length caliper that held his left leg together. 'A cobber was hit badly and we rolled into a shell hole. When daylight came I looked around and saw our mates on the barbed wire.'

As we tramped down the old stamping grounds, snatches of half-remembered songs were whispered:

If you want to find the battalion
I know where they are
They're hanging on the old barbed wire,
I saw them, I saw them, hanging on the old barbed wire.

Bert Field remembered the mud most of all: 'The earth was decayed from being fought over and back so long, beaten to pieces, falling apart. There were bodies in the mud. Limbs, hands jutted out, slime and stink and always mud and you fell over in it. Bodies buried in the trench from last month's, last year's battle . . . we walked over them.'

Jim Bryant (8th and 60th Battalions) survived Gallipoli, Belgium and France, and was taken prisoner by the Japanese at Singapore in the Second World War. 'I always thought I ought to sue them for restitution of conjugal rights' said Jim, aged 87 years.

A colour party was being drilled to take part in the cermonies that were to follow and the colour-sergeant was being, well, sergeant-majorish. 'Listen' said Kim Kimber (50th Battalion), 'they tried to teach us that sort of thing in 1914 and failed, so how in hell do you think you'll manage it now?'

They trooped colours first at Menin Gate, that portal at the entrance to Ypres in Belgium where the names of 56 000 men are listed, many of them Australian. When we had passed through Germany on our way to France we had been invited to dinner by the Afrika Corps and Manfred Rommel, mayor of Stuttgart and son of the 'Desert Fox'. One German asked Les McCarthy (7th Field Battery) where he had fought in the First World War. 'Ypres', said Les. The German threw up his arms and cried, 'Ypres, Ypres, Ypres,' in horror, and the men embraced.

Now they stood with colours furled, waiting for the town

clock to strike 8 pm. As on every night since 1928 when Menin Gate was built, a gendarme stops the traffic, a trumpeter plays 'The Last Post', the citizens hesitate for a moment, then life goes on. That night, the traffic was stopped for a little longer as four trumpeters sounded the call, the Anzacs lowered their flags, and we stood in zero temperatures beneath the names of Australian battalions who were lost here in the mud before I was born.

The young men killed in that battle are buried under Picardy roses in the large cemetery on the edge of the town. Those who lived through it were there these many years later; stoics all, no muscle moving on their faces, as we walked between the graves, row on row on row, up to the memorial. Past the rows marked 'Australian Soldier Known Unto God', past those identified by name. 'Some of my mob' Kim Kimber said. He was not quite 20 years old when he went into this battle. 'Oh, there's poor old Tom. A wonderful fellow. And Bob ... now there was a funny man! The stories he could tell! Ah, this boy. I was with him ...' No muscle moved. 'It's damned cold,' Kim said, shivering. It was a good excuse to blow a nose, wipe an eye. The eyes betrayed these men.

Tension was mounting, you sensed it in the old men as we drew nearer to Armistice Day. We were taken by buses to Villers Bretonneux. Armistice Day in Villers Bretonneux didn't so much as 'dawn' – it rolled a blanket of heather-grey mist and fog over the land. The lament began, the piper appeared and disappeared from view as the dark fog swept across like a ribbon and swept back again. The pipes came closer. As the chimes began to beat out the slow strokes of 11 am some of us glanced at the mist-swept scene, but the old men stared unblinking across the gap that they had crossed and can never forget, and we who were not with them can never fully understand. The old men will not come again. One had already died on this trip, one returned home unwell. Kim Kimber wrote:

And on this day of solemn things,
The bell within the tower rings
And just a little closer brings
The living and the dead.

We could hardly see the town for the Australian and French flags which the people put up in their streets. A French lady said, 'I was a young girl in 1918. The retreat was on. The Germans were coming.' I asked her, 'What did the Australians do?' 'Oh, they marched through us and we gave them some bread and a bottle of wine and ran after them with it. The Australians called out to us, "no need for you to go, we'll hold them!" And they did.'

The school in the town was *en fete* for *Australie*. Rebuilt with the help of the pennies collected by Victorian schoolchildren in the 1920s, the leitmotiv on the blackboard read in French and English: 'Never forget Australia'. Australian and French flags fluttered over the tables set for two-hundred people, both nationalities mixed together. We ate and drank and talked and laughed and sang for six hours and marvelled as the language barrier got smaller as the hours got longer. There was a lot of hugging. An old lady kissed and kissed me and her husband held my arms: 'Australia.' Like the rest of the group I bathe in the aura that spills over from the old soldiers. The only time we hush is when the children of the school troop in and sing to us: 'Once a jolly swagman ...'

On the following morning, 12 November, 12 km from Villers Bretonneux, we assembled in front of the steps leading to Amiens Cathedral. The French General in charge of the Picardy region escorted our leader, Major-General Sir William Refshauge, up the steps to the Bishop of Amiens. And so it began, the most remarkable hour, a unique experience. Every seat in the cathedral was occupied. As we entered, the huge congregation stood.

Sixty years ago on the day after the Armistice, the then Bishop of Amiens had spoken at a service here when the

Australians were leaving. The present bishop now reminded us of promises of sixty years ago – to care for the dead the Australians were leaving behind ('They are now sons of France'). Perhaps most poignant was the prayer that these dead youths would be taken without trial past the seat of judgement and into 'life everlasting'. In 1918 the bishop had then turned to the living and spoken of their exploits in Picardy: 'You made a rampart of your breasts behind which my diocese of Picardy sheltered, behind which my people were saved.'

For a moment the organ was silent and then, like the distant rumble of an underground train, there was a slow beat like muffled drums – or was it the sound of feet that would never march again? The silence in the cathedral was ear-stretching as we strained to catch the noise of the footfalls. Suddenly, the colours on the altar dipped, our starry cross spread out like a woman's dress on the scarlet carpet, and a thin cry rose and quivered and crept almost noiselessly down upon us – 'The Last Post'. It sounded not as a military thing, but more as the breath of a young boy's farewell.

Not in a lifetime of music have I heard such a thing; one could not expect to hear it again, surrounded as we were by the spectre of a generation whose endurance is tattooed on our folk memory. 'In the whole of history we cannot find an army more marvellous in its bravery,' the Bishop of Amiens had said in 1918. Marshal Foch had said, 'You saved Amiens, you saved France. Our gratitude will remain ever and always to Australia.' Now the present bishop said no less. Having thanked the Anzacs he bowed low to them. Our colours were brought down off the altar, three of our old men and a war widow led us back up the aisle past the standing French congregation as the organ played a slow march and 'Advance Australia Fair'.

I tell you, it was not a day to be wearing mascara.

Ceremony followed ceremony, flag followed flag, tear fell on tear; the French in Picardy asked us to as many remembrances as we could fit in. At 9.30 pm on the 12th we came on the lanterns of a group huddled in the cold by a small graveyard where Australians were buried. They were waiting for us. Beneath the starry Southern Cross of the flag of Australia there was a final brief prayer.

At the Arc de Triomphe, a French military band marched through off the Champs Elysees playing the 'Marseillaise' and 'Advance Australia Fair'. Looking at the old soldiers I wondered what Australia would be like today had their companions lived; if many of those who had come home had not been marked physically, mentally and emotionally. As 'Wolla Meranda' wrote in 1916:

> And beauty weeps in the land of the morn,
> For the flowers of love that will never be born.

Sixty years on we walked in the shadow of the survivors and saw people who still remembered and paid tribute to them and, through them, to every Australian.

My work with the Anzacs provided me with many valued friends and wonderful contacts. It also stirred in me a desire to honour those soldiers who, so often, receive little honour – the men who had been taken prisoner. Not just those who had been prisoners of the Germans or the Japanese in the Second World War – the Australian people had, finally, some inkling of the horrors endured by those prisoners – but those who had endured imprisonment in the First World War, and in the Korean War. After many years of gruelling and emotionally draining work, my book *Prisoners of War* was submitted to the publisher on the same day that I collapsed and was taken to hospital for major heart surgery.

Some say that today's generation of young men would not enlist for war as the generations before them have done. But this is peacetime talk. History teaches us that the panoply and mystique of war is most seductive. 'Which boy,' Jim Gordon, an old soldier of the First World War asked me, 'can resist falling in behind a drum? Which boy, bursting with the energy and excitement of youth, can resist the urgency of shrilling trumpets, of fluttering pennants? Particularly when they are poor or excitement is lacking.'

Add to this the almost irresistible magnet of the songs that have filled the 'ranks of death' with the 'bravest and the best'. These songs have not only seduced generation upon generation of men to battle, but have convinced those who stayed at home that it was a holy cause. Australians went to the Boer War singing 'Dolly Gray'. We went to the First World War singing:

> *For England, Home and Duty*
> *Have no cause to fear;*
> *Should Auld Acquaintance Be Forgot?*
> *No! No! No! No! No!*
> *Australia will be there . . .*
> *Australia will be there*

Soon we were singing:

> *What's the use of worrying?*
> *It never was worthwhile!*
> *So! Pack up your troubles in your old kit bag and*
> *Smile! Smile! Smile!*

a song with the most wicked of intentions. There was a time when cannons were called 'the queen of weapons' and young girls would place flowers in the cannons' mouths, but songs were more seductive than cannons.

American composers sold the war to that unwilling nation with even more brilliant songs, including 'Over There!':

> *Send the word! Send the word!*
> *We'll be there.*

For the Yanks are coming! The Yanks are coming!
They're drum-drum-drumming everywhere!

My generation sped out of the depression and off to war with
a song that had become a war song by accident. Gracie Fields
had made a film in 1939 *Shipyard Sally* and in it she sang 'Wish
me Luck':

Give me a smile, I can keep all the while
In my heart while I'm away,
Till we meet, once again, you and I,
Wish me luck as you wave me goodbye.

As the film was released, war was declared. The boys I danced
with were singing it as they disappeared to 'jump the rattler'
from the depression-hit bushlands to ride to the city to enlist.
They fled the depression that had tried to rip their pride out,
but that song helped them to escape. All day, every day, it
danced out of the big wireless in our home.

In two world wars we damned the munitions giants, Ruhr
and Krupps; perhaps we should have attacked the subliminally
seductive song-writers instead.

In the 1960s the media and most of the older generation
were throwing up their hands – and voices – because of what
they called 'four-letter words' being used publicly by young
people. 'Obscenities!' they accused. Obscenities? I always thought
that the greatest obscenity was a three-letter word – war – and
I still claim that war is the ultimate obscenity.

We seem not to have the answer that will stop fit young men
from going to war. No man goes to war thinking he will be
killed. Letters from men at two world wars show no horror at
death; wounds, yes, 'Thinking of a bullet, thinking if it hurts'
wrote a young Australian in 1917. But not death.

Untold hordes of the world's population love danger at a safe
remove – just look at the box-office takings for films such as

Rambo. The most popular books are still murder, mystery and horror. Those drums and flags have little trouble overcoming any resistance. Men who fought in the Boer War rushed to join up for the First World War, and First World War men joined up for the Second, and the Second World War men for Korea.

Perhaps those of us who later attempted to try to ban war did not address ourselves to the cause but rather to the effect of war. There were all our fine words, marches, attempts to ban war toys, shops attacked by us – the young mothers of the late 1940s and early 1950s – we wrote letters, told what the war had done to fathers of our children, to us and our homes. But the toy guns became even more popular as time went on. We had wasted our energy attacking ephemera instead of researching the alternatives to war. Are we as afraid of 'obscenities' as were our parents?

Society responds only as it has been conditioned, for fashions change, trends alter. It was always thus. But must it continue? The end of war has traditionally been signalled by mothers searching the battlefields for the bodies of their dead sons. Must our daughters and granddaughters creep out across the no man's land of their minds to the battlefields of the future, searching, anxious to spread ceremonial burial dust over a young body as did my generation (and as Antigone did 2000 years ago, near where the first great numbers of Australians died on Gallipoli)?

Some of us come from families whose mothers and grandmothers, until their dying day, searched wastelands of their hearts for their sons. We have weathered half a century without a 'world' war. Can we manage another fifty years? Can we keep our sons, our brothers, even our grandsons?

In 1985–86 I was engaged to work with the BBC (British Broadcasting Commission) for a year. It was fun, interesting, laborious, with good travel and good companions. I had been commissioned by the BBC to do a one-hour documentary for the Australian Bicentennial in 1988. The documentary was shown three times on the BBC and in Europe, and once in America. It was titled 'Australia Will Be There' and covered the fortunes and vicissitudes of the seventy-year period of my life.

The critics' columns in the English *Listener* carried two anti-me letters stating that I was anti-British. These were promptly replied to by a Welshman from Cardiff who wrote, 'If she was criticising the British for their poor treatment of the colonies then she was right and courageous to do it.' Another thought it all was 'Grand'. But the best thing that came my way was a letter from an English lady who had just returned from a journey to Australia:

I was just home and turned on the telly while I unpacked my case and I thought, 'I know that voice', and looking round to the telly it was you! I had seen your show first time round on BBC and it made me want to get up and go – so I did. I got the little money I had together and went down to Australia for as far as the money lasted but that two weeks was marvellous so when I got back home I began to save again and I'm just back again from Australia for the second time and there you are again on the telly and I sat down and watched it all again and it was right!

One doesn't often get fans as faithful as this. But I do regret that it was not shown in my own country. The ABC had, so the BBC told me, 'too much of the Bicentennial'.

I loved that year planning, writing and making 'Australia Will Be There'. The BBC film crew was a great team. We filmed on Gallipoli – with the English director expecting me to leap out of the boat at dawn and wade ashore and both of us forgetting I am only five feet tall. So they had to haul me back in when I came up for air – I can't swim.

A
Country Funeral

DAD HAD LIVED UNTIL HE was 86 years of age, and the cause of death was that common to old men: he was so modest that he hadn't even told my Mother that his bladder was in such a bad condition. Eventually, after operating, they realised there was no hope.

I wrote a memoriam for him but, at that time, it was just for my own eyes, not for the public or for the family. There was something I had wanted to say:

They are burying the old navvy in the bush by the track this morning. Listen, you railway repairers, raise your banjos – that is, if you still carry shovels in this day and age – in salute to all the old navvies who are buried out on the hills from one end of this continent to the other.

Give a pop on your whistle, all you Big-Wheel men, blow a cockle-doodle-doo for the men who kept the tracks in repair for your engines to ride safely when they were young and so was our land. Cry the traditional Banshee wail of the railmen – Wah, Waaahhhah – all you drivers of the goods, the coalies, the Ghan, the Bunbury Belle, the gippies, the lines that ran from north, south, east and west of this land.

Many is the time in the drought he has off-loaded half-dead sheep for you, watered and fed them until they were fit to travel on and that wasn't his job, or any navvy's job, but they just did what they thought was right and necessary and told no one of it.

Out of bed at all hours with the cow-cockies coming in whenever they could manage it in those hard times. 'Put a kettle on Mum, the poor bloke's hide is cracking.' Never again will you get men like these. Honest, loyal, modest.

Dad: remember the day we were in Melbourne, you and Kathleen and me, when we were young and we needed to phone the hospital where Mum had gone for an operation, and we went across from Flinders Street to where there was a telephone booth and we pushed the money in and this amazing thing happened? The phone box absolutely spewed out silver, two-shilling pieces by the score, one shilling, sixpence, it just poured out and we stood staring at it, trying madly to stop it all from falling to the floor.

Dad said without a moment's hesitation, 'You two girls stay here and watch that no one steals this money. I'll go and find a policeman to come and take it away.' And so we stood there as he'd ordered, and back he came with the policeman and the money, to the last threepence, was gathered up and then we walked away never having touched a penny of it.

When Dad became sick there was a nightmare drive to the hospital in the city. I dashed off to park the car, rushed back and found the old bushman in a four-bed ward with three down-and-out alcoholics for companions. He was in pyjamas many sizes too big for his wiry labourer's body, in a corner with his teeth out, cramped up in a chair by the wall looking like an old sheep cornered in a paddock. I rushed out shouting. Nurse said 'This is a public hospital'. Quickly I got the young resident on the phone. 'He was trembling. I thought it was the DTs. Can he speak? Or move?' Dad was a teetotaller.

'He is a bushman. Until last week he was working six days a week in his vegetable garden – no, not in a backyard, in a paddock.' He had rows of beans and pumpkins climbing the frames, with cucumbers firmly trained to head in the other direction; sweet corn you could eat raw with the milky flow running down your chin, red cabbage and green, tomatoes, silver beet, carrots sweet and young, celery, bright bell capsicums, zucchini, peas to eat by the handful every time you walked out to empty the teapot, turnips with purple tops and yellow swedes, little chillies brightly coloured, and over all the flowers of broad beans, staked up high, tattooing their unique perfume into the nerve of the garden. But now, there he was cornered. It wasn't right at all.

When we came back in an hour he had been taken to a ward with three younger men and the four were talking and laughing together, and the young medico had coaxed Dad to tell him how to go about planting a garden in loamy soil. Dad was chiacking the young men, but he was done for. After the operation, we knew.

He said, 'Take me home to Gippsland' where he was born. A terrible drive, sick all the way home. And so we crept as far as the West Gippsland hospital where he lay down on the first bed he saw.

Old, scholarly Monsignor Daly came to ask him if he would like Extreme Unction, a Catholic rite in time nearing death, and Dad said yes, and insisted on taking the oxygen mask off, with Mons saying 'Leave it on, Albert', but Dad calmly refused. The two men had been to the local races several times in Mons' car and as far as I know horses were their only mutual interest – until now, when they were both dying, Mons with cancer of the throat and only three weeks left to read the racing pages. Dad put out his hand and the two old men shook hands on death's doorstep. 'Thank you, Mons,' Dad said in that quiet way of his. 'Thank you for your company,' said Mons.

I stayed up country with Mum, within walking distance of the hospital. She was anxious, so was I. I wanted to see Dad right to the end of the road, give any aid he needed to assist him to finish his long and noble sojourn in the manner he had journeyed for nearly ninety years, *a long and noble time.*

Nobility is not the preserve of the rich and famous and any

who had come in contact with this man knew it. It was in his bearing, even when he was telling of the larrikin pranks of his early life in the wild mountains of tall timber, or when he related an incident he had observed, or when he came in, hat in hand, and tipped the contents out on the table to delight Mum: mushrooms he had walked far to find, the first of the year, this he did as a king might bestow jewels on his queen. And mostly his nobility shone out with his quiet acceptance when Mum, in her cruel, burning rages, harangued him, said awful things, although never the truth – that one thing that she had every right to feel bitter, cruel, hateful about she never threw that at him. I now believe that this was never mentioned between them. That she who was barren through no fault of her own body, and he who was the cause of the untitled, secret frustrations that demented and deranged her, had no discussion after his first and only announcement of his one fatal flaw. And there was her innocent, virginal acceptance of him as he was.

Dad had the calm dignity. When he got a free railway pass to go to Adelaide in the 1930s to watch a cricket match, he and I set off with our basket of food that Mum had prepared and when the fuss about bodyline bowling was going on, Dad just remained seated, his hand firmly on my shoulder, and he said, 'They shouldn't have done that'. And we sat back quietly until the hubbub had died down.

And now he had reached the top of the mountains. From where he lay in the bush hospital he could see the peaks of the beautiful Baw Baws where his childhood tracks petered out. He was ready to lie down there.

Mum and I drove into Warragul on a delicate mission we felt needed clearing before the death. Monsignor was dying and we thought he was too ill to officiate at Dad's funeral but we didn't want to broach the subject in a brutal way. The cancer had eaten Mons' jaw away, there would be no more operations, no prayers would help him, he was to die. He answered the doorbell at the presbytery. 'Well now! What incomparable company!' he laughed with joy. 'Come in, come in.'

'Albert is dying,' Mum said. 'I know, I know,' his voice was still beautiful with its Australian-broadened Kerry lilt. 'You'll be needing a drink.' 'Thank you, Monsignor,' Mum's anti-drink, icy-pole tongue spake, 'I don't drink'. 'Well, I'm sure young Patsy will join me,' Mons said, and young Patsy did. The housekeeper brought a tray of tea things in for Mum and after the two elderly ladies discussed the fine embroidery of the traycloth, the housekeeper retired. Mons motioned me to the drinks trolley to pour for the two of us while Mum looked everywhere else. 'It's Jamesons,' Mons said. 'Not to be spoiled by stinting.' The glasses were sparkling Waterford, as was the jug that was there for decoration only, not for water. It was going to be a session. 'You don't spoil good whiskey with water.'

And Mons gave us no opportunity to suggest he was not well enough to bury Dad. He had made up his mind.

We sat with Dad all night while he was dying: Mum, Johnny, who'd been brought up as his son, and me. We eased him during the night, held his hand, kissed him, kept his body comfortable, and just as morning came Mum said, 'I think he's leaving us'. And indeed he was. We embraced him, we stroked his loving hands and cheeks, we whispered our love.

When it was done, I walked out into his garden, that big vegetable garden he had in the paddock behind the house. The last cabbage was still there, and I knelt down, held it to my face. He used to sell the odd lettuce and cabbage to the publican's wife for money to put a 'two bob' bet on the horses. He still had a bit of the larrikin in him.

This was the last cabbage, and I laid my cheek on it again as though my heart was breaking in anticipation of the years to come without him. I was trying to take in his strength in adversity, the simple goodness of the man.

Blow the wild whistle through the hills, you Big Wheel men, over the plains, the Mallee, the valleys, up through Sunset Country, through all the miles he and Mum toiled; humble, unassuming, stoic – and laughing.

And weep for an age that will never come again.

Our family are country people, and we bury our people as we see fit. John, whom Mum and Dad 'brought up', became a Captain in the Country Fire Authority, as was his father-in-law. When his mother-in-law died her eulogy was read in the local Methodist church. 'She was', said the clergyman, 'never far behind the fire brigade wagon. And on two occasions that we know of she was in front of it, because the brigade had alerted her to where we would be making our stand to repel the oncoming flames. We have lurched back into her station many times in many years, and reached out for a steaming cup of tea in one hand and a scone in the other.'

The town was closed for her funeral. All shops shut, the mourners packing the church, and those who couldn't get in crowded outside. She was carried out on the shoulders of her kinsmen to the hearse through an avenue of Country Fire fighters in their uniforms. The point was made clear to us, who had deserted the bush for the city, that life out here was still real, the seasons, the triumphs, the tragedies, the lives and deaths were all recorded for eternity in the deep place kept inside each one of us.

When Cheryl, John's young wife, died the firemen again formed a guard of honour for by then she had taken on her mother's Fire Authority mantle. And as well, there was a guard of honour of scores of footballers because this girl had coached young boys and was their idol. Because her funeral was so huge there would not be room in their little church so, although it was not Cheryl's religion, the priest of the larger Catholic church in the next town offered his church – and still there was not enough room and mourners stood outside the door in great numbers. Never before had I seen so many young lads attend a funeral for a woman; nor had I seen so many boys and men weep for the loss of a member of their community.

The care we take in burying the people we love is not so widespread in this day and age, but it is the way our family still does it. I believe it is not only a sign of the deep respect for those we love to bury them with dignity, it is also a help to us when we see the six young kinsmen carrying the coffin aloft on their shoulders, the little children running around, laughing and playing as the sombre words are spoken over the grave and the handful of soil is scattered down, with the relatives and friends sprinkling their remembrances too.

And then it's time for tea. It's an old-fashioned way of going about it, having sandwiches, home-made hot dishes, cakes, tea and coffee, and the young men sit around the back where they won't be seen and have a beer or two, out of sight of those in the family who are teetotal. And we talk about the old days and the old ways. When Uncle Frank was buried we went back to the house. We were eating cake and my aunt Sarah happened to see some of the young boys getting around past the window into the kitchen. She promptly swept out, found that they had beer, stretched her hand out, and took two open bottles. And while talking to them about any old thing at all, she quietly tipped the beer down the sink and not a one of them had the courage to attempt to stop her. I remember the stunned look on the faces of these smart young men who had backed down to this little woman.

Of course, there is another side to funerals, and that is that they keep you in touch with the family. It is a great outing and you laugh, talk about things you all did when you were kids, what troubles you got into, what you're doing at the present time – and it makes for continuity in life.

The Royal Australian Navy did Dad proud. They sent men to clear the overhanging trees in the paddock-like cemetery in the bush where our family graves are. They sent the White

Ensign that would cover his coffin with his cap on top, and the cortege would be preceded by an officer and men in summer whites, and the bugler who was sent to play the final salute, including 'The Last Post'. My Dad, this old man, had been one of the first to join the Australian Navy when it was formed.

But it was Monsignor's day too. It was the last ceremony he would see and he knew it, and he dressed for it. After the church service he had gone back to the presbytery to change. The Princes Highway had been closed to enable the cortege and the hundreds of mourners' cars to slowly wind out of the town and down the bush road to the cemetery. We waited and waited. The police were getting fidgety and suggested someone might go up and see if Mons would soon be ready, but none had the courage. Finally, twenty minutes later he reappeared. He had changed. He was now wearing the fine vestments made as a farewell gift by the parishioners when he left Ireland as a 24-year-old. Now he was in his nineties. The people of this Gippsland town (not just the parishioners) had made a wonderful gesture: because of his long service to their community they had financed a small cottage in Ireland, and the town council had presented Mons with rod, reel and creel for the days when the salmon would be running.

But it was too late. I called on him several days after Dad's funeral, and we lowered a bottle of Jameson's enough to get us singing – to the obvious alarm of a young priest, acolyte?, who left swiftly when I was introduced to him by Mons as 'my pagan friend'. 'God save Ireland sang the heroes,' we sang with our arms round one another, each with a glass in our hand:

God save Ireland, cry we all
Whether on the scaffold high
Or the battlefield we die
Sure what matter if for Ireland dear we fall.

And I kissed Mons goodbye. He had been a good friend to my

Father, and neither encouraged nor discouraged him to become a Catholic.

Mons had once told me of his leaving Ireland and coming to Australia: 'I would ride my bicycle out over the hills to visit parishioners, and I'd be crying all the way I was so lonely for home, for Ireland.'

When my Mother died her 'effects' were put in my hand – only one hand was needed. The bundle included an old, much-battered cricket ball wrapped in a time-stained handkerchief with the legend '1913. Gone to Navy.'

Dad must have left it with his mother before he sailed off. There was a blue cotton bag as long as a pencil, holding my long black curls which were cut off in 1939. ('Your mother will kill me!' the barber in our country town had wailed.) The only other inheritance was wrapped in yet another stained handkerchief: a tightly rolled wad of letters. It took care and time to unwrap the fragile collection. The first group were letters from my Father to my Mother during their courtship.

'Dear Birdie' the first letter began. It was the pet name of my Mother, Bridget. Dad had been invalided out of the Navy, damaged, before the war ended, and he had met Mum at a dance in Gippsland. Only a short time later he wrote to her to say he would be 'no use' to her.

Dad was a country boy who had never been to a city or even a large town until he had gone to Melbourne in 1913 and was posted to the first flagship of the Royal Australian Navy, HMAS *Australia*. Five years later, when he was invalided home, he got a job on the cable trams in Melbourne for four weeks but sped to his home in Gippsland every chance he got. He was the youngest of a family of thirteen and his mother doted on him. The first letter was from his mother, the Scots lady, my Grandmother Isabella Adam-Smith, and it exposes her lack of schooling and her love of family which included even me.

Satrday nigh

My dear son Albert and daughter Birda,

Heir I am a gain in good helth so is Ted he is still working on the railway. Tonight he was going to a uca party yes they are talking about rising the pencions again but they take their time about it. No letters from the west oh well I dont care dear Birda I wish you could have seen your lilick bush it was lovely. I inclose a small sprae well my children I close with love to you & Birda and Katran & my littel friend Jean. So God bless you all loving mother

I Smith

xxxxxxxxxxx

(Birda = Birdie; Ted was one of her sons; uca = euchre; west refers to the fact that three of her sons were in Western Australia; lilick = lilac; Katran = Kathleen; Jean = me.)

The letters weren't in chronological order, and in the next one Dad writes in a splendid hand from 'Bourke Street, Melbourne'. 'To dear Birdie. I wonder what the devil young Birdie thinks of this chicken now.' It seems he had promised to meet her at a dance and didn't turn up (although he had ridden to Neerim, many miles past her lodgings). 'Can you swallow that excuse Birdie? It's the best one I have thought of. Are you going to the dance at Darnum tonight? I am going by train, so come, thats a good *kid*. Believe me to be, as silly as ever, Albert Smith.'

The next letter says that he will not be going out until she returns from a visit to her parents, but 'I think the heavens have been torpedoed the way the rain is pelting down and I hope there will be better days ahead – both for you and me.' He writes love letters denying that he is the 'wild devil' she claims him to be, and *not* the 'out-law', nor is he 'past redemption'. 'I wonder what she really thinks of me?' he asks in the letter and, no doubt, asks of himself. Could Dad ever have written this? In that era?

Dad went to war with his nephew Jackie Pearce, who was his best friend as well as being two years older than him. Actually, by the time he was born Dad had several nephews and some called him Uncle! Dad and Jackie remained the happiest of companions till the end of their long lives, both of them outrageous pranksters and teases, and both were joyous company and brought laughter with them as if they had been put on earth to cheer up everyone, including those who daily watch for the sky to fall on them.

But Jackie, who had been in hospital in France for five months with gunshot wounds, 'had his eye on' a dour young lady (who later aged to an even more dour older married woman) and Dad's letters of 1918 make it clear: 'Dad and I had the pleasure of beating Jack and the famous *Miss Ada* last night at cribbage.' The two young men, invalided home from war, had not lost their knockabout larrikinism. On New Year's Eve they removed a jinker and horse that was tied to the horserail at the front of the Neerim Hotel, took the horse to one side of a gate, locked the gate, and put the jinker shaft through the panels of the gate and reharnessed the horse. It would have been seen merely as a New Year's Eve prank had the owner not been drinking heavily. He staggered out to go home and said 'Gee up!' to the horse who was waiting patiently on the other side of the gate. As it was, the two young men, still in uniform because they had no other clothes, had to 'scarper' and gallop hell-for-leather the 18 miles home.

There's another letter, written when 'Birdie' is again visiting her parents: 'Jack is playing cards with my father and he looks over to me now and again and smiles. I guess he knows who I am writing to.' Dad is love-sick, he writes every day his 'Birdie' is away from him. 'I could write a long diary every day to you.'

A vast amount of loving comes through in these letters and it makes me wonder if there was more time to be loving in those days when we had time to write.

I would like to do something desperate today to cause some excitement, it's a very mad feeling. I love to see things stirring and to be amongst it. I wish I could be different and tear away these feelings, but I am always happy when I feel like that. But tonight will be dull. I am going to tackle *Comin' Through the Rye*. (If I get lost in the rye I hope someone I am always thinking of will come to my rescue.)

He must have given her a bit of a run-around according to his letters because three times he failed to meet her at dances where she'd ridden at his request. But his letters were doting: 'I am writing this in bed, so it ought to be sweet. Awkward as it is to write in this position, I have managed to scrawl more than you do.'

My Mother, 'Birdie', had six sisters and three of them at various times 'worked' for Mrs Gay, although both my Mother and Mrs Gay's daughter spoke of it not so much as mistress and maid but as giving country girls from a good family the opportunity to learn another way of life and work. As wife of the man who surveyed and built many of the early roads in Gippsland, Mrs Gay entertained and in this way, the Adams girls learned a style unlikely to come their way otherwise.

My Mother met Dad when Mrs Gay said 'Mr Smith's sailor son is come home. You go down and ask him if he'd sell me one of his lettuces.' And so, 21-year-old Mum went down, Grandfather sold her the lettuce and suggested to his sailor son that he should carry it back to the Gay's house. Thus began the loving relationship that lasted for sixty-four years.

In 1918 when my parents were discussing marriage they decided on the Presbyterian church for the ceremony as Adam Smith was a Scottish Presbyterian. But Mr and Mrs Gay were opposed to it. 'Birdie,' they said. 'Your parents, isolated back in the wilderness where priests rarely could venture, still tried to teach you the faith of their fathers. You might well have regrets if you go into this lightly.' And so they wed in a Catholic church, but down at Nar Nar Goon, well away from their own area. Religious bigotry in all Christian religions at that time was disgusting. This pure young couple could not marry in front of a Catholic altar because my Father was not a Catholic. They were wed in the sideroom of the church where the vestments and accoutrements of the service were kept and where dusters and Brasso were stored in a cupboard. The only time the bride appeared in the church was as she walked out after the marriage service. With them were my Grandmother and Aunt Anastasia who came as witness.

The wedding took place in 1919 and by 1921 Mum was away, writing to Dad, and this time she mentions Mickie, the 2-year-old red-headed orphan they had recently acquired. Her christened name was Kathleen Rita, but she was most often known as 'Mick', or 'Red-haired Micky'. Dad's letters to Mum on her visits down to Grandmother Adams are as loving but not as cheeky as those of his bachelor days. He writes of having ridden his horse 12 miles to the football. From boyhood, Dad had been a good rider. He ends the letter with forty-two crosses, one kiss for every day she will be away.

In 1931 in the heart of the depression he wrote from Waaia: 'You have no idea the heat it was here today. The sweat simply rolled out of me at work.' Still during the depression:

Thorntons are being sold up here on the 11th March – They have a terrible lot of big, heavy horses and everybody reckons they will go for nothing as nobody about has got any money.

My pay is hardly worth drawing now and next pay, we are informed, will be worse. [It was cut to £2/17/6.] Tea has gone up a penny ha'penny. [And by now, there were Kathleen and me to be supported.]

Dad asked for the following letter to be burned, but as Mum did not do so neither will I. All the frustration, sadness and pain of his life since 1917 was in this letter:

Waaia
22.5.32

My own Darling Wife

Just a scribble to let you see that I am still capable of expressing on paper just a very small portion of my very deepest love that exists within me for you dear girl. Sometimes my actions may appear to you as though I care nothing, indeed my sweetheart that is when I feel most although at times I am very cruel and remark things that I know cuts you to the heart but remember dearest they cut me deeply to say them but that is a thing that I am going to try and cut out but the way that you over-look them is still further proof of the great love that exists within you for me. Although I myself love do not need any proof as far as that is concerned. I can honestly say that from our first meeting you have always been uppermost in my thoughts and will be till death doth part. You are still capable of bringing a tinge of jealousy within me. You to me dear girl is just like what petrol is to a motor car, without the petrol the car is useless. Well now dearest Birdie, how precious that name is to me – I must close. With all my love to you dear child. I am Your very sincerest husband, Albert XXXXXXXXX

(Would you please burn this when finished.)

The night before she died my Mother said to me, 'What would I have done without you?' She spoke firmly as she had used to do. 'The life, the everything. Part of me to the end.' I was embarrassed – or whatever it is we experience when we cannot reply. So I put my hands under the bedclothes and rubbed her old legs and stroked her tummy with the flat of my hand and she went to sleep.

It was like her to wind up affairs, even affairs of the heart. Few mothers and daughters have had the rapport we had.

During the depression, Mum booked up bills in every town we went to, and if she had had a car she would have had overdue accounts from one end of the State to the other. Only once was pressure put on her and that was at the grocery shop in Penshurst, and then it was only a hint that no more could go on the slate until her £18 account was erased. Shopkeepers were generous in that time but they, too, had bills to pay and were down on their uppers, as were we all. This in no way inhibited Mum. She had a family to keep and that meant keeping them well.

A navvy in Dad's gang had a small farm and Mum suggested to Dad that he ask Jack for a loan. Dad was embarrassed, but he had to do it. He later told Mum, 'Jack said if two poor buggers that staggered back from the war can't stick together, who can?' In time Mum always paid her bill, but she was like the dairy farmers she had descended from, and always believed they needed to buy yet another cow and the bank could wait. What was a bank for if it wasn't to lend money? That was Mum's principle.

Near the final years she had moved down from the country to the War Widows' Hostel near my house and for the first time in ninety-three years she lived in the city. But it was hard. Apart from me there was no one she could converse with – talk, yes, but there was no one her age who could talk about events all those years back, into another century and its warp. She was better than most elderly ladies; there are few (none that I have known) who can converse, tell a history, an anecdote or sing a song of long ago as she could do, with all the warmth of joy or tears.

We buried Mum with Dad, in the paddock among the hills where four generations of us have been buried, in a little graveyard with a caretaker who has known three generations of us. He told me he always cared for our graves, 'She was a wonderful woman'. It seemed strange to hear that from a grave digger.

A country girl did as I had asked and created a whole art form – not a wreath, but a coffin-cover the length of the box, 15 inches high, and including every flower, wattle, eucalypt bush and tree twigs from plants grown in Gippsland. She had even gone to find the rare little bush orchid, and knew which would be open by the day they were needed. 'I picked them at daylight with the dew still on them.' Boughs of gum nuts trailed over the sides of the box which my son and five of her many nephews and grandsons carried to the grave. It wasn't dramatic so much as being a complete farewell, there was time for tears, prayers, time for reunions, and the meeting of new babies and then, back to the cars and off up the narrow road into the little town of Drouin where the women who had known her had prepared food and drink and talk flowed and often her name was spoken. 'God her temper was vicious.' 'But she was the one of the family I really loved.' 'She was a giver.'

There were ninety-five red roses piled around her grave. At the service, the young priest said, 'Any who wish to take communion in the sacred spirit of which it is intended are welcome to the altar.' I moved to all Mum's children around the various pews. 'Come on!' John, Albert and their children, Kathleen and Adrian and Robert, and my own family. 'I don't think I'm allowed,' Kathleen said. 'No, no. We're not,' said Adrian. 'Are you?' 'I'm giving out the permits,' I said. The poor young priest was breaking bread into little pieces to get round us all. I think the whole congregation fronted. It took a long time to get done.

I don't know what the others thought of that act of communion, but to me it was not only a way of continuing to walk with Mum in the way she would have loved, it was also a mark of respect for what she had independently believed and followed for over ninety years while often living in a wilderness. Before the Catholic church made its sweeping changes in the 1960s she couldn't read the Latin mass but had to follow the English translation. But she believed. I knew the Latin but I didn't relate to belief, only to beauty, and I knew Mum had lots of that.

Before the service I had asked the young priest to do something for me and he did it well. He read aloud from the altar of the injury my father suffered in 1917, while away at the war. Dad not only could never make babies, he could not have sex, he could only give love, and this my Mother had never told a living soul. I learnt it from his naval discharge documents. That passionate woman (who had seven sisters who each bore more than six children) and the passionate man who had lived with her and loved her for sixty-odd years, sharing the same bed, had been unable to fulfil their urgent needs. And she had shouted rage and vitriol and we girls heard through the thin walls and wondered that he never replied, but not once did he do this.

The pain of these star-crossed lovers touched all of us and many wept in the church. Cousins came up and said, 'I never knew. I couldn't understand.' 'She gave each of us a wristlet watch for our sixteenth birthday,' the boys remembered. 'She was cuddly and generous and then her tongue was so bitterly cruel and it bewildered all of us.' Many spoke of her violent rages and that night I wrote it all down, I didn't want to forget any of it for it evened up the harsh, cruel times our family had survived. Once I had come home from school when she was at work at the rail station at Monomeith and our cat was in the yard, squealing, and something was flapping round its backside, and with some odd terror I ran up to the station and yelled for Mum to come. Full of concern for me she ran down thinking a snake had got the cat, and then she saw the kitten being dragged along, only half out of the birth opening, unable to get out. She went mad: 'Get away, get away, this is what you wanted to see, isn't it?' I was backing off, it was a sight that was horrendous and I truly didn't understand what was happening. 'No,' she said. 'Stay and watch, that's what you want, oh yes, you'll like this thing, won't you. Oh yes, look, look! Female cats have babies.'

I ran around the back and huddled in the little wash house. There I planned the most absurd thing for a small girl who never had pocket money – I huddled thinking, trying to work out how many years it would take to pay back the money she had spent on food for me in the nine years I had already lived. And my brain, which had not handled money, worked out that it would take three years. But I would do it. I was sure. And then I would disappear.

Of course, I didn't. Mum came looking for me, took me in her arms and carried me back to the station. And after the last train came and went, she took me, still in her plump arms, down to the house and consoled me. 'You shouldn't have seen that' she said, knowing that it had shocked me as much as it had done her. I never knew what happened to the cat or the kitten. Probably Dad handled it when he got home and found Mum sitting in front of the stove with me in her plump, homely arms, singing softly and rocking me.

All this I thought of while I spread a handful of soil over her grave. And then, that night on our way back to the city, we detoured to drop a flower on the stone monument at Longwarry where the names of her two brothers – 'lost' at Lone Pine, Gallipoli, in 1915 – were recorded. This was the warp and weft of our family life.

Our
Conundrum

WE WERE A DANCING FAMILY and danced right to the end. At family gatherings, Kathleen comes to me and she leads. Our kin-folk stand back for us to do one 'turn of the floor' before they join in.

Our parties were laughing, dancing, feasting times with kids dancing with adults, and calls of 'Ladies and Gentlemen, please change your partners!' We sat down to great dinners and followed that later in the evening when we had supper. We 'put up' gorgeous decorations. There were Golden Weddings and Diamond Weddings for Birdie and Albert, and we hired halls and the same dance band – Nortons – we'd danced to all our days.

I try not to bewilder people by explaining my family. It is not difficult for me: 'My sister, whose parents were not mine, had two brothers, neither of them mine, and two sons who were sort of my nephews and later became sort of my brothers.' I knew that my Mother had never been pregnant and our Father had had no children. My Father's mother wrote of me as her 'dear littel frend Jean' not as her dear little grand daughter. However, my maternal Grandmother, even though she was indeed entitled to that title, wished I had never been born and knew that my Grandfather, her husband, intended to shoot me as I was being carried in the womb.

It was clear to all of us in the family, and few families could have knitted so well. We each loved one another and still do. And in particular, each of us still revere Mum who, when it became necessary, became mother to boys who had been her grandsons and thus changed me to sister from aunt. We had lived as the happiest family that could be made, and we were never backward at making fun out of the whole damned thing that life is.

My 'Christian' or given names were Patricia Jean but my family and old friends have always called me Jean. Almost everyone else outside the family has called me something else. When I joined up during the war, the first time I walked into a ward the Matron said, 'Girls, here is the new nurse – what's your name?' I looked up at her, she looked down on me – God! Matron had spoken to me! 'Patricia Jean Adam-Smith' I mumbled in what was meant to be a smart military manner, and she said, 'Pat'.

And there it was. I was Pat. It remained Pat until my daughter was born, and her first spoken word was 'Patsy'. And so I have remained (with minor detours such as 'Mrs Pat' when I was at sea). There are still some who call me Jean or Jeanie, but they are thinning out with the years. I love hearing the old name from them, but I keep it just for them. It is a reminder of the bonny times of long ago and I have a fierce protective feel for the name I was first known by.

Until I began this book I hadn't realised how many aliases I have carried. I got 'Paddy the next best thing' as a small child, at about the same time as Kathleen got 'Mick'. *Paddy the Next Best Thing* was a book of the day and the young girl in it seemingly got into as much mischief as I did, so the joke was as corny as the period. The nickname was outgrown and had died away until it popped up years later in a book about Australian women biographers that had a section about me. The writer suggested it was a crude and cruel jibe at me because, you know, I was adopted, not a *real* daughter, therefore just a 'next best thing'. As though those gentle parents could ever be so cruel.

It was such a misreading of my Father's character that I felt shame that I had written a book about his love and yet could be so misinterpreted. I was very disturbed. Perhaps some man in that writer's life could have tagged a little girl with such cruelty, but coming from my Father it was a laughing, loving sort of game that we indulged in during that period. It worried me also as an indication of how history can, and is, distorted by each generation.

One is afraid to use the slang of an earlier age in fear of what some smart-arse says (and what would they say about that word?). 'Look me in the eye and say that.' 'Go on, say it to my face'; or, 'I won't take any more of your lip'; 'Would you like a taste of the razor strap?' (the common punishment of the day – a whack around the legs with that thick, long lump of leather). One spoke of 'a poor old codger' and maybe bamboozled him by giving him 'a bit of scran', but these expressions should not, perhaps, be exposed to folk who did not grow up with them or, worse still, make a guess at what an expression of another era meant at the time it was in use.

After my first two books were published, a publisher sent air tickets for me to fly to Adelaide to discuss my doing another book. This book was the first that let me know an author must fight for the right to a decent living. That day I fought and won, and never again did I let a publishing house get away with anything. I fought hard and argued and coaxed when it seemed a viable thing to do and, for all my books I have been given a decent deal. In return I have tried to deliver my manuscripts as close to the delivery date as I could (even if some got in by the skin of my teeth). But I did pay a penalty. From the day I refused to accept the rate that was offered I was considered 'mean', 'hard as nails', and to have 'lost her loveliness'. (Oh God! Let's lose it if it means making men pay us the same as men get!)

Like all born writers, I know when one work is better than another, though the book may seem just as good to a reader. But a *writer* knows. You can see where and how you could have selected your words even more delicately, moved the drama of life to a section where it may have had more impact, clarity; you can see how you could have moulded the descriptive paragraphs that were necessary pieces of information or continuity, even if the reader may not care to leave the high alps for the plains of a book.

And that self-criticism can come after three drafts; one book of mine took nine drafts, the colour out of my hair, stole my social life for the many years of its gestation (as opposed to the six to twelve months a book usually takes for the hard slog before you begin to rewrite). You resurface after writing a book feeling like Rip Van Winkle because you've been cut off from the world, don't answer your gate buzzer or messages on your answering machine. You resent your secretary or typist turning up even though they are part of your team. I once found myself writing a note to my housekeeper-cleaner, even though I was home when she was there. A writer would live in cardboard cartons in derelict warehouses if someone didn't keep an eye on you and your dwelling and food cupboard. I wrote *Folklore of the Australian Railwaymen* on a diet of Weeties and powdered milk. The first edition sold out in four days so you can't deny it was a great diet. And the empty Weeties packets doubled as filing cabinets on my big, billiard-table size working area.

At that time, my children were teenagers so I gave them money to buy food for themselves. They'd wander in of a morning and night, and I'd surface and we'd enjoy talking in front of the open fire and we always seemed happy with our life together. However, I do notice that even now, when they are both married and each has a child and homes of their own, that they never, not ever, when staying with me move a piece of paper, no matter how scrappy it looks, from the floor, the beds, the walls, the window frames or old cartons. Some of the notes are valuable, some valued by the donor or lender, some are 'may-be's' or notes I write 'in case of', and of course, there are the hundreds of diaries and letters sent to me from all over the world.

Yet there is a system. I can't think how to describe it, but it must be good because (cross fingers!) I have never lost one page, one letter, diary, illustration or book.

Books cost an author money, health, even life itself, but short of having your hands tied behind your back and your brain quick-frozen there is nothing a writer can do about it. Friends remain only if they know how to fit into the writer's lifestyle. If not, they go, and there is little regret.

Friends have played a great part in my life, much more so than if I had been in a lifetime partnership; some of my friends have been backstops as well as friends.

A totally involved author has only one goal: to tell the story. There is no escape, you are engaged for life, like it or lump it you are shackled. When one works on huge concepts like some of my books, such as *The Anzacs* and *The Shearers*, one cannot afford to lose the thread, the impetus. You must give it your whole life or give it up. I cannot imagine how I would live if I was stopped from writing. I have never wanted to do any other thing.

When I collapsed after completing *Prisoners of War* the publisher's book designer was with me. I made it to the last page and then let go. I came to the next day to be informed by the surgeons at the end of the bed that they had 'tried but failed'. So now I wait. Nothing more can be done. My legs are hideous, one scarred in an unbroken line from ankle to pelvis with a horizontal wound across the shin bone and another scar on the thigh; my left leg is scarred even more so, with a shattered ankle bone plus a foot-to-knee wound that became gangrenous and opened up, vast and wide. It ate deep into flesh until bone was exposed and prevented me from walking at all for two months. I was in a wheelchair, and then hobbled on a stick for seven months. And there was more. I have been in for open-heart surgery three times (the third time hardly counts as my heart stopped when I was on the slab and the operation was aborted). There were six other operations. My bosom is no longer the pretty sight it once was. None of me is. And to cap it all, three lesser but still termed 'serious' operations and two separate large 'donor grafts' were necessary to patch up open wounds.

And you think I don't smart when a reviewer mocks 'She speaks of her "wounds".' What else are they if not wounds?

There is no point in trying to describe the pain gangrene causes on a body because the pain is such that one lies whimpering like a dog beaten near death but afraid to draw attention in case worse is inflicted. When it was being discussed as to whether or not amputation could be the final relief it was not to me they spoke but to one another, as if this gibbering, near-to-collapse patient was no part of the scene. A surgeon came to the end of my bed, ordered two sisters to hold me down, and debrided the gangrenous leg – with no pain-killers at all although the sisters begged him to give them. He just pulled my legs apart and stood in my crotch with his scalpel, making one sister hold my open legs, the other hold my body down.

Only one month previously I had climbed the Kokoda Trail and the mountains, and been photographed on the way by the BBC crew who had been photographing me from Anzac Cove to Egypt, France, Darwin and stockmen riding in Kimberley – but now I was no more than a piece of meat. The effect was lasting on me, and I believed I should speak up.

Much of this could and should have been avoided and, with the advice of many professional people, I sued the hospital – and won. Sick as only the very sick know with the vast debilitation that comes with such a long and overwhelming battering to so many parts of the body, I went through the trial by fire of being sent by lawyers to separate surgeons for assessment of the damage done to me: some were furious at my 'temerity' in questioning the surgeon's behaviour. They showed this by not even reading the reports their own 'side' had sent ahead and always, without looking at it, dismissing the material my lawyers had collected. One prominent man put me in his surgery, banged the door shut behind him and I never saw him again. I waited until it grew dark before I gave up hope and tried to get out of the building but there was no one there, the rooms all empty. It was eerie; I was frightened. Later a cleaner came, she wasn't happy and at first thought I was a thief on the prowl, but she did realise I was very ill and turned the key and let me out. Another man lectured me on the temerity and 'thanklessness' of anyone questioning a man – him or any other surgeon – 'who had given up his life to save others'. Of course, all this was after the worst of my condition had lessened and I was able to hobble along on a stick.

The nurses were splendid. When it was thought my leg must go this team began dressing it every two hours for forty-eight hours. I would feel them gently removing the cradle and inserting tiny pipettes along the gangrenous wound. And they hated having to inflict more pain. As soon as I could put one foot to the ground I was wheeled out and my son, who had returned from Canada (where he had lived for a year), and my daughter cared for me and slowly, painfully, with specialist surgical dressers visiting twice a day, I was able to stagger around.

I now walk upright. I am scarred like a road map, but I am here. And sometimes I don't feel so bad. However, I am always conscious that I am here because of the work of one, great, caring physician who took over when my faith in surgeons was quite destroyed.

As fortune strikes a mother I've been lucky in that my two children and grandchildren are close-knit, loving and each quite free to develop whichever way suits. Tragedy has struck our little family twice, cruel and unyielding and unending to death, and we close in even tighter with love, while living as if this is what life is about – and it is: the good, bad, sad, the unbearable that you have to bear.

Near the end, Mum had said 'You've run a good race, you've run a long way and you've taken me with you.' The run I began when I was born didn't impress or dismay me, but I was pleased Mum recognised that it was a part of me, not a conscious thing. I couldn't be anything other than what I was, am. If Mum had repressed this birthright we would have lost the bond we had – and it was an amazing and deeply loving bond.

Luck? I've had it all my life. It began at my birth when I fell into the arms of a mother few could have excelled or could have suited me so well. The only trauma I have about my birth is the fear of the poor thing life would have been for me had I been accepted by a dour, non-dancing, non-workingclass, proselytising family, weighted down with wealth and dreams of more wealth and fame, and weighted down damnably, silent, lest the secret leap out and shame them for eternity with the unspeakable weight of me in their midst.

While they lived with the fear of my birth being exposed for what it was, I lived on with Mum and Dad and my sister with love, fun, whacks when I deserved them (and sometimes when I didn't and Mum felt like letting off steam). Life has been good to me. Few could have had better.

A journalist once asked me if I was fearful of death. He wrote:

She is a fighter and has no fear. 'I always was a fighter. I want to get the best out of everything. Even death. There's a lot I still want to do, and to say, and if the man with the sickle comes for me before I've got it all on paper I'll be very disappointed because, as the old saying goes, I have played the game fair and square and taken the bad with the good. I haven't asked anyone to share my tears; perhaps that was a fault but they burnt so fiercely I was afraid friends could never understand and they would be embarrassed. I was too proud to expose the pain.'

The journalist asked if I shared my Mother's Catholicism. My reply was 'I haven't got the necessary grain of mustard seed. I envied my Mother who was certain there was *something* after life. You can't help but envy people who believe this. But I can't.'

It doesn't worry me one way or another but it would be great fun if there was a hereafter, and I could sit again with Mum and Dad, and Kathleen would come in calling, 'How ya going, eh?' And Dad, who loved her, would say, 'By Joves, look who's blown in!' And we'd yarn and laugh together and have a game of crib on the kitchen table, and pots of tea and home-made cakes . . .

With the great good luck I've had all my life I wouldn't be at all surprised.

Other Works by Patsy Adam-Smith

Rediscovering Tasmania: the North-West Coast (1955),
  with Piet Maree
Hear The Train Blow (1964)
Moonbird People (1965)
There Was A Ship (1967)
Tiger Country (1968)
Hobart (1968), with Max Angus
The Rails Go Westward (1969)
Folklore of the Australian Railwaymen (1969)
Across Australia By Indian–Pacific (1971)
No Tribesman (1971)
Port Arthur (1971), with Max Angus
Tasmania (1971), with Max Angus
Footloose in Australia (1973)
Romance of Australian Railways (1973)
The Barcoo Salute (1973)
Launceston (1973), with Max Angus
The Desert Railway (1974)
Trader To The Islands (1977)
The Anzacs (1978)
Islands of Bass Strait (1978)
Victorian and Edwardian Melbourne from Old Photographs (1979)
Romance of Victorian Railways (1980)
Outback Heroes (1981)
The Shearers (1982)
When We Rode The Rails (1983)
Australian Women At War (1984)
Heart Of Exile (1986)
Australia, Beyond The Dreamtime (1987), with Thomas
  Keneally and Robyn Davidson
Prisoners Of War: From Gallipoli To Korea (1992)
Trains of Australia (1993)

Hear the Train Blow *The classic autobiography of growing up in the bush*
Patsy Adam-Smith

Hear the Train Blow is the true story of a remarkable young girl growing up in the bush during the Great Depression – Patsy Adam-Smith, now one of Australia's best-loved and most successful authors.

Patsy Adam-Smith was a child of the railways, moving from place to place as her stationmistress mother was relocated. *Hear the Train Blow* tells of yabbying and rabbiting, of childhood excitements and sorrows. It is also a celebration of the ordinary people of Australia and of a life that no longer exists. Not one station where her mother was stationmistress still stands.

There Was a Ship Patsy Adam-Smith

There Was a Ship is the story of Patsy Adam-Smith's years at sea. From the moment she saw a little coastal trader on the Bass Strait Patsy was bewitched. She eventually spent six years on the *Naracoopa*, and was the first woman to be granted signed Articles in Australian waters. As radio officer, she shared the hard life of a small ship's crew and was rescued from the sea three times in some of the most hazardous waters in the world.

The Anzacs   Patsy Adam-Smith

Gallipoli was the final resting place for thousands of young Australians. Death struck so fast there was no time for escape or burial. And when Gallipoli was over there was the misery of the European Campaign.

In *The Anzacs* Patsy Adam-Smith tells of the men who gave birth to a legend. Winner of the Age Book of the Year Award when it was first published, it remains unrivalled as the classic account of Australia's involvement in the First World War.

'If you have not read *The Anzacs* there will always be a part of Australia you will never understand.'

Les Carlyon, *Australian*